The Evolution of the South African System of Innovation since 1916

The Evolution of the South African System of Innovation since 1916

By

Mario Scerri

CAMBRIDGE SCHOLARS
PUBLISHING

The Evolution of the South African System of Innovation since 1916, by Mario Scerri

This book first published 2009

Cambridge Scholars Publishing

12 Back Chapman Street, Newcastle upon Tyne, NE6 2XX, UK

British Library Cataloguing in Publication Data
A catalogue record for this book is available from the British Library

ISBN (10): 1-4438-0160-7, ISBN (13): 978-1-4438-0160-7

To Rooha, my mother and my sister, and the memory of my father.

TABLE OF CONTENTS

List of Tables ix
Preface x
List of Abbreviations xiii

Introduction 1

Part 1: Theory

Chapter One 18
National Systems of Innovation

Chapter Two 69
South African Economic Historiography

Part 2: The History

Chapter Three 100
The Path towards Modernity

Chapter Four 148
Science and Technology Policy under Apartheid

Chapter Five 182
The Emergence of the Technological Growth Sectors

Chapter Six 209
The Post-Apartheid System of Innovation

Endnote 252

Part 3: Appendices

Appendix A: Patterns of R&D 260

Appendix B: Industrial groupings by SIC category 273

Appendix C: Notes on R&D Data 275

Bibliography 277

Index 295

LIST OF TABLES

Table 1: Share of Applied R&D by Sector (%) in Total Applied R&D .. 257
Table 2: R&D/Sales (%) by Industry: 1991 259
Table 3: R&D/Sales (%) by Specific non-MEC Industries: 1991 261
Table 4: Share of MEC R&D in total Manufacturing R&D, by Performer 263
Table 5: Electronics R&D/Total Manufacturing R&D, by Performer..... 264
Table 6: Change in R&D/Sales and Performer Share (1977-1987)......... 265
Table 7: Change in R&D/Sales and Performer Share (1977-1987): Non-MEC 267
Table 8: Share (%) in Total Applied R&D by Performer 269

PREFACE

The origin of this book lies in a sense of disquiet with the relatively sudden exclusion of discourses on the economic history of South Africa from the centre of economic planning shortly after the election of the country's first democratic government. This may have been due to an overwhelming concern that the focus of economists and economic planners should shift definitively to the more standard economic concerns of a now "normalised" economy that had suddenly entered the global economy. The inherited economic distortions of apartheid were indeed factored into the post-apartheid economic planning paradigm but at a peripheral, rather than a central position. In a way there was a dissonance between the overwhelming political imperative to redress the massive injustices of the previous three hundred odd years of South African history and the economic prescriptions of how this redress was to be effected. Effectively, political reform was divorced from economic reform and this led to deep rooted contradictions in policy.

The analysis of South African economic history has always been problematic, specifically because of the phenomenon of apartheid which was, unlike the more common cases of colonialism, quite exceptional in the history of economic development. The debates around the foundation of the political economy of apartheid had been rich and highly contentious, and had evolved and matured considerably over the thirty odd years before the advent of democracy. While the post-apartheid political agenda recognised the complexity of the problems which the democratic government faced, the economic planning paradigm did not. Post-apartheid South Africa was, at least implicitly, analysed as a post-colonial developing economy requiring orthodox macroeconomic planning in line with the neoliberal paradigm which ruled supreme in the mid-nineties. The mid-nineties marked the zenith of neoliberal economics and this approach to economic planning in South Africa left little room for history. Partly because of this exclusion this paradigm appeared at the time wonderfully appealing in its apparent ability to render the analysis of, and the planning for, complex actual cases of economic development so simple.

Concurrently, the nineties saw the emergence into the public sphere of a new approach to economic analysis and economic planning, in the form of a new paradigm, popularly labelled the "national systems of innovation" approach. Indeed, this term was adopted early in that decade by politicians and international economic organisations world-wide; perhaps it was adopted too glibly and without sufficient attention to the implications of the new approach to policy. Certainly, in the case of South Africa, while widely used, the application of the term was restricted to the science and technology sector and did not enter the core of economic planning. As the relevance of science and technology to the growth and development process was increasingly recognised, the status of this sector of public policy increased. This shift was aided by an increasing world-wide sense of uneasiness at the wisdom of neoliberal policy proposals, exemplified in structural adjustment programmes which were increasingly seen to impoverish developing economies, especially across Africa. In South Africa, the growing perception that the neoliberal policy approach had failed to deliver on its redistribution targets has, since the turn of the new century, led to sporadic but largely fragmented attempts to find more relevant economic policy frameworks. In this regard I feel that the systems of innovation approach can provide a viable and useful alternative policy framework.

The scope of this book is to re-examine the history of the South African political economy from the early part of the twentieth century until the present day, with the specific aim to try to understand the nature of structural continuities and ruptures in this history. Most of the critiques of the current economic policy framework are based, explicitly or implicitly, on the proposition of structural continuities from apartheid to the post-apartheid economy, which had been ignored in national economic planning. While the general approach to this history that has been adopted here is an innovation systems approach, the specific version of this approach has to be articulated clearly since the numerous versions of this approach are rarely made explicit in the literature. The one that I have followed in this study is the broadest possible rendition of innovation systems theory, one which has the possibility of becoming an alternative general theory of economics, and which has certainly brought old development theory back to the forefront in the analysis of developing economies.

This book has been long in the making. I had planned to finish it by the year 2000 and its coverage was supposed to end with the 1996 White Paper on Science and Technology. Essentially that book would have been a study of the evolution of the system of innovation until the end of apartheid, with a relatively short coda on the setting of innovation policy within the new overall planning framework. In 2001 I took on the post of executive dean at a tertiary education institution which was shortly to become part of a large higher education sector merger and my work for the next six years was almost entirely managerial. I resumed the writing of the book when I stepped back into academia in mid-2007. The delay was fortuitous in its effect on the book. The passage of time, a huge portion of the short history of the post-apartheid South Africa, enabled a significantly improved perspective on post-apartheid economic performance and planning. The privilege of hindsight and a number of critical reviews of post-apartheid economic planning that had emerged in the meantime allowed for a more informed assessment of the post-apartheid system of innovation and have resulted in what I hope is a more finished text and one that holds more relevance for the development challenges faced by South Africa.

In the course of writing this book I had the benefit of the assistance of a number of associates. Dave Kaplan from the University of Cape Town and Michael Stettler from the University of the Witwatersrand, both read a very early draft of a part of the book and offered a number of cogent critiques, which enriched the progressive re-writing of the work. Towards the end of the work Mammo Muchie from the University of Aalborg, Denmark and the Tshwane University of Technology, South Africa and Rasigan Maharajh from the Institute for Economic Research on Innovation at the Tshwane University of Technology both gave valuable feedback. I am especially grateful to Mammo Muchie for his extensive critique of the final draft of the text. The last chapter of the book was written while I was on an Erasmus Mundus fellowship at the University of Trento. An early draft of that chapter was presented to faculty there and here I need to thank Bruno Dallago and Italo Trevisan for making that period most conducive to the completion and revision of the book. Finally I need to thank my wife, Rooha Variava, for opening up for me various sources of early twentieth century South African history and for providing a critical insight into the race-class debate which has dominated most of the post-war South African economic historiography. I also owe her a great deal for the much needed emotional support during the writing of the book.

LIST OF ABBREVIATIONS

AEB .... Atomic Energy Board
AEC .... Atomic Energy Corporation
AECI .... African Explosives and Chemicals Industries
AE&I .... African Explosives and Industries Limited
ANC .... African National Congress
ARC .... Agricultural Research Council
ARMSCOR .... Armaments Development and Production Corporation
AsgiSA .... Accelerated and Shared Growth Initiative for South Africa
CIS .... Community Innovation Survey
COSATU .... Congress of South African Trade Unions
CPSA .... Communist Party of South Africa
CSIR .... Council for Scientific and Industrial Research
DACST .... Department of Arts, Culture, Science and Technology
DNE .... Department of National Education
DOE .... Department of Education
DST .... Department of Science and Technology
DTI .... Department of Trade and Industry
ESCOM .... Electricity Supply Commission
FRD .... Federation for Research Development
GDP .... Gross Domestic Product
GEAR ... Growth Employment and Redistribution: a Macroeconomic Strategy
HSRC .... Human Sciences Research Council
IDC .... Industrial Development Corporation
IDRC .... International Development Research Centre
ISCOR .... Iron and Steel Corporation
JIPSA .... Joint Initiative on Priority Skills Acquisition
MINTEK .... Council for Mineral Technology
MRC .... Medical Research Council
NACI .... National Advisory Council on Innovation
NCRL .... National Chemical Research Laboratory
NEERI .... National Electrical Engineering Research Institute
NIAST .... National Institute for Aeronautics and Systems Technology
NIDR .... National Institute for Defence Research
NITR .... National Institute for Telecommunications Research
NMERI .... National Mechanical Engineering Research Institute

NPRL..National Physical Research Laboratory
NRDS ....National Research and Development Strategy
NRIMS ....National Research Institute for Mathematical Sciences
NUCOR........................Nuclear Development Corporation of South Africa
OECD.............. Organisation for Economic Cooperation and Development
R&D ....Research and Development
RDP......................................Reconstruction and Development Programme
S&T... Science and Technology
SABS...South African Bureau of Standards
SACP.. South African Communist Party
SAMES......................................South African Microelectronics Systems
SAIMR .... South African Institute of Medical Research
SASOL ....South African Coal and Oil
UCOR...........................Uranium Enrichment Corporation of South Africa
UNDP.. United Nations Development Programme
UNESCO... United Nations Educational, Scientific and Cultural Organization
VFP..Victoria Falls Power Company Limited

INTRODUCTION

The history of South Africa's economic development, especially through the second part of the twentieth century, constitutes one of the more unique stories in the annals of economic history. It has followed and led, through complex sets of causalities, a political development path which was highly idiosyncratic. It has consequently rendered the study of the various aspects of the country's economic history through the twentieth century progressively less amenable to comparative analyses which are rooted in the assumption of commonalities. Thus the dominant historical studies of the South African case, and apartheid in particular, which have adhered too rigidly either to a Marxist or to a liberal paradigm have tended to be didactic and reductionist. South African historiographies, both economic and political, in their dense and complex intertwining, must surely constitute a dangerous source of disillusionment with distinctly structuralist analytical approaches. The potentially disastrous consequence in the post-apartheid era has been an ensuing disillusionment with historical analysis. This disillusionment, especially when set within the increasingly globalised world economy that has emerged since the nineties, has to a large extent eliminated history from post-apartheid economic planning.

The particular history that is the subject of this book is the innovation path of the South African economy and the various processes that fed into the development and formation of South Africa's national system of innovation. This area of study involves two distinct and highly contentious analytical fields and the variety of possible combinations of alternative renditions within them makes for a rich, albeit often contradictory, interpretation of South Africa's technological development path. The first is the theoretical placing of technology and the broader concept of innovation within economic discourse, with a multitude of often conflicting definitions competing for the status of the definitive explanation. The second concerns South African economic historiography, with its various renditions and the political ideologies which inform them. The polemics which have arisen from debates on the fundamental determinants of the economic structure which developed under apartheid set the overall context within which any applied analysis has to be placed, even though a perturbing facet of contemporary debates on South Africa's economic policy is that they seem in general to be immediate and ahistorical.

When compared to the large histories of South Africa over the twentieth century-the evolution and implementation of apartheid, the complex development paths of the various resistance movements, the history of the labour movement, to list a few-a recount of the evolution of the country's system of innovation may seem insignificant and of interest only to those few whose area of interest lies specifically in the economics of innovation. When set within these larger histories, however, and when the ramifications of its contextualisation are explored, it can open up another source of engagement with the complex phenomenon of apartheid. The basis for this claim lies in the employment of the concept of national systems of innovation, which is a relatively recent arrival in the economist's lexicon and which is noteworthy for its uncharacteristic definitional breadth and for the unprecedented theoretical challenge that is poses for conventional economics.

The main debate over the role played by innovation in the analysis of economic growth and development is between the neoclassical paradigm, which in general assumes knowledge to be a free good that is available to all economic agents in any context, and that stream of theory, stemming from List and explicitly addressed by Schumpeter, which assigns property rights to knowledge and places innovative activity at the core of economic development. Although neoclassical theory has become the reigning paradigm since the war, the polemic has been revived in the later part of the twentieth century by the stories of a number of nations whose development paths repeatedly confounded conventional economic wisdom. The economic successes of the South East Asian economies starting with the early emergence of the Japanese post-war economy were, from the perspective of mainstream neoclassical economic orthodoxy, quite unpredictable and consequently they have provided the main source of empirical raw material for alternative explanations of economic development.

The various expositions which have emerged in opposition to neoclassical economics have coalesced, relatively recently, under the broad rubric of evolutionary theory. The main concern of the wide and often disparate group of theoretical and empirical studies which form the basis of this approach has been the analysis of the nature of innovation, its determinants and the role it plays in the process of economic development. Even more recently the concept of systems of innovation has emerged as the most coherent theoretical construct to date to define the perimeters of the evolutionary approach to the relationship between innovation and economic development.

National systems of innovation can be loosely defined as networks of institutions within the borders established by nation states which determine the economy's ability to develop and to absorb innovations. These systems are postulated on the basic assumption that technology and innovation, which are defined to include the rules and practices which govern problem solving within a specific social context, are to a significant extent tacit and hence imperfectly transferrable across societal and national borders. Thus innovation is seen as partially context specific and idiosyncratic and it is this approach, in contrast to the orthodox economic view of technology as universally available information, which has been able to address in a systematic and meaningful manner the divergent growth and development paths of nations. National systems of innovation are therefore seen both as the product of the broadest context of economic development processes and as symptomatic of it.

One of the main defining characteristics of the evolutionary approach, the one which differentiates it fundamentally from the neoclassical orthodoxy, is the focus on the historical specificity of the development paths of nations. The abandonment of the neoclassical postulate of technology as a universally available stock of knowledge through the broadening of the definition of technology to include practices, routines and institutions, invokes a concept of innovation as a cultural product contingent on the context wherein it originates. However, the rejection of the postulate of generalised sets of economic laws does not mean a total renunciation of structuralism by evolutionary theorists. The imperative to design policy within most schools of thought in economics necessarily checks the definite move of the theoretical foundations of most approaches to a post-structuralist base. Thus, simultaneously with the emerging emphasis on specificities, there has arisen within the evolutionary approach a recognition of the need to identify commonalities in patterns of technological and economic development as a counterweight to the concern with specific histories and in order to provide a basis for a qualified normative position.

In the search for commonalities, the South East Asian success stories have obviously provided a rich empirical source for the isolation of the preconditions for those quantum leaps in development paths which defy the predictions of the economics orthodoxy. Accounts of the presence and relative importance of various conditions have varied considerably but there is a broad agreement on which conditions are necessary, though not by any means sufficient, for the set of structural transformations required for high and unprecedented growth rates. Among those prerequisites which have been identified as common to most of the success stories are high levels of investment in human capital formation, a broad accord between state, labour and capital within the context of a loosely defined capitalist framework, a large and growing internal market, and the political will and ability to focus on selected sectors of the economy as the basis of the kick start for the growth process, regardless of the current state of those sectors.

There are, however, preconditions to these conditions and here the analysis for the economist grows murkier as the borders of the discipline as they have been defined by the dominating neoclassical paradigm are transgressed and explanations are sought in fields of study which themselves fall into the interdisciplinary interstices. One such field is the study of nationalism, its various definitions and manifestations, and the contextual determinants of its emergence. Lall (1994) argues that the one common characteristic of the Asian "tigers" has been the absence of common economic policy blueprints. This in itself points to the need to find a deeper layer to the explanation of their immediately obvious commonality, which is their unanticipated success. This layer may consist of specific manifestations of a nationalist drive operating within a context of a broad internal consensus and motivated by the will to attain a standing and a voice in the international political and economic arena. From this perspective it would then be profitable for the analyst to examine the conditions under which ethnic affirmation, transmuted into nationalism, can foster the set of conditions which enable the shunting of the development process into the fast track. Gellner (1987: 15) proposes that the prime requirement of a modern (as opposed to a traditional) society is a "realistic and well-based expectation of economic growth ... which, over time, allows everyone to become richer". This, Gellner argues, is the binding glue of the nation state which, he is at pains to point out, is not based on "natural" ethnic determinants, such as race, language, or religion, but instead actually requires a willed and forced amnesia of diverse and potentially infinitely divisible, and divisive, ethnic origins. The implication of this proposition is that a slowdown of the growth process, and worse, its reversal, sets up the conditions for the breakdown of the nation state, with the consequent deleterious feedback effects into the development and growth process. The second half of this century is littered with such cases, the most dramatic of which was the Soviet Union and its various satellites. Where the economic slowdown and the threat of recession appear, divisive ethnic affirmations often re-emerge to threaten the recently formed nation states. Even rapid growth rates, when accompanied by unchanging or even worsening income inequalities, can pose a significant danger to the stability of the nation state. The unpredictable economic success stories, on the other hand, consist of those nations, the newly industrialised countries, which managed to attain, against the expectations of orthodox economic theory, unprecedented growth rates in the economic well-being of their general citizenry. However the rapid set of political and societal crises engendered by the series of international financial crises starting with the collapse of the South East Asian economies in the nineties are a cautionary reminder of the fragility of the newly emerging nation states and the contingency of their stability and permanence on economic success.

The emphasis on growth allocates a central position to innovation within the evolution of the modern nation state and Gellner lists the prerequisites of sustainable innovative efforts as ultimately residing in the political freedom of the general populace to attain economic power within a context which is characterised by the absence of constitutional and institutional constraints on the drive to equality[1]. Thus, the various characteristics of systems of innovation can be useful as a taxonomic device to identify the positioning of specific nation states in the global drive to modernity. At the same time this approach would draw out those conditions and circumstances which could transform the nationalistic drive into an insurmountable obstacle to development or which may be a source of crisis in the future development path of those economies which have already managed the quantum leap to the fast growth track. Nationalism and especially a nationalism which has powered economic miracles can also engender xenophobia and a consequent rigidity which may prove

1 Gellner (1987: 15) points out that

> "Innovation ... presupposes unceasing occupational mobility, certainly as between generations, and often within single life-spans. [This] requires that members of such a society must be able to communicate in speech and writing, in a formal, precise, context-free manner - in other words they must be educated, literate and capable of orderly, standardised presentation of messages. ... Men cooperating on complex tasks involving high technology must be able to read, and to be able to read the same idiom. Men on the move between diverse jobs, in enterprises with distinct and independent hierarchies, can only cooperate without friction if the baseline assumption is one of rough equality: all men as such are equal, and ranking is *ad hoc* and task-specific. Inequality is temporarily vested in individuals, in virtue of wealth, role-occupancy, or achievement; it is not permanently vested in entire hereditary groups."

In the South African context none of these conditions could be attained within the framework of apartheid.

disastrous in the face of dramatically changing global conditions. However, the liabilities of "successful" nationalism and the newly defined national affirmation are not the main concern of this study. What is pertinent to the South African case is the examination of the preconditions for the leap into a high growth path rather than the consequences of those conditions once the leap has been made.

In the case of South Africa, apartheid, in a manner that was distinct from the segregation model that predated it, constitutes a particularly extreme example of an ethnic and nationalist agenda which determined the development path of the country and the evolution of its national system of innovation. This statement does not imply a one way causality, as liberal economic historians propose. That would be as simplistic as the alternative explanation stemming from the extreme Marxist revisionist position that apartheid was the product of the tension in the relationship of power between imperial (English) and indigenous (Afrikaner) ownership of the means of production and that its shape was the result of a resolution of this conflict through an intra-white redefinition of the ownership base of capital. One of the main defining features of apartheid, and of particular concern to the study of its particular imprint on the country's emerging system of innovation, was that the affirmation of national identity on the basis of racial dominance was enacted in a country where the oppressed constituted the vast majority of the country's population. It was not simply the case that the South African polity failed to attain the Gellner's pre-condition for the emergence of a modern nation state. Apartheid was premised on ethnic difference as its defining feature and was therefore by definition anti-modern within the post-colonial context. This uniquely reactionary aspect, the rejection of the requirements of modernity, constitutes the foremost defining characteristic of the system of innovation that emerged under apartheid, a feature that was largely absent in a pre-apartheid segregation period that could still be located within a colonial set of references.

As an ideology, apartheid, and racist tenets in general, could not possibly constitute the basis for a modernising economy. It did not provide a revolutionary construct of interconnected premises about human relationships on which a concerted and complex programme of political and economic policy could be formed. It had the one conservative, and at the time already reactionary, premise of racial superiority as its core "truth". In a way it was this very simplicity of its value underpinning that permitted a high degree of flexibility in the political and economic programmes which were devised to maintain racial dominance.[2] Simultaneously of course this also implied a lack of consistency in such programmes with frequent and often disruptive alterations in economic policy.

The development of the capitalist sector in South Africa's history also manifests a remarkable flexibility in its interaction with the state and certainly a high degree of durability.[3] Around the turn of the century the requirements of the mining sector determined the fundamental and traumatic reshaping of the rural-urban economic relationship for black workers and black peasantry, not only in South Africa but throughout a substantial portion of Southern Africa. Mining interests virtually dictated the various acts of legislation which affected the labour supply for this sector and it was only when the pursuit of these interests infringed on the existing privilege of white workers, that political tensions arose between state and capital. This tension was eased progressively under apartheid as the wave of successful Afrikaner nationalism motivated policies that effectively eroded the inherited correspondence between white ethnic groupings and the command over the means of production. The archaic nature of the system of innovation which emerged under apartheid does not therefore necessarily imply that it was not viable or that it was contrary

---

2 The move from an essentialist assumption of racial superiority which rested on faith and could not therefore be refuted through rational arguments to the model of "separate development" as designed by Verwoerd can be construed as a shift to rationality within the apartheid agenda. Separate development was premised on distinct cultural differences which could be cited as an evident observable fact which only required a convenient amnesia of the origins of such differences and of their attendant hierarchical ordering in state policy to be used as the empirical basis for the justification of apartheid on 'pragmatic' grounds.

3 Adam (1971, 1972) argues that the conflict between state and business was on issues of strategy, rather than on the "basic principles of white rule" (Adam, 1972:147). He identifies the basis of the accord between these two sectors as follows

> "Only economic strength enables the government to defy external pressure and to control the sounding board of internal opposition. The entrepreneurs on their part are aware that only the Apartheid order, and especially the prohibition of effective non-white unions, ensures a relatively cheap labour force. Any political advance of the non-whites would enable them to force economic concessions to the detriment of white profit rates. Thus far, Apartheid has not been an obstacle to the present boom, but one of its important prerequisites." (Adam, 1972:148)

Adam does point out that at the time of writing (1970) there was already evidence that the requirements of secondary industry for skilled workers was starting to pose a serious obstacle to future growth prospects.

to the interests of the principals of the apartheid regime, whether these were whites in general or white capital in particular.

The success of apartheid,[4] the fact that it was able to survive for over forty years in the post-colonial period, was due to two main related factors. In the first place there emerged during apartheid a convergence between the interests of the Afrikaner nationalist movement and the colonial and neo-colonial owners of the means of production within an inherited structural context. This convergence ratified the economic exploitation of the disenfranchised mass of the population. The association between intra-white ethnic divisions and the ownership of the means of production was thus effectively eroded and a new dominant correspondence between ethnicity and economic power emerged. Economic power became irrevocably determined by race within a resource rich economy where the beneficiaries of a predatory state constituted a small proportion of the population. This provides the source of the rapid development of specific technological core competencies within the context of a national system of innovation that in its entirety was ill suited for development. It was a system with some salient features that, within the post-apartheid context, still strongly inhibit the transformation of the country into a globally competitive modern economy. The second factor was the integration of South Africa's industrial structure within the western capitalist system and the concomitant political linkages in the cold war era. These linkages served to mitigate extensively the efforts of the international anti-apartheid movement to isolate the South African economy. Concurrently the overtly capitalist nature of the South African economy, especially within the context of the cold war period, served to reinforce the specific technological development paths which emerged within the unique setting of apartheid.

The focus on ethnicity as a basis for the study of South African economic development may perhaps be construed as a liberal argument for the distortions imposed by a racist "ideology" on the otherwise efficient functioning of markets. This would be a fallacious association emerging from the race-class debates which have dominated South African economic historiographies. Thus within the context of the debate between the liberal (race) account of the economic history of apartheid and the Marxist revisionist (class) account it may be thought that this stand falls within the liberal camp. However, this debate has long ceased to be

---

4 In this regard, Adam (1972: 16) argues that

> "The Apartheid system has been viewed as simply the most outdated relic of a dying colonialism, yet possibly it is one of the most advanced and effective patterns of rational, oligarchic domination."

reductionist and more complex assessments of the interrelation between apartheid and capitalism have emerged as a consequence. Class distinctions and class conflict have always been associated with ethnicity within the South African context. Throughout the pre-apartheid segregation period this was manifested in the struggle over the access to economic power between English and Afrikaans speaking white South Africans and provided the motive power behind Afrikaner nationalism. The highly effective strategy of the apartheid mandarins after the 1948 elections accomplished the successful resolution of this conflict through the democratisation of the access to economic power within the white population. This was achieved through the interpenetration of capital across ethnic divisions among whites which generated a realignment of the social division lines within that group.[5]

After that, and throughout South African post-war economic history until 1994, ethnicity as the effective qualifying basis for access to economic power was explicitly defined in racial terms. Thus, while the country's various subjugated populations became subsumed within the general category of 'non-whites', constitutionally excluded from equality with whites, the policy of separate development aimed at the fragmentation of opposition by the granting of differentiated sets of political and economic rights to different racial groupings within the disenfranchised majority. Apartheid was premised on difference and the core of its strategy, primarily through its education policies and its restrictions on economic and spatial mobility, was to deepen the correlation between ethnicity and economic power. This is the heritage that the country's first democratic government faced and still faces, an enduring effective differentiated access to economic power rooted in ethnicity. It constitutes

---

5 The transition from ethnicity to class as the primary intra-white differentiating criterion is identified by Adam (1972: 179), when he argues that

> "... the historical division between the English- and Afrikaans-speaking populace is rapidly being replaced by class contradictions between the two groups. As an entrepreneur, an Afrikaner has more in common with his English speaking counterparts than with his poorer fellow Nationalists. ... With their growing economic control over a relatively powerful industrial state, with increasing urbanization, and diminishing isolation ... the dominant interests of the political rulers have come to resemble those of the formerly hated industrialists."

The erosion of the identity defining prowess of ethnic differences with the liberalisation of the access to economic power across ethnic demarcation lines fulfils Gellner's condition for a modernising society. Of course, the oddity of the South African case is that this process occurred within a wider context which flouted, through legislation, this requirement.

the most formidable block to the attainment of Gellner's prerequisites for a modern economy and encapsulates the whole plethora of other, essentially secondary, obstacles to the development of the type of national system of innovation that is required for a rapid growth path. The success or failure of economic policy in the post-apartheid era, whether it can lay the foundation for another economic success story, will rest on its ability to redefine ethnic identity in terms of nationhood through an effective plan to redress the inherited inequalities of income, wealth and opportunities.

The particular history developed in this work contains little reference to actual inventions or innovations developed or adopted in South Africa since 1916. In that regard several thorough reviews already exist.[6] This recount concerns, rather, the evolution of the institutional context within which innovation occurred in South Africa. In the process it is hoped that it also opens up the space for some reflections on the nature of the context itself. This should contribute to a rigorous assessment of the continuities and rupture in the evolution of the South African system of innovation. In turn that assessment should enable the development of a new perspective on the assessment of post-apartheid economic policy formulation. The rest of this book is roughly divided into two sections, one theoretical and the other applied.

The following two chapters review the theoretical space within which this study is set. The first deals with the concept of national systems of innovation, its genealogy and domain. The main focus of this chapter is on extent of the areas of concern which are addressed by this term and the wide range of inter-related disciplines which are enlisted in its service. The definitional and operational breath of this concept which is seen by its adherents as analytically rich can also constitute a threat to its theoretical integrity, especially when compared to the clear delimiters which demarcate the neoclassical paradigm. This is one of the issues that will be addressed in this chapter.

The second chapter deals with alternative renditions of twentieth century South African economic history in order to anchor this study within the prevalent debates that have occurred in this field. Broadly speaking the debates fall in either of two camps. The first is based on the

---

6 Brown (1977) and Kros (1993) offer South African histories of technological innovations in a number of fields. Kingwill (1990) intersperses a history of the Council for Scientific and Industrial Research (CSIR) with that of technological achievements. Landgren (1989) details the history of technological development within the military sector. Kaplan (1990) and the series of Industrial Strategy Project reports published in 1995 offer a series of detailed industry studies which include detailed chronologies of the courses of the relevant technological changes.

assumption of racial domination as the core explanation of the course of South African history. Within this account, which has been largely appropriated by liberal economists, economic rationality is judged to have been perverted by the requirements of racial discrimination, especially during the apartheid era. The recurrent pronouncement of the liberal camp is that market rationality would not have tolerated the costs imposed by segregation and apartheid through "distortions" such as compartmentalised labour markets and international isolation and that in the absence of state coercion market functioning would have inevitably moved to eliminate the discrimination inherited from the colonial era. The second camp, which emerged on the basis of a rejection of the assumption of some optimally efficient market organisation whose rationality was perverted by the requirements of ethnic affirmation, deals more cogently, albeit in a theoretically restricted fashion, with the exercise of power. Marxist historians point out that the origins of state intervention in the labour markets arose from the requirements of the business (mining) sector and that until the seventies low labour costs generated exceedingly high profit rates. From the perspective of this approach the increasing pressure on the state to relax the constraints of job reservation and to provide better skills development programmes for black workers from the late seventies onwards constitute evidence that capitalism was the principal behind apartheid. The shift from a Keynesian to an overtly market friendly macroeconomic planning framework and the rift between the state and organised labour in the transition to democracy is also quoted as incontrovertible evidence of the dominating role that capitalist interests have played over the course of South Africa's history.

The attraction of the second approach lies in its counter-intuitive stance, its semi-deconstructive erosion of what appears to be the prime characteristic of apartheid and its antecedents. It does however share two characteristics with the opposing camp. The first is its claim to provide a totally deterministic explanation of the phenomenon. The second is its simplistic discourse on power. Power is seen as a means to an end, however that end is defined. Power is thus purely instrumental and it is denied the possibility to be an end in itself, to alter the nature of the agent who exercises power. The extreme versions of both the liberal explanation and the Marxist revisionist approach thus fail to open up the analysis to the consideration of the myriad idiosyncratic nontrivial manifestations that emerge in specific contexts. Technology and power are two closely interrelated discourses. Technology choices proceed from sets of power relations, within the scientific community, within factor and commodity markets, within the relationship between institutions which pertain to state and market and from the relationship between the local and the global economy. Technology endows power, almost inevitably in a non-equitable fashion, thus reinforcing or eroding current power relations in a multitude of relevant contexts. Moreover, the outcome of innovation is never fully predictable, especially with respect to the distribution of power.

The commonalities between the two accounts also imply that the association between the discourse on race and liberal account of economic history could be accidental. A Marxist historian could easily adopt a race position and bewail the fact that apartheid impeded the progression of the country's broad economic base from a pre-capitalist to the capitalist stage which would have set the basis for a socialist revolution[7]. However, if we move away from the glib race account of South African economic history and abandon the inherent presumption of the efficiency of untrammelled markets, the analysis of ethnic affirmation can provide the basis for the understanding of the development of South Africa's innovation system. Here we therefore open a new discourse based on the evolution of systems wherein the interplay of ethnicity, race and power within a specific historical context can enable the analyst to understand the nature and viability of the South African system of innovation.

The rest of this book deals with a selective narrative of the institutional development process within which the innovation base of the South African economy evolved. The choice of a starting point for any particular account is inevitably arbitrary to some extent. In the case of this particular history a convenient commencement date is 1916, the year that saw the first concerted attempt at the formulation of a national science and technology policy framework for South Africa. This emerged from the combination of a changing global context and the set of conditions peculiar to the South African political economy. This first science and technology plan emerged shortly after the formation of the Union of South Africa and during the First World War which heralded the end of colonialism and ushered in technology as the main determinant of the fortunes of nations.

---

7 In his essay "Nationalism and Marxism" Gellner argues that Marx was in favour of free trade since it would eliminate the obstacles posed by national boundaries and national identities to the emergence of a world wide proletarian consciousness. Gellner (1994: 13) quotes the *Communist Manifesto* as evidence of this position:

> "The nationality of the worker is neither French, nor English, nor German, it is *labor* ... His government is neither French, nor English, nor German, it is *capital*. His native air is neither French, nor German, nor English, it is *factory air*."

The history of the evolution of the South African innovation system over the period considered in this work is treated in three parts. The first period between 1916 and 1948 sees the state, with some interruptions, proceeding on a path which had the potential to eventually establish a science and technology base appropriate for a modernising economy. This section covers the period of segregation which preceded apartheid and concerns the internal conflicts which, along with a dependence on the policy making centre of the British Empire, determined the vagaries of policies on science and technology as well as industrial and trade policies which had a direct effect on the development of South Africa's system of innovation. The end of this period marks the failure of the state to resolve these contradictions and the fossilisation of the country's technology base in an evolutionary cul-de-sac. It is difficult to envisage the progression towards modernity, hesitant though it was that was initiated in the years preceding 1948 within the apartheid context which emerged after the victory of the National Party. This incompatibility is not proposed because authoritarian regimes and modernisation are assumed to be mutually exclusive, but because the specifically racist nature of domination within South Africa where the oppressed constituted the large majority of the labour force eventually posed insurmountable structural obstacles to the development of a modern economy.

The second part of this history, which covers the period of apartheid between 1948 and 1994, looks at the erosion of comprehensive national science, technology and innovation planning, in spite of accelerating drives on specific technological fronts. This occurred precisely because of the incompatibility between the requirements of a process of modernisation and the exigencies of apartheid. In the process the state relinquished the role of a prime mover and shaper of the evolutionary path of the nation's system of innovation. Some technology initiatives during apartheid were intensive and achieved successes but these initiatives were specific and their success was evaluated within the paradigm of apartheid. They were mostly driven by the perceived national strategic needs of an increasingly embattled regime and were key constituents of the rapidly growing military-industrial complex.[8] The abandonment of control, at a

8 Fine and Rustomjee (1996: 246) object to the validity of a "military-industrial complex" as an explanatory framework for the analysis of the power relations underlying South Africa's industrial development under apartheid on the basis that "the existence of security and industrial imperatives do not in themselves explain the extent and composition of the defence industry. Rather, the development of the defence ministry has been intimately related to the interests and evolution of the [minerals-energy complex]". I do not use the notion of a military-industrial

certain aggregate level, over this component of a nation's development path may seem incompatible with a regime which was in the process of laying down the details of the complex edifice of grand and petty apartheid and which had no reservations about imposing extreme control measures over the populace in the process. This is the question that will be explored throughout this section.

The third part of the history starts off with the publication of the White Paper on Science and Technology in 1996, in order to locate it within a set of oppositions and continuities *vis-à-vis* this history. The analysis of the evolution of the South African system of innovation since the demise of apartheid is predicated on the assumption that over time structures develop a momentum and that the cultures which inform policy endure, especially when divested of opprobrious racist connotations. In this part the role assigned to science, technology and innovation policy is examined within the context of the rapidly changing nature of the state's macroeconomic planning vision and the determinants of that change.

The White Paper of 1996 was drafted shortly after the collapse of apartheid and within a global context which, in the aftermath of the collapse of the Soviet Union, was in a process of radical flux and redefinition. The White Paper is itself the resultant of a wider economic policy discourse whose identification was, and still is, is the source of a current highly acrimonious debate. In the final part of this work the implications of this study for the future of South Africa's innovation system are discussed. The underlying argument presented here is that the South African economic system was grievously unprepared for the world into which it emerged from apartheid and that the shock of the transition in conjunction with the policy options that were adopted have been damaging for the prospects of creating a viable system of innovation suited to the country's development requirements.

This discussion is located within a global context especially with regard to the increasing empirical irrelevance of the concept of a specifically "national" system of innovation. In this section the concept of regional (supra-national) innovation systems is used to explore the possible evolution paths that the South African system faces in a global context which is marked by the emergence of economic blocs. South

complex as the overriding explanation of the shape of the industrialisation process but rather as arising from the recognition that the military imperatives of an increasingly embattled and isolated apartheid regime did stimulate specific patterns of investment and innovation, no doubt generating unprecedented rent seeking opportunities for established capitalist interests which would otherwise not have occurred in the process.

Africa's economic fortunes have become crucial to the future of sub-Saharan Africa and the relationship has become reciprocal.

As a study of twentieth century South African economic history this particular exercise is at some levels a "top down" narrative. State policy on science, technology and innovation was too rarefied an area, given the glaring inequities and the overt and extreme nature of the political and economic oppression which were to be combated, to become a significant focus of the liberation struggle. It becomes therefore a history of the oppressor, but even then it is a history rendered more in terms of an account of what is ignored and omitted and which gains meaning within the context in which it is set. In contrast to the plethora of racist policy formulation affecting the rights to work, to education, to freedoms of speech, association and habitation, there were no overtly "apartheid" science, technology and innovation policies. In fact if such policies, both formal and implicit, that were enacted in South Africa before the advent of democracy were to be de-contextualised the uninformed reader would find it difficult to discern the country of origin, except to conclude that it was rich in mineral resources and had a small highly skilled population. Even the level of R&D spending on defence would not raise eyebrows since the proportion of the total defence budget that was allocated to R&D fell in the same category as a number of medium sized economies across the world[9]. It is this very rift between official policy and the realities of the conditions to which it was meant to apply that constitutes the defining characteristic of planning in this field and requires the conceptual breath of a system of innovation analysis to capture the essence of science and technology planning within the South African context.

The apparent innocuousness of this particular part of the apartheid heritage renders it perhaps more problematic in the debates on post-apartheid policies for reconstruction and development. Generally speaking, the development of the country's system of innovation was affected, but not fundamentally addressed, by the successful outcome of the liberation struggle. The low priority placed on science and technology policy formulation in particular and on policies to enrich the country's system of innovation in general by its first democratic government, in contrast to policies adopted by newly industrialised economies, is partially

9 Landgren (1989: 51) points out that

> "...(b)y 1983, two per cent of the South African defence budget was spent on research and development. This is approximately the same level of spending as in Canada, Switzerland, Italy, Japan and Norway ... in 1971 ... South Africa was on par with such countries as Spain, Portugal and Greece as to the proportion of GNP spent on R&D."

a heritage of the history that is recounted in this study. It is also symptomatic of the tenacity of the ubiquitous structure which evolved since 1948 and which has successfully reproduced itself and the power relations that it serves.

PART 1:

THEORY

CHAPTER ONE

NATIONAL SYSTEMS OF INNOVATION

Both theoretical and empirical analyses within the innovation system approach have, until relatively recently, lain largely on the fringes of the conventional language of economics. As a methodological tongue such work was not a dialect, as the language of development economics had become in the eighties, but a language of revolt that revisited the foundational arguments of classical economics. By the early nineties the conditions for a Kuhnian paradigm shift in the economic analysis of growth and development seemed to be in place. The body of evidence of the failure of mainstream economic theory to explain or predict economic growth and development paths had become overwhelming and the new approach was being advocated by theoreticians who carried weight within the discipline. And indeed the 1990s was the decade that saw the term "National Systems of Innovation" enter the documents of policy makers on both national and international fora.

The origin of the concept of national systems of innovation lies in the work of the evolutionary school[1] which, in the late twentieth century, owed a significant resurgence to the growing scepticism regarding the adequacy of the neoclassical account to explain the nature, sources and effects of economic change (Hodgson, 2007). Since the neoclassical paradigm constituted the dominating discourse in post-war economic theory, any other discourse which sought to locate itself within the discipline was perforce constituted as an alternative and was necessarily anchored in the role of a counter discourse. In the case of innovation this was particularly unfortunate in its wastefulness since neoclassical theory was never designed to account for technological change, let alone

1 The concept of a national system of innovation can be traced back to List as the basis of his counter argument to Adam Smith's position on free trade. In the late twentieth century its revival was first articulated specifically by Lundvall (1992), but its antecedents are diffused across time and authors. Nelson (1993) locates its origin in the contributions of a number of authors in Dosi et al. (1988). See also Freeman (1991).

innovation, except in a most cursory and highly stylised fashion. In her comprehensive survey of game-theoretic models covering the timing of research activity, the licensing of innovations and their adoption and diffusion, Reinganum (1989) concludes that such models are highly stylised and counterfactual[2]. The broadening of the definition of innovation beyond technological change to cover most of the sources of change weakened the suitability of neoclassical economics to address dynamic systems even further.

Generally, within the neoclassical analytical framework technology and technological rationality are treated as universally applicable and as equally available across time and space. When combined with the assumptions of a common rationality and optimising behaviour, this articulation implies that while technological specifications differ across industries there is a necessary uniformity of technology across geographical and institutional boundaries. Until relatively recently, technology and technological change were treated as exogenous to the neoclassical general equilibrium model and optimisation models in general. The effects of technological change in neoclassical growth models were represented by the classification of such changes as labour-biased, capital-biased or neutral. However, the increased consciousness of the role of technology in economic growth led to attempts to endogenise technological change, especially in the analysis of firm behaviour. These attempts have however been severely constrained by the assumption of uniformity in neoclassical analysis which extends to institutions and institutional networks across contexts. Without this assumption, the predictive and prescriptive prowess stemming from the internal logic of the neoclassical approach would be severely compromised. It does however severely impair the explanatory power of the paradigm with respect to the analysis of dynamics in general and of innovation in particular.

In contrast, evolutionary analyses of innovation focus on contextual contingencies as a crucial determinant of the development of innovation and this is the core assumption that gave rise to the concept of national systems of innovation. In the process, such analyses shift the focus of the enquiry to include specificities, thus significantly reducing the capacity for

2 Reinganum (1989: 905) states categorically that the game-theoretic model has

> "...not had a significant impact on the applied literature in industrial organisation; its usefulness for policy purposes should also be considered limited. For these purposes, one needs a predictive model which encompasses the full range of firm, industry and innovation characteristics."

generalisations, be they at the analytical or at the prescriptive level. Simpson (1995:16) identifies the two common general features of technology as "the separation of means and ends" and "the rationalization of the means for the efficient procurement of the ends", while grouping the contextually contingent attributes as those which are "situated within a particular institutional framework of a particular set of social arrangements". The consequence of this shift in focus on the scope of the evolutionary approach is defined succinctly by Dosi (1991: 354) when he says that

> "...evolutionary theories attempt to model economic systems rich in positive feedbacks (that is, self-reinforcing mechanisms such as dynamic increasing returns in innovation). Relatedly, such systems tend to exhibit non-linear dynamics and multiple dynamic paths, *also dependent on their history*." (emphasis added)

Evolutionary theorists have therefore set themselves a double-pronged research agenda, with an often uneasy tension between the focus on specific cases of national development and the imperative to identify some underlying common principles governing the mutation of various innovation systems over time. The search for commonalities is required particularly for prescriptive purposes, but is prejudiced by the fundamental assumption of contingency which renders cross-national correspondences problematic.

The core differences between the evolutionary and the neoclassical accounts of the economy stem from the different conceptions of the type of information on which various economic agents base their allocation decisions. The radically different definitions of information in the two accounts determine the respective definitions of economic agents, such as consumers and producers, which are consequently virtually unrecognisable as we move from one paradigm to the other. The neoclassical economic agent makes allocation decisions on the basis of full and perfect information; future events also fall into this definition by assigning probability values to different possible outcomes. This assumption is necessary for the derivation of equilibria. Marginalist analysis which constitutes the all pervasive optimisation tool in neoclassical economics would be impossible without the assumption of continuous constraint and objectives set functions, and these in turn depend critically on the assumption of full and perfect information. Evolutionary theory, on the other hand, assumes ignorance as a permanent and non-trivial feature of the information sets within which economic agents operate. Moreover, ignorance is assumed to grow as the planning horizon of economic agents extends into the future. It is this assumption that makes evolutionary theory so much more suitable for the analysis of economic dynamics. Given that static analysis has become increasingly irrelevant, both empirically and theoretically, evolutionary theory has emerged as the as the dominant paradigm, in terms of explanatory prowess.

The assumption of ignorance as an indelible property of the decision space brings in the issues of the imperfect mobility of knowledge, knowledge property rights and tacit knowledge. Together these aspects allow for the introduction of imperfectly mobile knowledge and of specificity into economic analysis. While knowledge property rights allow for the consideration of knowledge as a tradable commodity, tacit knowledge, which refers to that component of the stock of knowledge which cannot be codified,[3] entrenches the specificity of systems as a permanent defining feature. Tacit knowledge lays the theoretical foundation for the concept of core competencies and competitive advantage.[4] Core competencies which derive from technological capabilities are seen as historically determined and, at least partially, unique to specific systems.

Technological capabilities can be broadly defined as the capacity to innovate and utilise innovations. Nelson (1990a) identifies the two components of this capacity on the basis of the roots of the word technology - the *techni* and the *logi*, the mastery of the "how" and the "why" of a technology. Each of these components is crucial both in the development of new technology and in determining the absorptive capacity for existing technology. However, while the latter enables the adoption of techniques and new production methods in the short term, the development of technological capabilities requires the enhancement of the understanding of the principles underlying new processes. Pietrobelli (1994) and Lall and Latsch (1996) define technological capabilities in terms of requirements, i.e. the pool of skills that are needed to utilise technology efficiently. The range of skills that are considered is wide,

---

3 Marglin (1990b) calls this type of knowledge *technic*, i.e. deriving from *techne*. He contrasts this with his definition of *epistemic* knowledge, i.e. theoretical, fully codified knowledge. Freeman (1991: 502-503) stresses the importance of tacit knowledge in the process of technological acquisition:

> "It is now very generally recognised that in the technology accumulation process within firms and other organisations, tacit knowledge is often more important than codified formal specifications, blue-prints, etc."

4 See Nelson (1991) on his discussion of tacit knowledge as the explanation for variability among firms within the same market.

comprising both technical and organisational capabilities, and pertain to different levels of aggregation from the firm to the broadest macroeconomic level. Technological capabilities are, of course, a stock variable. The flow counterpart is the learning process (see Archibugi and Lundvall, 2002) which again is context specific and constitutes the main determinant of the competitive advantage of firms and of systems.

The incorporation of tacit knowledge, technological capabilities and core competencies in the analysis of economic systems has therefore led to a growing appreciation that the idiosyncrasies of the diverse economic histories of nations have progressively precluded easy generalisations and hence generalised prescriptions. The concept of a national system of innovation is founded on the premise that the prime characteristic of technological capabilities is that they are essentially local. This is due to the incorporation of the histories of the structures which generate technological capabilities, thus rendering systems of innovation specific to time and place. In consequence, the shape and nature of technological capabilities may be expected to differ significantly across nations and through the histories of nations. The analysis of national systems of innovation is thus an attempt to map out the web of complex institutional relationships that constitute and determine the context within which a nation's "stock" of technological capabilities and the consequent nodes of core competencies are shaped. Nelson (1993) circumscribes the concept of national systems of innovation by defining the domains of each of the three components of the term and it here that a degree of definitional confusion becomes possible. The concept of innovation itself is amenable to a wide range of definitions from the narrow sense of science and technology to any alteration of economic relations. The definition of those institutions that may be incorporated into the system may also vary dramatically in its inclusiveness in a manner that is to some degree related to the particular definition of innovation that is adopted. Finally, the relevance of the nation state as the delimiter of a system of innovation has been questioned repeatedly. The various combinations of the definitions of these three sets of parameters give rise to a number of possible, and significantly different, conceptualisations of national systems of innovation.

Moreover, in terms of the application of the concept, it is important to emphasise the obvious point that the analysis of national systems of innovation bears two distinct, albeit strongly related, aspects - the taxonomic and the historical. Taxonomies are constructed in order to provide an intelligible "snapshot" of a specific national system. Those studies which emphasise a taxonomic approach are especially useful for comparative purposes. Historical analyses would be more pertinent for an understanding of a specific system and an assessment of possible future evolution paths for that system. The two approaches are, of course, not mutually exclusive. A taxonomy which has no reference to the evolution of particular systems would be a woefully sterile analytical device while a historical analysis which ignored commonly used definitions and measures would be so specific as to divest itself of a (global) context wherein it can become legible.

In the construction of a taxonomy pertinent to a national system of innovation the different categories and indicators which are developed should, as far as possible, be applicable to different national systems, thus enabling comparative analyses. Taxonomies are, however, dependent on how systems are construed, specifically with respect to degree of focus that is adopted. This defines the relative weighting assigned to the various parameters that are eligible for consideration. One can think of sets and subsets of parameters, with the narrowest addressing specifically those activities which are directly related to innovation and broader ones which contain most of the determinants of economic activity and the specific economy's development path.

Measuring innovation

The concept of innovation can cover a vast set of changes which can range from the trivial to those which alter the very foundations of economic, social and political organisation. In most of the literature on innovation the focus is on technology. In the evolutionary tradition, however, innovation can be extended to incorporate all sources of economic change. Furthermore, if economic behaviour is analysed from the perspective of political economy, change and the sources of change can be extended to cover social, political and organisational change. This is enabled by the wide definition of institutions[5] which is discussed further down in this chapter. Innovation in its broadest definition can feasibly be accepted as the definitive identification of human economic behaviour. Even in the most static of contexts economic activity would be based on the utilisation of a stock of knowledge that is the result of past investments

5 North (1990) defines institutions as "...the rules of the game in society ...the humanly devised constraints that shape human interaction." (p. 3) and to "...include any form of constraint that human beings devise to shape human interaction. They can be ...formal constraints - such as rules that human beings devise - and ...informal constraints - such as conventions and codes of behaviour. Institutions may be created ...or they may simply evolve over time" (p. 4).

in learning, invention, adaptation and absorption. Should this wider definition of innovation be adopted, it can provide the basis for a general theory of economics.

From the perspective of this wider definition of innovation any change that is novel within a specific context would be termed innovative. This would apply to both technological and institutional changes which are seen as resulting in a better allocation of resources, however that is defined. This context specificity means that a new product or process is innovative regardless of its origin, as long as it represents a practice which had hitherto been unknown or unutilised within the specific context under consideration. In this case the term "innovation" includes the ability to adopt (and adapt) an existing body of knowledge to a new context as well as the invention of new technologies or organisational modes.[6] Freeman and Perez (1988) propose a taxonomy of innovations consisting of four categories. These are (a) incremental innovations which tend to occur continuously, often outside the ambit of formal R&D structures, (b) radical innovations which are discrete breakthroughs resulting from formal goal-oriented R&D programmes, (c) changes in the prevalent "technology system" which affect several related sectors and require a new configuration of coordination among various firms across sectors; these are similar to Schumpeter's "constellation" of innovations and to systems development as discussed in Nelson (1993), and (d) "techno-economic paradigm" shifts,[7] which are the result of a change in technology that is so fundamental that all sectors of the economy are affected.

The choice of indicators which are used to assess the incidence of innovative activity depends on the manner in which such activity is defined. As discussed above, this is informed by alternative definitions of

---

6 Schumpeter (1954) adopted the broader evolutionary approach to innovation when he defined innovations as any alteration by an economic agent to the context within which it operates, when stating that

> "(t)he fundamental impulse that sets and keeps the capitalist engine in motion comes from the new consumers' goods, the new methods of production or transportation, the new markets, the new forms of industrial organisation that capitalist enterprise creates." (p. 83)

7 Freeman and Perez (1988) substitute the term "techno-economic paradigm" for Dosi's "technological paradigm", which owes its origin to Kuhn's (1970a) formulation, to shift the emphasis away from the purely scientific realm to a consideration of those technological paradigms whose effects extend throughout the economy. Perez (1988) defines a techno-economic paradigm as "... an interrelated system based on a set of shared principles" which forms the "... 'common sense' of engineers, managers and investors ... a(n) ideal model for best productive and most profitable practice." (p.86)

technology arising from the two main contending schools in this area. Since Solow's (1956) claimed discovery that total factor productivity growth which he ascribed to technological change "accounted" for the greater portion of American economic growth, neoclassical theorists have tried to render technological change endogenous to the paradigm.[8] Given the requirement within the neoclassical tradition for models to be translated into stochastic specifications amenable to econometric testing, economists from this school required a quantitative measure to represent this ephemeral but pervasive variable which had come to be accepted as the overwhelmingly significant determinant of the economic fortunes of nations.

The most commonly used measures of innovative activity are restricted to technical change and are provided by R&D statistics. These data are attractive because they permit apparently easily comparable measures between countries and sectors and over time. However, a number of serious objections have been advanced against a simplistic application of R&D statistics. Their employment should therefore be qualified and, where necessary and possible, complemented by other data. It is worthwhile to discuss the main qualifications of R&D data since in the process alternative and supplementary measures can be explored and through these discussions a measurement classification can be developed.

R&D statistics generally tend to under-report actual innovative activity and distort its spread across sectors. In the first place, since not all firms report expenditures on R&D, the sample choice cannot be assumed to be representative. Secondly, innovations can and do occur outside formal R&D departments. Thus the estimated relationships in empirical analyses, especially where econometric techniques are used, are often largely relevant to the largest firms which contain formally organised R&D

8 The two areas where these efforts were most pronounced were the analysis of the firm's decision making (optimisation) mechanism and the refinement of total factor productivity analysis through the extension of the production function to include technology. In both cases there are serious theoretical and logical shortcomings. As argued above the full information requirement of constrained optimisation analysis denudes the analysis of technological change from its crucial characteristic, i.e. that it concerns the less than fully known or predictable. In the case of the introduction of a variable representing technology as an input on the right hand side of the production function equation, the logical basis of the neoclassical production function itself is violated since technology is the fabric that defines and determines production relations and cannot therefore be included as a variable. Within the neoclassical formulation, technological change requires a re-specification of the production function, a redrawing of the isoquant map, and cannot therefore itself constitute a part of the function or the map.

departments. Moreover, the incentives to provide data on R&D expenditure differ, often being most pronounced in industrialised economies. This feature can thus render inter-country comparisons of innovative activity based on R&D data problematic.

Other input measures can be added to R&D expenditure figures in order to capture better the incidence of innovative activity and the extent of technological capabilities. In the process the focus shifts from activities to capacity and capabilities. The employment of scientists and engineers is often used as an alternative indicator of the capacity to engage in R&D. This variable may also capture that part of innovative activity which is undertaken outside formal R&D programmes. A general measure of the skills profile of the labour force can be used to assess the capacity for implementing new technology on the shop floor. This, in turn, has implications for general and technical education policy which determines the human capital stock of the labour force and has a direct impact on the absorptive capacity for new technology.

One of the more serious objections to the use of R&D expenditures and statistics on the employment of scientists and engineers is that they measure the inputs of innovative activity and, unless knowledge is available regarding the "productivity" of R&D programmes, little can be inferred regarding the contribution of R&D expenditures to "knowledge stocks". Griliches (1979, 1980a, 1980b) and Griliches and Lichtenberg (1984) argue that the relevant decision variable for the firm undertaking R&D is the accumulated stock of knowledge. This is the factor whose services enter the firm's production function and R&D activity is only a partial determinant of it. Unlike most other forms of capital, however, the stock of R&D capital is liable to serious measurement problems since it is essentially "unobservable". For one thing, the depreciation rate associated with the stock of knowledge is difficult to estimate. Pakes and Schankerman (1984) argue that the depreciation rate relevant to the stock of knowledge is considerably faster than that of physical capital because of difficulties of excluding non-payers from the benefits of knowledge. Moreover, current R&D activity adds to the stock of knowledge only after a time lag. Griliches (1980b) proposes that a further time lag between the increment in the stock of knowledge and its translation into a successful market innovation should be included. The length of this lag varies widely according to the specific definition of knowledge that is adopted and the type of R&D that is undertaken. A further determinant of the lag is the extent of the complementary managerial functions that are required to market and implement the innovation.

A further measure of the innovation potential of specific industries is provided by a decomposition of R&D expenditure. Gross R&D measures obscure the high degrees of heterogeneity of both R&D activity and the resulting contributions to the stock of knowledge. A clear distinction needs to be made between the stages of R&D (basic research, applied research and development)[9] and between the goals of R&D programmes (product and process innovations).[10] Data on the mix of R&D activity - basic research, applied research and development - within a particular industry can provide an indication of the depth of the science base of that industry and can thus be used to chart the "innovation profiles" of specific industries from the input side[11].

One of the functions of innovation profiles is to assess the development potential for technology, or technological opportunity. Within the context of the neoclassical theory of production, technological opportunity may be seen as the technology governing the "technology production function". Rosenberg (1976) broadly defined technological opportunity in a manner based on the criterion proposed by Phillips (1966) for the potential for product differentiation in the following manner:

> "The productivity of R&D activity depends in part on the firm's ability to develop and use new innovations. Some industries, given the characteristics of their products, tend to encourage rapid technological change such as the introduction of new products which are significantly different from the previous product mix." (p. 105)

---

9 While the term "stages" may imply chronological linearity, it is now recognised that any one of the "stages" may precede others; technological breakthroughs often lead eventual expansions in scientific frontiers.

10 Mansfield (1984) articulates the implications of this deficiency as follows:

> "For both analytical and policy purposes, the total R&D figures are hard to interpret because they include such a heterogeneous mixture of activities. Basic research and applied research are mixed up with development. Long-term projects are mixed up with short-term projects. Projects aimed at small product and process improvements are mixed up with projects aimed at major new processes and products. Process R&D is mixed up with product R&D. To answer many important analytical and policy questions, it is essential to disaggregate R&D." (p. 128)

11 The interpretative significance of this classification is now less clear with the abandonment of the assumption of the linear progression from basic to applied research to development. The complex interrelationships among the various classes of R&D activity with numerous feedback mechanisms and uncertain directions of progression that are now accepted render the simple classification of R&D less meaningful to the analyst.

The state of science underlying specific technologies thus becomes a major determinant of technological opportunity. Jaffe (1986) defines technological opportunity as the combination of the

> "...exogenous variations in the cost and difficulty of innovation in different technological areas. These variations may be due to intrinsic characteristics of the technology, or they may be due to the state of exogenous scientific knowledge at a particular point in time." (p. 984)

Most approaches adopt the hypothesis that a strong scientific base reduces the cost of innovation. If R&D is defined as a search process in problem solving, then a strong science base narrows the search scope along a given research trajectory, thus reducing cost. The exploration of the implications of this definition of technological opportunities was pioneered by Scherer (1967a) who classified industries on the basis of the strength of their association with specific scientific fields. Although crude, this technique proved highly powerful in explaining inter-industry variances in innovative activity (measured in terms of patenting activity).[12] Nelson (1982) defines knowledge as "capability to focus search efficiently" (p. 455) and the basic research which produces it as the activity which "enhances the productivity of applied research and development" (p. 465). Nelson (1959) was among the first to define the outstanding characteristic of basic scientific research - its high content of external economies - and to advocate the ensuing policy implications. He argued that the low level of appropriability of this type of research necessitated extensive public support of the activity. This policy implication was set well within the value framework of a capitalist system. If left to the private sector the socially desirable level of basic scientific research would only be attained in a market structure composed of " large firms with a wide technological base, with virtual monopolies in several markets" (p. 305) - the antithesis of the competitive economy. Only under such a market organisation would the external economies inherent in basic research be internalised and the private rate of return approach the social one. This is effectively a re-statement of the Schumpeterian postulate.

An alternative to the input measure is provided by an industry (product) classification system. Since industries differ dramatically in their science and technology base, the sectoral mix of specific economies can be used as an indicator of the "innovation potential and impact" of systems. There are a number of ways whereby an innovation profile of

---

12 See Levin et al. (1987) on the derivation and measurement of variables which are commonly used to estimate technological opportunity within an industry.

specific industries can be constructed. The one adopted by Nelson (1993) provides a classification of industry outputs which serves to assess the technological ripple effects of innovations through an estimation of the nature and extent of inter-industry linkages. Eventually, these estimates should enable an evaluation of the spread of technology multipliers in an economy. This enables a ranking of product groups on the basis of their spillover effects across the economy. From this perspective products can be classified as complex systems products, discrete products and bulk commodities. The development of complex systems requires a large coordination role drawing in different agents from components and materials production and systems design. The specific nature of the coordination nexus (market functioning, sub-contracting, government facilitation, etc.) is one of the comparative parameters. Once introduced, the new product is subject to a long process of improvements based on feedbacks from producers and users. In the case of discrete product development, once the product is introduced there is no room for product improvement. The strategic leeway is then usually provided by the discovery of new uses for the product. The development of the product requires interaction with process equipment suppliers rather than input suppliers. It is often the innovation of process equipment required to produce the new product that is the subject of continuous innovation, rather than the product itself. In the case of bulk commodities the specifications of the product are usually unalterable. Here the scope of innovation lies almost entirely within the equipment and input suppliers with the aim of producing the same product at a lower cost.

Given that knowledge usually contains a high public good component, the spillovers of knowledge generated by other agencies offer a significant contribution to R&D capital. Since direct R&D measures exclude spillovers as a source of technology, Palda (1986) argued that a realistic indicator of technological intensity cannot be based simply on in-house research activity but should incorporate spillovers of technology through backward linkages and through government agencies and universities, as well as research by foreign affiliates. No explicit payment is made for this source of new knowledge but its utilisation depends on the absorptive capacity of the performer, which in turn depends partly on the level of in-house R&D activity.[13] Sources of spillovers would include other firms (both within the same industry and from other industries), non-market

13 Nelson (1990b: 73) points out that

> "(a)n industrial R&D laboratory tied to a firm is both a source of new technology for that firm and a vehicle through which that firm stays up with advances in technology made elsewhere."

agents such as government institutions and tertiary education institutions, and transnational information flows. The impact of these various sources of in-coming knowledge is not easily amenable to generalisation or to any accurate estimation. R&D spillovers are usually estimated by an examination of input-output coefficients, which, again, is an input measure. Since knowledge *per se* cannot be directly measured, spillovers of new knowledge are represented by the research intensity incidence of intra-industry and inter-industry linkages.

The consideration of technological spillovers also raises the issue of appropriability. The appropriation of the returns from an innovation by the innovator is rendered difficult by the ease with which the knowledge embodied in new processes, but especially in new products, may be copied or imitated. The possible means of securing appropriability include patents, some specific characteristics of the innovation which make it expensive to copy and investment in complementary activities, such as marketing, sales effort and customer service. A further incentive effect may be due to the presence of complementarities in R&D activity. In such cases, where the competitive aspect of research activity is not so pronounced, the absorption of outside knowledge would exert a positive effect on the productivity of the recipient's R&D.

One major problem in the empirical analysis of the issues of technological spillovers and appropriability is posed by the fact that the same measure can represent both phenomena. Thus, while extra-industry spillovers tend to enhance technological opportunity within an industry, the effect of intra-industry spillovers is ambiguous, since they may reduce the incentive to engage in R&D by reducing the ability to appropriate the returns on innovative activity. A low level of appropriability might therefore make it worthwhile for the average firm to let others bear the (often high) initial costs of exploratory research and then to imitate the resulting innovation. The phenomenon of intra-industry spillovers is therefore indissolubly bound with that of appropriability, each inducing contradictory effects. Empirical analyses in this area largely differ in terms of how the relationship between the two phenomena is specified and the in terms of the assessment of the relative weights that are assigned to each. A major concern in both theoretical and empirical analyses in this issue is the "efficiency effect" of spillovers - their net effect on R&D spending. Cohen and Levinthal (1989) specify the effects of spillovers on the recipient firm's R&D such that two countervailing forces are present. The first is the standard (Nelson, 1959 and Arrow, 1962) argument that an increase in spillovers diminishes appropriability and hence the incentive to innovate. The second arises from the recognition that the absorption of technological spillovers cannot be treated as costless to the receiving agency, in the same manner as most other externalities. Cohen and Levinthal (1989) noted that the exploitation of knowledge spillovers is contingent on the level of own R&D activity. Thus increased spillovers provide the firm with an incentive to spend on R&D in order to increase the absorption rate and capacity. This effect is applicable to both extra-industry and intra-industry spillovers.

Spence (1984) first provided a badly needed simplification in the empirical treatment of spillovers by adopting Lancaster's (1966) conceptualisation of consumable goods and services as a bundle of inputs into the consumer's "utility production function" at a cost. This simplification also enabled researchers to treat both product and process innovations as cost-reducing activities. In this vein Bernstein (1988, 1989) and Bernstein and Nadiri (1988, 1989) include the R&D capital of other firms as a determinant of the cost functions of the recipient. While Bernstein, and Bernstein and Nadiri, represent the spill-over effect by the unweighted sum of other firms' R&D, Jaffe (1986), loosely following Griliches (1979), weights other firms' R&D by a "measure of proximity" to the receiving firm, based on a distribution of patents across patent categories to determine the "technological position" of firms. A similar use of patent statistics had been adopted earlier by Scherer (1982) in the construction of an inter-industry technology flow matrix for the purpose of estimating the impact of R&D on productivity. Goto and Suzuki (1989) measure spillovers as R&D expenditure of other industries weighted by a measure of their capital goods flows to the receiving industry. Scerri (1993) measures technological spillovers by combining the inverse coefficients table in the input-output tables (showing the total requirements, direct and indirect, per rand of delivery to final demand) with data on real R&D expenditures.

Finally, local R&D statistics fail to capture technology transfers within multinational corporations, across national borders. Mansfield (1984) argued that in the case of multinational corporations, R&D activity should be disaggregated into that component undertaken locally and R&D carried out in overseas branches. Foreign direct investment statistics can be used to assess the mix of national and trans-national ownership. This information can be used as a rough proxy measure of the incidence and interface of trans-national technology with the local innovation system and the degree of openness of an economy to foreign direct investment and intra-firm technology transfers.

The OECD and a number of countries, as well as other country blocs, now regularly conduct innovation surveys which seek to capture a broader definition of innovation than that reflected by unqualified R&D statistics. It does however seem implausible that neoclassical methodology, however unsuited it may be to the analysis of innovation and of economic change, would have been displaced from what is rapidly becoming the central concern of economics in such a short time span. Indeed the methodology underlying the OECD Innovation Surveys that started in the nineties is so rooted in the predicate set of neoclassical economics (Scerri 2006a and 2006b) as to violate the fundamental premises of the new approach. The main flaw of such surveys, especially with regard to comparative analysis is that they tend to assume a common institutional context for innovation.

The assessment of the relevance of any specific innovation survey depends on an examination of its emphases, its inclusions and its omissions. These are partially determined by the degrees of generality and specificity of the survey. They also reflect a particular definition of systems of innovation as well as the core characteristics of the systems that meant to be covered by a specific survey. Thus, for example, the core questionnaire of the Eurostat Third Community Innovation Survey (CIS III) which follows the *Oslo Manual*,[14] surveys only business enterprises. This choice of respondents is based on the standard assumption that firms are the main source of innovation and that the role of the state is that of a legislator. However, this assumption is contingent on the economic context for its legitimacy. It can be assumed to be most valid in the case of developed industrialised economies with a developed market for innovations, where an efficient infrastructure for innovative activity can be safely assumed. The role of the state in industrialising economies should be quite different. In developing economies the role of the state should be to set up appropriate structures for the development of the type of national system of innovation which is most suited for development[15]; ironically, of course, in most cases the presence of the state is often significantly more

---

14 The CIS III covers basic information on the firm, labour skills, information on type, sources and effects of innovations, the funding of innovation, the strategic objectives of innovation, cooperation in innovation, sources of information, perceived bottlenecks to innovation, information on innovations that have been generated, patenting activity, expenditure on innovations, organisational changes related to innovation programmes, and state support for innovation programmes.

15 A report (Ogbu et al., 1995) quoted in the IDRC (1999: 16) study identifies a "..need for the state to display a more interventionist role in the underdeveloped countries than in the industrialised ones. Implicitly what is being argued for is a set of national systems of innovation with the state actively laying down the regulatory, physical, human and social infrastructure."

notable in the market for innovations in developed industrialised economies than it is in developing economies.

In the Eurostat survey a good part of the questionnaire addresses business perceptions about a number of aspects of the national system of innovation. Again, the significance of business perceptions differs widely across countries that are in different stages of development. We can assume that the private sector in a mature economy with a relatively stable institutional framework and an established history of innovation is intimately aware of the functioning, deficiencies and requirements of the national system of innovation. In the case of developing economies business perceptions are less of a reliable reflection of the nature and prospects of the country's system of innovation. At best, a survey of such perceptions may be useful in assessing the probable reception of policy directives by the private sector. This one factor, the implicit assumption of a common underlying relationship between the private sector, the state and the national system of innovation is required for the assumption of a continuous range within which any innovation system can be placed. It is however an invalid assumption and its adoption for comparative purposes may be fundamentally misleading both for analysts and for policy makers. This problem can be addressed through an ongoing questioning of the underlying assumptions of the various innovation surveys. Through this the delimiters of the applicability and the explanatory value of specific surveys can be calibrated to ensure various degrees of relevance to specific cases.

This brief discussion of the measures of innovation should give some indication of the complexity of the phenomenon in question, even when the definition of innovation is restricted to technology. The more generally applicable the indicators that are sought, the less precise they tend to be in their definition of what they are supposed to measure. This is largely due to the fact that general indicators tend to conflate several interrelated but distinct phenomena. The alternative to this type of measurement is a shift to specific case studies based on field research in the tradition that was started by the Science Policy Research Unit at the University of Sussex some forty years ago. This main objective of this type of research was initially to understand how firms actually make decisions on R&D and to assess the various origins of innovation within the firm and the context within which the firm operates. The vast body of research that has emerged over the years from this approach has laid the empirical foundations, in a piecemeal fashion, for the development of the systematic critique of the orthodox approach to technology and for the sets of hypotheses and ensuing alternative policy implications which constitute the national innovation system approach.

Systems of innovation

The core component of innovation theory rests on the analyses of the systemic basis for innovation. Nelson (1993: 4-5) defines an innovation system as

> ".. a set of institutions whose interactions determine the innovative performance ... a set of institutional aspects that, together, plays the major role in influencing innovative performance."

This definition implies that the systemic interaction of institutions generates an object of analysis that is more than a simple addition of the various economic agents. Nelson concedes that the definitional breadth of innovation may make the choice of the relevant institutions problematic and that consequently a number of innovation systems may be identified for the same context. Another source of confusion arises from the various definitions of institutions. Neale (1987), among others, identifies the confusion in the definition of institutions as one of the main deficiencies of orthodox economic theory. Neoclassical theory, in particular, with its focus on constrained optimisation and the drive to abstract to excessive limits to attain unique solutions, has virtually assumed away any consideration of the institutional underpinning of the economic system that it seeks to explain. The neoclassical general equilibrium model is the epitome of this peculiar depiction of the multitude of complex systemic relationships of the economy and its trade-off for the sheer elegance of this model is the complete exclusion of institutional analysis. Within the neoclassical paradigm this is a necessary trade-off since the solution of the general equilibrium model would be impossible once institutions, with their specificities, norms and sign-posting functions as the determinants of behaviour in a less than fully certain world, are brought in. The context would then move to one of bounded rationality where unique solutions become impossible and even irrelevant.[16]

---

16 Neale succinctly identifies the core difference between institutional economics and neoclassical theory as follows:

> "(n)o universal aim, no universal method or logic is assumed. Rather, what people want to achieve and how they go about it - the institutions that govern provisioning - become the subjects of study." (Neale, 1987: 1180)

Within orthodox economics, the incorporation of institutions has been primarily in terms of their transaction cost reducing function.[17] In this light, institutions themselves can form part of neoclassical economics, subject to the dictates of constrained optimisation. However, the introduction of systems of institutions moves the analysis of institutions definitively outside neoclassical theory. A system assumes an own identity which acquires specific characteristics which render it different from other systems, in spite of the commonalities. In the case of knowledge systems, the institutional web can be viewed as simultaneously determining and determined by the production of knowledge.[18] The multitude of systems that are made possible by the acceptance of bounded rationality and historical specificity requires that criteria for the location of systems within a comprehensible and useful taxonomy be developed. Marglin (1990b) proposes four categorical parameters which can be used to classify specific knowledge systems - their epistemology, their modes of transmission and inter-temporal self-perpetuation, their modes of innovation which determine their adaptability and dynamism over time, and the expression of power, both within a specific system, in terms of the power concentrations and relations among its constituents, and with respect to other knowledge systems. Thus a knowledge system needs to be identified in terms of its constituting principles and its ability to survive and evolve. This ability can be charted through an examination of the location of the specific knowledge system within a power grid relative to other existent or potential knowledge systems.

Discourses on institutions and their development are inevitably discourses on power since the rationale of institutions is necessarily to leverage power in pursuit of stated and implicit objectives.[19] Apart from

---

17 See Coase (1937) and North (1981). Johnson (1988) defines institutions terms as those

> "... sets of routines, rules, norms and laws, which by reducing the amount of information necessary for individual and collective action make society, and the reproduction of society, possible." (p. 280).

18 Simpson (1995) explains this dichotomy in terms of the tension between the autonomy of technology in terms of its internal logic which renders it potentially formative of human needs and technology as instrumental, i.e. as subservient to needs. In the latter aspect needs, mediated through social institutions, form the constraints on technological development paths, but needs are themselves affected by changing technological opportunities.

19 Thompson (1995: 13) argues that

> "...(i)n exercising power, individuals employ the resources available to them ... by accumulating resources of various kinds, individuals can augment their power ... While resources can be built up personally, they

the founding principles, institutions also develop their own unstated power dynamics which are rarely perfectly congruent with the explicitly stated objectives that informed their formation. In the overall institutional framework within specific delimiters, be that the nation state, sub-national or supra-national entities, asymmetrical distributions of power are inevitable. The emergence of new institutions will either reinforce or challenge the existing power asymmetries in pursuit of the expansion of the power base that they represent. Within any institutional framework and within institutions there is always a tension between the imperatives of stability and of adaptability to a changing environment with innovation as the main strategic tool to gain more power over that environment. Within the overall institutional framework, stability is assured by various means. These can range from a general acceptance of a social contract, due to effective socialisation processes, to an overtly coercive dominance by one power base over others. Thus, innovation paths and the production of specific types of knowledge are fundamentally power/knowledge discourses wherein we can analyse the manifestation of power, with coalitions and revolutions, in order to understand better the underlying power bases of, for example, established current technology regimes. From this analytical perspective we should also be better able to assess the ramifications, across various groupings of agents of the evolution of specific innovation paths at the expense of alternative ones.

A specific innovation path may reinforce the power base of certain sections of the body politic to the detriment of others. A rapid rate of innovation on a broad front will alter the power relations among various skills bases. It will alter the power relations among different competing societal goals; a good example is the environmental debate. A change in the power relations in any society will necessarily result in a reordering of priorities and hence a reclassification of alternative knowledge sets as more or less appropriate. The linkage of knowledge to power brings in the issue of conflict as the inescapable attendant of innovation and the consequent danger for the stability of societies also brings in control mechanisms as a necessary corollary of innovation. These control mechanisms, whichever form they may take, are therefore necessary to limit the potentially dangerous consequences of explorations whose outcome is not perfectly predictable.[20]

---

are also commonly accumulated within the framework of institutions, which are important bases for the exercise of power."

20 Foucault (1970: 52) argues that

"..in every society the production of discourse is at once controlled, selected, organised and redistributed by a certain number of procedures

A system of innovation may be identified by its topography of diverse "knowledge stocks", a mapping of the concentrations of power, of the distribution of knowledge and of the relationships between the various power/knowledge nodes. If the broadest definition of innovation is adopted, this topography becomes all encompassing, covering all economic sectors and institutions, both formal and informal. This topography is, however, fluid and perforce has to account for history as the basis for an understanding of the direction of its alterations. This is where the term "evolutionary" becomes relevant, where the correspondence is far removed from the vulgar pseudo-Darwinian "survival of the fittest" rendition which has been appropriated by extreme neoliberal proselytisers. It is rather a systems development analysis with the acceptance of contingency, dead ends and calamities as inescapable properties of the development paths under consideration.[21] It is from this perspective that the viability of specific systems of innovation can best be assessed. Viability in this case refers to the capacity of systems of innovation to reproduce, to grow and to evolve. Reproduction is essential for the survival of a system, while (steady state) growth implies that the current shape of a specific system of innovation is well suited to its broader environment. There are various measures that may be used to assess these two dynamic processes, depending of the breadth of the definition of systems of innovation. They may range from those pertaining specifically to systems of science and technology to those which reflect the wider political economy. The evolution of systems takes two forms. The first is essentially reactive in the sense that the mutation of the system is responds to a changing environment. To use the biological analogy, this type of

---

> whose role is to ward off its powers and dangers, to gain mastery over its chance events."

21 Dosi clearly specifies that manner in which the biological metaphor of evolution is applied to innovation theory:

> "... (the) economic and social environment affects technological development in two ways, first selecting the 'direction of mutation' (i.e. selecting the technological paradigm) and then selecting among mutations, in a more Darwinian manner (i.e. the *ex post* selection among 'Schumpeterian' trials and errors)." (Dosi, 1982: 156)
>
> "... 'evolutionary' does not imply a notion of necessary gradualism: it is also consistent with abrupt changes, instabilities, revolutions (even in biology, evolutionary theories allow for discontinuities). Moreover, an 'evolutionary' theory should not be merely equated to simple Darwinian metaphors on selection tournaments based on near-tautological criteria of differential fitness. ... in the social domain, evolution is certainly quite Lamarkian, involving both learning and selection." (Dosi, 1991: 354)

evolution is Darwinian. The other type, drawing on a Lamarckian analogy, is a conscious mutation, based on feedback effects, which alters the environment within which the system is set; it is initiative rather than reactive.

Generally, the appraisal of national systems of innovation, based on the restriction to technical innovations, can be formed through an understanding of four broad constituent categories. These cover an understanding of whom the innovators are, of the power relations within the system of innovation, of overt science and technology policy and finally of other policies which affect the context within which innovative activity occurs.

The providers of innovation

The focus of most of the studies on innovation systems is on the firm since in most economies the bulk of innovative activity is carried out by firms and firms are the main users of new technology and knowledge. Firms, however, are not homogenous. Apart from the different legislated ownership structures of fully private-sector owned, directly state owned or parastatal firms, different contexts generate radically different corporation cultures. It is difficult to place the old lifetime employment Japanese model, the "hire and fire" American corporation, the South Korean *chaebol* and the modern Chinese corporation within the same general category. The main overt determinant on the nature of the firm within specific contexts is the relationship between state and market, through the legislative framework and the facilitation mechanisms provided by a wider interaction of extra-market institutions with firms.

The neoclassical concept of profit maximisation is useless for the analysis of the strategic decisions of firms, specifically with respect to innovation. In an imperfectly known decision making environment this concept is operationally meaningless in the strategies of real corporations. The alternative assumptions of limited knowledge and bounded rationality place the consideration of security, expansion and competitive advantage as the more realistic guidelines for strategy than the highly abstract neoclassical concept of profit maximisation. This understanding was reflected in mainstream theory in the early shift in theoretical and empirical work from decision-theoretic models, which consider the firm as the decision making agent in isolation, to game-theoretic models.[22] However, while game-theoretic models have grown quite complex and

22 See Cohen and Levin (1989) and Reinganum (1989) for comprehensive reviews of decision-theoretic and game-theoretic models.

varied in terms of the assumptions on the nature of the interaction among firms and on the context within which R&D is used as a competitive strategic tool, the unavoidable assumption on the nature of information that is required to solve such models still renders them too simplistic for empirical applications or policy formulation.[23] Moreover, the neoclassical treatment of non-technical innovations is non-existent, given the necessary assumption of optimal decision making based on full information sets. Moving away from the neoclassical construct of the firm, we can find a richer analytical tool in behavioural and organisational theories of the firm. It is in these approaches that we can locate in a more intelligible manner the intra-firm allocation decisions among various possible alternative strategies, the search processes which firms undertake in a decision making space littered with pockets of ignorance, and the development and entrenchment of distinguishing sets of core competences.

The public sector also engages directly in R&D. However, the evidence from the results of econometric analyses of the impact of R&D carried out in the public sector on private R&D is contradictory and generalisations are impossible. Thus Levy and Terleckyj (1983) concluded that the relationship between R&D actually performed by government (and universities) and private R&D expenditure was weak. In a similar analysis for Belgium, Holemans and Sleuwagen (1988) conclude that government-funded R&D does not substitute for private R&D and hence does not displace private research efforts. Lichtenberg (1984), on the other hand, obtained negative and highly significant coefficients when regressing changes in company R&D/sales on federal R&D/sales, indicating a displacement effect of federal R&D activity, which seriously reduces its effects on productivity. The largely inconclusive evidence from empirical studies of this nature stems from a disregard of the type of R&D undertaken by the public sector. The closer it is to applied R&D the greater is the chance that it can displace private R&D activity. This

---

23 Cohen and Levin (1989: 1096) state that such models

> "... depend upon typically unverifiable assumptions concerning the distribution of information, the identity of the decision variables and the sequence of moves."

and Reinganum who is one of the foremost contributors to the game-theoretic literature on R&D endorses this position when she states that this approach has

> "... not had a significant impact on the applied literature in industrial organisation; its usefulness for policy purposes should also be considered limited. For these purposes one needs a predictive model which encompasses the full range of firm, industry and innovation characteristics." (Reinganum, 1989: 905)

probability would obviously diminish as public sector R&D moves towards basic research. However, as public sector R&D moves towards basic research its relation to the more applied R&D undertaken by firms becomes increasingly complex and less amenable to stochastic estimations. When it comes to non-technical innovations - macroeconomic policy shifts, the re-configuration of the civil service, the re-organisation of delivery mechanisms, etc. - there is a notable gap in analysis, mostly due to the general restriction of the definition of innovation to technological change. The analysis of this type of innovation is mostly relegated to public management studies or general economic theory and is implicitly treated as an environmental determinant of innovation, rather than innovation in itself. This restriction is partially due to the history of the study of innovation as science and technology. It is also due to the virtual impossibility of measuring organisational innovation in its myriad possible forms.

The type of R&D performed by tertiary education institutions is often biased towards basic research whose effects are impossible to capture through the estimation of regression models. Most of the relevant studies in this area have been case studies. In his study on the relationship between university R&D and firm R&D intensity and the contributions to technical advancement of materials suppliers, equipment suppliers and research equipment suppliers Nelson (1986) concludes that

> "... university research rarely in itself generates new technology; rather it enhances technological opportunities and the productivity of private research and development, in a way that induces firms to spend more..." (p. 188).

In the case of basic research activity the role of tertiary education institutions is perhaps most succinctly defined by Feller (1990) at the conclusion of his lucid criticism of the growing tendency in American universities to commercialise faculty research:

> "..whether profitable or not, these ventures serve to shift academic researchers from the social roles in which they are most efficient, as suppliers of a collective good -scientific and technical knowledge." (p. 347).

Globally, this shift of university research towards corporate sponsored, and other commercially viable research programmes, has increased considerably. The implicit definition of university research as a collective (public) good constitutes the major problem which is most often confronted when trying to incorporate university R&D in an empirical analysis of the determinants of private R&D. Though empirical research has been done on the determinants of the research output of universities (Johnes, 1988 and Hare and Wyatt, 1988), such studies have been placed entirely within the context of academia where output is measured in terms of peer reviewed publications. Otherwise, analyses of the contribution of university R&D to industrial and economic performance have been mostly of a descriptive anecdotal nature.[24] It is impossible to quantify the output of basic research which had traditionally constituted the bulk of university R&D before the increasing requirements of financial viability forced the shift towards money generating R&D programmes. The distinctions between the performers of innovation have been consistently eroded with the progressive "privatisation" of the public good R&D.

This re-positioning of tertiary education institutions itself constitutes a shift in the role of universities not only in terms of R&D but as the providers of the higher end of the human capital spectrum. In this sense universities can be seen as "process" innovation suppliers and changes in tertiary education sectors are themselves innovations. In the South African case, for example, the massive structural re-configuration of the tertiary education sector with mergers between traditional universities and "technikons" has fundamentally altered the manner in which university education is provided. Another shift which is less explicit is the progressive increase in the provision of "job ready" graduates from the tertiary education institutions to the private sector. This has affected curricula, teaching and the general nature of a university education.

Concentrations of power

Earlier I argued that the discourse on the generation of knowledge is interlaced with a discourse on power. From this perspective, the analysis of systems of innovation is also, at least implicitly, an analysis of the relative strengths and the relationships among various power bases within the system and between the specific system and other systems. A quick assessment of the power base which underlies an innovation system can be provided by an analysis of the concentrations of ownership and control throughout the economy among the business sector, government, organised labour and consumer bodies. Given globalisation we would also have to look at the various local/global power relations, covering transnational corporations, international aid and financial institutions and

24 See Schimank (1988) and Waissbluth et al. (1988).

other governments. Innovation which affects and alters the relations of production is one of the main sources of conflict and the main power bases that are most often in conflict are labour and capital. The analysis of this conflict has obviously become complex, primarily because technological change and innovation in general have altered production relations in ways that could not possibly have been foreseen by classical economists. The accelerating demand for skills in a context where the obsolescence rate of human capital is unprecedented in history fundamentally affects the homogeneity of labour and has a significant impact on the traditional power relations between labour and capital. This effect, which tends to fragment organised labour, tends to be more pronounced in those economies that are increasingly based on the development of broad based human capital. Globalisation has also fundamentally affected this relationship by creating new global class rift lines dependent on the access to global citizenship (Bauman, 1998). The permutations and combinations of the various possible linkages within and between systems of innovation are obviously vast and can only be imperfectly captured by statistics. Often a mosaic of specific case studies would have to be constructed in order to provide an intelligible picture.

The relationship between the state and the market is one of the more important foci of innovation studies for a number of reasons, both analytical and prescriptive. The very definition of a system of innovation, whether it is national, local or global, determines how the role of the state is analysed. If systems of innovation are, as often is the case, premised on state macro planning, the role of the state becomes paramount and quite amenable to relatively easy normative generalisation. From this perspective the absence of the state would mean the absence of a national system of innovation. Alternatively, we can uphold the original biological metaphor and look at systems of innovation as the necessary organising and coordinating mechanism of the economy, whether or not the state is present. This latter approach is more suited to assess the specificity of systems, but it constrains generalised policy prescriptions. If this approach is adopted, the analysis of national systems of innovation can accommodate the widest gamut of state/market relationships, ranging from the most extreme forms of *laissez faire* to various versions of command economies.

The interface between the local and the global economy adds a further degree of complexity to the analysis of the power base of a national system of innovation. A crude indication of the degree of integration of the national system within the global economy can be provided by the incidence of foreign direct investment and the devolution of decision making capacity from the planning seat of the foreign investor to the host country. The stance taken by particular states regarding the determining power over the nature of industrial development allotted to foreign enterprises is a crucial defining factor of the context within which the internal industrial development process interacts with foreign capital and technology. This position has varied widely across countries and through history and is always the resultant of diverse lobbying powers, both within the economy and with respect to external agencies, whether they are firms or institutions such as the IMF and the World Bank. State policy in this regard is often the main determining factor in the reversal of centre/periphery positioning, as happened in the cases of Japan and South Korea and as is presently happening in China, or in the reinforcement of a current positioning, as is the case in most of post-colonial Africa. Policies regarding strictures on foreign direct investment can therefore play a major determining role in circumscribing the process of technology transfers from abroad in order to maximise the enhancement of technological capabilities. This will occur if safeguards are installed to ensure that an indigenous decision making space is enlarged by foreign direct investment, rather than displaced. Where such a policy stance is adopted the tension lies between overly protective protectionist policies and the requirement to participate in the global knowledge markets. As Lall (1987) argues in the case of India prior to liberalisation, isolationist policies, while successful in the generation of a sound base of technological capabilities, ultimately suppressed internal competitive forces and isolated the economy from leading edge technological developments in the global context. In the case of South Korea, on the other hand, a tempered approach to foreign direct investment and to the transfer of knowledge successfully altered the rules of the game to enable a poor economy to emerge as a leading industrial power. The globalisation of the economy in general tends to reinforce existing power configurations when governments adopt a neutral role in the development process. In this case it is comparative advantage, rather than competitive advantage, that becomes a more relevant determinant of the development path of a specific national system of innovation.

Science, technology and innovation policy

Government may influence private sector spending on R&D by acting as a client, thus providing a sinecure market for the innovator. The major impact of state expenditure on the R&D activity of firms in most countries has often been related to armaments and associated industries but this indirect means to generate an indigenous technological capabilities base has also been used in a number of sectors whose development was seen as being in the national interest. The secure market for steel assured by the state administered railways in South Africa during the inter-war period constitutes one such example. The effects of the shift from the minerals-energy complex to the military-industrial complex on the industrial structure in during apartheid, as documented by Fine and Rustomjee (1996), constitute another.

As discussed earlier, the state can also enter into the role of an extra-market performer of R&D. State institutions can, through the addressing of bottlenecks in public good provision in basic research either as a direct performer or by subsidising university research and that of public institutions, enhance the scientific base of particular industrial sectors. In this case the public sector acts as a substitute for private R&D and, depending on the type of R&D activity, may run the risk of inducing a crowding out, or displacement, effect. This effect may be avoided through the encouragement of state-university-industry research partnerships that maximise complementarities in R&D.

Finally, the state may try to induce private R&D effort through the provision of fiscal incentives. The evidence regarding the effects of these diverse forms of government intervention is contradictory and thus indicates that generalisations in this respect are invalid. In an early study Howe and McFetridge (1976) formulate and test a marginalist optimisation model for firms in which they include government R&D incentive grants (in the form of cost sharing) along with sales, after tax profits and depreciation as a determinant of R&D expenditure. Mansfield and Switzer (1985) and Mansfield (1986) found that tax credits and other allowances had minor importance in stimulating private R&D expenditure in the cases of the United States, Canada and Sweden. These fiscal incentives were judged inefficient in the sense that the R&D expenditure that they generated was significantly lower than the loss in revenue that they cost. In his review of a grant system in Australia, MacDonald (1986) finds little evidence that this type of incentive has stimulated private R&D to any significant level and no evidence that it has altered the nature (in terms of risk content) of R&D programmes in the private sector. Other studies are not so dismissive of the value of incentives for R&D. While supporting the evidence of earlier estimates of the low ratios of induced increases in R&D expenditure to government revenue foregone, Cordes (1989) objects that the omission of spill-over benefits from the induced R&D data may have led to serious under-estimations of the benefits from tax credits. Levy and Terleckyj (1983) found a strong positive relationship between government-funded R&D contracted out to industry and private R&D expenditure.

The general debate on the appropriate degree and the nature of government intervention in a developing economy is divided between the respective arguments for neutral and strategic intervention. The rationale for the liberal case for neutral intervention stems from an uneasy conflation of Smith's "invisible hand" and the neoclassical efficiency criteria from which emanates the premise that the untrammelled market is the best possible coordinating mechanism. In the case of what Lall (1994) termed "moderate neoliberals", the role of government should be the correction for market failures of a general "public good" nature without altering inter-sectoral price ratios. Examples of this would be the provision of pre-university education and of infrastructure such as transport and communications. Extreme neoliberal proponents would argue that even this function should be left to the market. The often unstated assumption is that the state should be the guarantor of a legal system that includes property rights. Wade's (1996) account of Japan's challenge to the World Bank's neoliberal programme and its championing of a strongly strategic interventionist industrial policy provides a fascinating narrative of the contending views on state intervention and of the power play underlying the adoption and implementation of a specific approach by international institutions. Japan quoted its own economic history and that of the South East Asian tigers as the empirical justification of the theoretically sound countervailing argument to neoliberal economic policy. In spite of a campaign that lasted several years over the 1980s and the 1990s and of Japan's standing as a major contributing member in the World Bank, the Washington Consensus survived largely unscathed but sufficiently fine tuned to guard against future attacks.

The case for strategic intervention can be made from two distinct theoretical bases. The neoclassical paradigm does allow for this type of intervention where there are externalities evident in specific sectors. The foremost example in the case of technology is where social returns exceed private returns due to spillovers and the consequent appropriability problem. The main limitation on this approach lies in the problem of assessing spillover effects and the appropriate type and degree of intervention. Most assessments are based either on *ex post facto* case studies or on industry linkage measures. Both refer to existing structures and, unless data pertaining to other extraneous structures are used as a reference frame, they are inadequate in assessing the spillover potential of an industrial mix which is marked by significant gaps in the industrial chain.

The alternative rationale for a public sector strategy based on "picking winners" arises from the premise that markets, especially in the case of developing economies, are inherently inefficient in the sense that they are inappropriate mechanisms for structural transformation. This constitutes the broader theoretical setting within which the evolutionary approach to science, technology and innovation policy emerged. Given that the *raison d'être* of development policy stems from a dissatisfaction with the adequacy of a given economic structure to address the country's development needs, the role of the state should be driven by the concern with structural change. In pursuit of this goal, specific sectors are targeted as having a higher growth potential than others and policies are designed to encourage their development, perhaps at the expense of other sectors. In this pursuit industrial development policies can be designed to ease bottlenecks in specific sectors and stimulate investment and technology transfers. The earliest rationale for strategic intervention is provided by the infant industry argument, pioneered by List (2005), which assumes that burgeoning sectors need a learning period before they can be feasibly exposed to international competition. The case for strategic intervention also owes a debt to Hirschman' (1958) advocacy of an unbalanced growth and development strategy which relies on industrial linkages and industrial multiplier effects as the criteria for state intervention. Picking winners in a development and transformation context does however require substantial planning and implementation capabilities from the public sector. In such a context, this policy usually requires the ability to build scenarios that may have only a limited congruence with the current structure of the economy and the political will and administrative capacity to alter the structure.

Broader contextual parameters

Apart from those activities within the public sector and tertiary education institutions which directly enable R&D activity, there is a multitude of other contextual factors which have an effect on the specifics of a particular national system of innovation. In consequence, the impact of policies which affect directly the incentives to engage in R&D can be extremely limited if they are pursued in isolation of the broader economic policy framework. The development of a country's innovation system can be enhanced or inhibited in specific directions by complementary economic policies. One of the important perspectives on the specific science, technology and innovation policy under consideration is therefore the degree to which it is integrated with other facets of the national economic and social planning agenda. Furthermore the development of the national system of innovation depends on the overall level of integration among all the various aspects of the national planning framework. This integration of policy depends to a large effect on the development paradigm that is adopted *vis-à-vis* innovation. If innovation is defined solely in terms of technical change then science, technology and innovation policy is subsumed within a larger policy framework. If, on the other hand, innovation is defined broadly to include any source of change in the economic structure then the conceptualisation of the national system of innovation would encompass all facets of the economy and development policy transmutes into innovation policy.

Given the lessons learnt from the numerous case studies of the post-war success stories, the central role in the development of technological capabilities has been assigned to human capital formation. The widely adopted determinant of this is education, but the concept entails a wider range of contributing processes and education policy has to be embedded in a broader policy framework before its effects on human capital development can be properly understood. Systems which assure the secure provision of basic needs to households and which cater for the child rearing requirements of single parent families, for example, provide the appropriate setting for lifetime planning which sets a specific context for the long term sustainable and adaptable education for the general population. One of the complementary determinants is the provision of job security, enhanced through various measures by the provision for retraining. Within this setting the provision of free education at various levels has a higher impact on human capital development. Then there are the numerous debates on the degree to which education curricula should be targeted to the requirements of the job market. Central to this debate is the assumption regarding the degree of certainty with which specific future skills requirements can be predicted, weighed against the need to ensure flexibility in order to guard against unforeseeable obsolescence of skills and unemployment.

On a more specific level, measures which directly affect the rate and direction of industrial development have a more immediate impact on the contour of the national system of innovation, especially in those countries which are still industrialising. As far as industrial development programmes are concerned the debate again comes back to the neutral vs targeted intervention argument. The wide array of possible investment incentives can be brought into the service of one or the other stance. The debate is carried over to trade policy and policies on foreign direct investment. Thus, apart from direct fiscal incentives for R&D and the provision for bottlenecks in the formal innovation chain, a wide array of other measures can be brought to bear so that the incentive schemes for innovative activity can be embedded within export promotion schemes and protection from imports for high tech industries.

Locating innovation systems

The focus on national specificities in the analysis of national systems of innovation is perhaps the most problematic component of this concept and the associated methodology. In Nelson (1993) the term "national" is implicitly equated with the nation state since the case studies in that work all refer to established nation states. However, there is nothing that is historically immutable in the nation state (see Anderson, 1983). While a sovereignty that is internationally recognised as a binding legal definition constitutes a *de facto* national system of innovation, the historical specificity of the evolution paths of specific nation states is a crucial core component of the analyses of national systems. The acceptance of historical specificity introduces a degree of instability in the concept of national systems of innovation as given units. Different national systems have different vintages and exhibit varying degrees of stability, and their integrity can be vulnerable both from within and from outside forces. Civil wars and invasions by other nation states are only the more dramatic instances of such threats to the stability of national systems of innovation. Other, more ubiquitous and subtle, threats are posed by the diverse and complex effects of globalisation. Given the historical contingency of national systems, we then need to identify and include other systems at the intra-statal and the supra-statal levels as legitimate objects of analysis.

At the intra-statal level we start off with the acceptance that the modern nation (or multi-nation) state is generally composed of several nations, with different ethnic specificities, however these may be defined, with different institutional networks and development paths (see Gellner, 1983 and Cooke et al., 1997, among others). The main difference in the analyses of national and sub-national systems of innovation is that while sovereignty provides a usually unquestioned premise for the existence of a system, there is generally no such a relatively immutable one for sub-national systems. Within the state, spatial legal demarcations are negotiated and negotiable and do not therefore necessarily constitute the basis of local systems of innovation. This basis has to be sought in those historically determined networks of relationships which through inclusion and exclusion identify a specific innovation system as distinct from others. The recognition and analysis of sub-national systems therefore enrich the understanding of national systems of innovation and introduce a more sophisticated understanding of the nature and behaviour of specific national systems. In the process it also enhances the analysis of specificity. The relationship between national and local systems of innovation is determined legally and establishes the degree of the governance autonomy of local systems.[25] This defines the explicit relations of power between the local and the national systems. The actual nature of the relationship between local and national systems can best be assessed by means of various measures of the convergence of viability indicators among the various sub-national systems. This process of convergence itself provides an important determinant of the viability of the national system as a whole.

On the other hand, those critiques which are based on a consideration of the supra-statal economy, emerging from the accelerating rate of globalisation, tend to erode the claim to the specificity of national systems of innovation. The rapidly growing ease of the trans-national coordination of production processes, due to the rate of technological change in information and communications technology, lowered transport costs and the dramatic erosion of barriers to the mobility of goods and services, labour, and financial capital, has significantly weakened the relevance of national systems of innovation as an object of analysis.[26] Moreover, the increasing incidence of systemic technological programmes often requires cross-border alliances and partnerships because of the scale and scope issues of such programmes. This phenomenon has revitalised the ubiquity of the universality premise of neoclassical economics through the assumption of a convergence of the diverse innovation paths of diverse

---

25 Cooke et al (1997) assess various configurations of the institutional relationships between specific legally defined sub-national entities and the central government as the determining factor of the relative autonomy of different localised innovation systems within the borders of the nation state.

26 In this regard, Thompson (1995: 253) points out that

> "... the globalizing tendencies of modern social life have rendered territorial delimitation increasingly problematic. Particular nation-states are increasingly embedded in networks of power ... which extend well beyond their boundaries and which limit, to an extent which varies greatly from one country to another, the room to manoeuvre of ... national governments. ... there are a range of issues - concerning, for instance, the activities of transnational corporations, problems of pollution and environmental degradation, the resolution of armed conflict and the proliferation of weapons of mass destruction - which cannot be satisfactorily addressed within the political framework of the nation-state."

economies towards some general model which represents "best practice" regardless of the context.[27]

The counter argument is based on the fact that, as Kozul-Wright (1995), Asheim and Gertler (2006) and others point out, the concentration of knowledge intensive industries still lies in first world economies and this concentration is growing over time. Maskell and Malmberg (1999) propose that within the framework of globalisation which, through its rapid erosion of formal institutional barriers to the movement of resources, including knowledge is levelling down national boundaries, the tacit, geographically "sticky" (Asheim and Gertler), component of knowledge becomes the prime determinant of the competitive advantage of nations.[28] Thus, context specific core capabilities, and their grounding in specific locations due to the significant role played by the non-transferrable determinants of their underlying capabilities sets, become the main differentiating factor in the understanding of the economic performance of nation states.[29] In this vein, Nelson (1993) proposes that national borders

---

27 Kozul-Wright (1995: 152) points out the effects of globalisation in this regard when he says that

> "... a new best-practice set of global rules for designers, engineers, entrepreneurs, managers and marketing agents is emerging ... The resulting product (of trans-national corporations) is ... a complicated bundle of inputs, produced in a variety of locations, assembled in home or host countries for sale in those countries or anywhere in the world." (parenthesis added).

28 Maskell and Malmberg (1999: 167) state that

> "... the knowledge-based economy is characterised by three elements: the growing importance of economic transactions focussed on knowledge itself; rapid qualitative changes in goods and services; and the incorporation of the creation and implementation of change itself into the mission of economic agents."

29 The importance of geographical location is stated by Maskell and Malmberg when they say that

> "... knowledge creation of even the most globally oriented firms or sectors is, at least to some extent, influenced by differences in the economic properties of their place of location. Firms are progressively stimulated by and dependent on localised technological capabilities in order to maintain and increase their competitiveness *precisely* because of the drive towards globalisation and the resulting homogenisation of formerly critical factors of production." (ibid.: 168, emphasis added)
>
> "... a logical and interesting consequence of the present development towards a global economy is that the more easily codifiable (tradable) knowledge can be accessed, the more crucial does tacit knowledge become for sustaining or enhancing the competitive position of the firm. If all

still impart a specificity to the nature of technological capabilities, due to a range of determinants of tacit knowledge which are imperfectly mobile across national boundaries. The analysis of tacit knowledge and its institutional setting places human capital development at the core of economic dynamics and this is highlighted by Lundvall's (2002) analysis of the transition from the knowledge-based economy to the learning economy. Insofar as learning processes are to a significant degree local, they provide a strong rationale for the tenet of the partial immobility of capabilities, since the structures that can successfully support the human capital investment requirements for growth vary substantially across economies. While codified skills development programmes are transferrable across national borders, a substantial portion of the learning processes and of the consequent human capital development paths emerge from the political economic histories of countries and their capacity to provide the required investment for development is often contingent on such histories.

From the perspective of innovation theory, the positive welfare implications that have been attributed to globalisation by the neoliberal agenda have to be treated with caution. Market forces do not *per se* usually alter the structural underpinnings of the various economies in which they operate and, if unaccompanied by targeted initiatives by host countries, they often reinforce current international inequalities in the development of innovation systems. The ease of the transnational location of enterprises and the transnational sourcing and allocation of resources with the accelerating process of globalisation may easily have intensified the enduring global inequalities among nations and regions, as well as between communities within specific economies.[30] On this basis, Kozul-

---

> factors of production, all organisational blueprints, all market information, and all production technologies were readily available in all parts of the world at (more or less) the same price, the market process of competition between firms would dwindle." (ibid: 172)

30 Kozul-Wright (1995: 159-160) offers the following sound rebuttal to the neoliberal prescriptive *non sequitur* that the emergence of the trans-national corporation and the weakening of the nation-state in the era of globalisation will lead to the attainment of Pareto efficiency across national borders:

> "The presence of these firms, in itself, is testament to discontinuities in the economic environment and there is no *a priori* reason for assuming that the activities of TNCs, any more than international trade, will by themselves remove inequalities between and within regions. ... weak states are more likely to establish weak, and ultimately unsustainable, growth paths and reinforce global segmentation."

Miyoshi (1997: 50) argues that

Wright argues that national policies still have a significant role in determining the context, the set of rules, explicit or implicit, within which trans-national corporations operate. Kozul-Wright further argues that unless the appropriate global regulatory regime to ensure convergence is established, the adverse effects of globalisation for the weaker economies will continue to escalate. Globalisation can also be calamitous for power relations within specific economies through, for example, the erosion of the bargaining power of trade unions and the increasingly differentiated access to the global economy for different sections of populations. This differentiation is usually negatively related to the degree of development of national systems of innovation and therefore further widens the gap between developed and developing economies.

Since the power of individual nation states on the world markets has dwindled, the negotiation of a global regulatory framework which would facilitate effectively a process of equalisation of development prospects will occur only through the strong lobbying by groupings of states which belong to roughly similar development categories. There are however strong asymmetries at a global level in the nature and power of the economic blocs that have emerged or can emerge and the implications of the formation of economic blocs for the enduring relevance of nation states can be contradictory. On the one hand this phenomenon may be seen as a progression towards a fully integrated global economy, since, by definition, barriers to trade and to resource mobility are dismantled within the confines of economic unions. On the other hand, the path towards the effective unification of markets can be tortuous, as evidenced by the experience of the most successful bloc, the European Union. In most areas, especially among developing economies, this phenomenon is still in its early stages. Again, taking the case of the European Union, the obstacles that have been encountered in the attempts to integrate former Soviet Union satellite countries indicate that effective economic unification requires a high degree of similarity in the development levels of member countries. Without a modicum of symmetry in the distribution of economic power within the prospective bloc, the prospects for convergence would be poor. This pre-condition for the emergence of successful economic blocs will tend to intensify the current division of

---

"Capital can move freely in time and space as long as the target area guarantees: (1) a stable political structure (often meaning dictatorship); (2) viable labour conditions (that is, cheaply trained or trainable labour plus the absence of unionism, feminism, and human rights); (3) reasonable infrastructure; (4) lower tax rates (favoured treatment by the host governments); and (5) indifference to the environment."

power, through the elimination of rivalries among economies in the industrial centres, without a corresponding increase in the power wielded by blocs of weaker economies.

The crucial paradigmatic difference between the neoclassical and the evolutionary accounts is therefore not one of emphasis on one or the other of the two aspects of generality and particularity. It is rather the fundamental one between the neoclassical language which, complex as it may be, still offers a total, and hence essentially simple, explanation of the world against that of the evolutionary school which has eschewed such explanations and concentrates on difference as the ineradicable feature of the systems that are studied. The former explanation cannot logically allow for empirical approximations to the ideal narrative. Indeed it cannot even perceive itself as a narrative. The evolutionary approach, on the other hand, does allow for the development of diverse sub-narratives some of which can conceivably invalidate the premises on which the original research programme was launched. Thus, within this analytical framework it is possible to examine the proposition that increasing globalisation may progressively render national differences in technological paths increasingly irrelevant. In this case one may consider "regional innovation systems" (where regional is defined in terms of a collection of states rather than in the intra-statal manner used by Cooke et al.) as a fruitful analytical terrain in a world that is becoming increasingly characterised by the formation of economic blocs. The focus of the next stage in the associated research agenda would then shift to a consideration of the tensions between national specificities and the convergence of national systems of innovation. Of especial interest would be the transition phase from national to regional systems where the reference frame, the definitional backdrop, of core competencies, and the associated nodes of competitive advantage, would shift, with some dying out and new loci emerging through the combination of new technological complementarity matrices and the economies of scale and scope which are rendered accessible due to the larger internal markets.

Historical specificity and the evolution of systems

A particular system which evolves in a specific economic context is a historical product subject to historical analysis. However, any historiography is subject to various treatments. The emphasis informing any particular analysis can oscillate between continuities and ruptures, between key figures and moments on the one hand and the evolution of structures on the other. In this section I examine alternative approaches to the analysis of the relationship, specifically the tension, between technological and institutional change.

For institutions to fulfil their role of reducing transaction costs efficiently their value and norm structure must be legitimated and accepted by the actors within the domain of the institutional web. Merton (1957) argues that the stability of a system depends on the internalisation on the part of its members of both societal norms and values. A deficient internalisation process diminishes legitimacy and results in different manifestations of deviance, with deleterious effects on the system's stability. In this eventuality social cohesion can only be secured by increasingly overt interventions by the state, including explicit acts of violence. North (1981) argued that a substantial portion of general education is devoted to the transmission of what he termed as "ideology", i.e. the set of societal values and norms, through a process of socialisation that forms an integral part of the legitimating process. Legitimacy imparts stability to institutions, which, in turn, reinforces the legitimate status of institutions.

In a changing environment all institutions are caught in the tension between stability and flexibility (Johnson, 1988) and it is the resolution of this tension that often determines the viability of innovation systems. A degree of stability is obviously necessary for the survival of institutions, since one of the prime aims of institutions is to provide the signposts and norms for behaviour in a less than perfectly known decision space. Almost by definition, these norms and signposts must remain relatively set over time if institutions are to be effective. Stability is obtained by numerous means which vary according to the type of institution under consideration. In the case of formal institutions stability is assured by explicit, formal rules and regulations which may be enforced by several means. In the case of informal institutions that govern practice and routines, stability is more often assured by an internalisation of a system's values in its members. Here the coercion, by virtue of being implicit, is rarely overt and is thus often more effective. Informal institutions therefore tend to be more stable over time and inherently more rigid and resistant to change. Innovation poses one of the main challenges to the survival of institutions and as we extend our understanding of innovation to encompass most human behaviour this challenge itself becomes a part of the nature of institutions. The manner in which the institutional framework comes to terms with innovation then helps define it. Neale (1987) argues that innovation is inextricably intertwined with institutions and that it simultaneously poses a major stimulus to institutional change and a threat to the stability of institutions. The degree of the stimulus and the threat depends on the nature of specific innovations. While all institutions are able to adapt to change, unless we assume a perfectly static world, one of the main generalised ways to differentiate between institutions is provided by an assessment of the limits of radicality of innovation that they can adapt to without running the danger of collapse. Johnson (1988) identifies three approaches to the relationship between institutional change and innovation, each of which has different implications on the ability of institutional frameworks to adapt to, and provide a stimulus for, innovation.

The first approach is essentially an extension of the "invisible hand" proposition to institutional change wherein institutions adapt continuously and efficiently to the changing environment generated by technological change. While orthodox economics *a la* Becker (1993) has expanded the theorist's consideration of the goal sets informing economic agents, thus significantly enriching the explanatory power of neoclassical analysis, the optimising agent still remains as the pivotal ordering mechanism of the systems which are analysed. The difference is that now the premise of a universal rationality no longer applies to the components of an objective (utility) function but has been restricted solely to the logistics of constrained optimisation. When applied to the study of the development of systems over time, analyses based on the extended constrained optimisation model almost inevitably become an exercise in postdictive rationalisation where human capital accumulation combined with the now (post Becker) fluid objective function can be adjusted to correct for the shortcomings of the predictive model. Thus, for example, whereas traditional neoclassical analysis could only explain international differences in such areas as income levels and trade patterns on the basis of factor endowments, Becker's innovation allows systems to differ according to political/ideological goal sets. In this manner, history is brought into neoclassical analysis. However, since an analysis of goal formation is abjured, and given the assumption of perfect information, or at least agents acting under the illusion of perfect information, the explanatory power of the historiography that emerges from this approach is still extremely limited. Goals are taken as given and institutions are seen as the structures that emerge and fluidly adapt to fulfil these goals. A marginalist analysis approach is assumed wherein optimisation implies a pursuit of goals up to the point where marginal "cost" is equated to marginal "returns" and where returns are specified in terms of the utility generating capacity of the planners' goals. Changes in the return and cost functions are exogenous to the analysis, but once they happen institutions adapt policy in order to retain an optimisation path. Becker's departure from the strictures of the mainstream neoclassical treatment of utility functions opened the space for variation among systems on the basis of differing goal sets, but still required the process of institutional adaptation and development to remain common to all settings.

The abandonment of the assumptions underlying constrained optimisation analysis is the final step towards the disavowal of claims to universally applicable analytical approaches. The further away we move from a neoclassical account of development, the greater is the degree of specificity that enters our depiction of particular systems.[31] Nelson shifts the analysis of institutional change into the evolutionary camp when he proposes that

> "... devising and learning to use effectively a significantly new organizational form involves much the same kind of uncertainty, experimental groping, and learning by making mistakes and correcting them, that marks technological innovation and invention. New modes of organisation are not simply 'chosen' when circumstances make them appropriate as neoclassical economists are wont to argue. They, like technologies, evolve in a manner that is foreseen only dimly." (Nelson, 1991: 351).

The second approach also proposes a unidirectional causality between the two processes but introduces the concept of institutional inertia due to the trade-off between the stability of an institution and its flexibility. Along with Perez (1988) and Freeman and Perez (1988), Johnson (1988) proposes this relationship as an explanation of economic fluctuations through the lags between technological change and institutional adjustment. The strength of the relationship depends on the combination

---

31 Neale (1987) draws the distinctions between neoclassical and institutional economics succinctly as follows:

> "Standard economists regard economic behaviour as universal over time and space. Institutional economists regard it as specific to time and space. The standard economist holds that economic behaviour is maximising (and *vice-versa*). The institutional economist thinks of the economy as the ways in which a society provisions itself. The standard economist derives his explanation in large part from the assumed motive of all individuals: ... maximising something good ... The institutionalist focuses upon the rules and opportunities for action and the limits to action ... motives are ... the reasons why an individual acts in any particular case, but the person's specific aims or passions do not determine specific acts. What specific acts are chosen depends upon the institutional context: the particular 'rules of the game' in a particular system that each individual tries to manipulate to realize his goals. (Neale, 1987: 1180-1181)

of the radicality of the technological change, which determines the extent of the shock to the system (with techno-economic paradigm shifts obviously being the most disruptive), and the degree of flexibility of the institutional framework. Freeman and Perez list the dimensions of the structural change that a techno-economic paradigm shift would entail and require. These include, among other areas, changes in output and investment mixes, new infrastructural requirements, altered skills requirements, changing consumption patterns and possibly even changes in the industrial concentration. Obviously such an extensive structural change requires a corresponding adaptation and even a redefinition of the institutional framework. When, as is inevitable within this formulation, the rate of institutional adjustment lags behind the requirements of the new emerging paradigm a slump period is experienced and continues through the period of transition to the stage where the parameters of the new institutional framework match the requirements of the new paradigm.

The third approach to the relationship between technological and institutional change considers the causality in the relationship as running in both directions. Although institutional inertia is obviously a necessary conjunct of the transactions costs reducing function, institutional change, responding to a perceived need, can lead the required technological change. A dramatic example of this phenomenon was the emergence of "big science" which was due to the military requirements of World War II. The post-war development history of those countries which, starting off with Japan, have been labelled as the "Asian tigers" is one where national economic objectives generated the transformation of countries' institutional framework within a total strategy which moved the economy through a number of techno-economic paradigm shifts.

The first account virtually eliminates the possibility of discontinuities in the evolution of institutions. The second account, with its reliance on institutional inertia as an explanation of economic fluctuations, opens the space for the possibility of breaks in the development of institutions, especially in the case where the disturbance in the relationship between the institutional setup and technology is caused by a techno-economic paradigm shift. In the case of the third account, the possibility that a rupture in technological development can be caused by a shift in the objective set informing the current institutional framework is introduced with the premise of multi-directional causality. The last two accounts, whether applied to technology, institutions or a particular society's *weltanschauung* focus on discontinuities in the process of structural change and transformation and localise continuities within specific technological paradigms, institutional norm sets and epistemes.[32]

From the foregoing discussion it should be clear that the two threads, the two arguments which are ever present, whether stated or not, and which permeate any evolutionary account of technology are ignorance and power. It is the interaction of these two factors which generates the phenomena of irreversibility, cumulativeness and path dependency and it is that interaction that renders them central to the evolution of systems of innovation. The underlying proposition behind these concepts is that once a specific path of scientific, technological or institutional change is chosen out of a number of options, successes along that path reinforce the incentives to move further along it. Moreover, as the stock of knowledge pertinent to that path accumulates relative to other stocks the feasibility of switching to alternative paths diminishes, thus reducing progressively the range of inter-path choice. Thus technologies, as well as institutions, have a tendency to lock in, a tendency which increases with time. This means that even if alternative paths are seen, in hindsight, to have been preferable to the ones actually taken, the cost of switching to them tends to become progressively prohibitive over time. Marglin (1990a: 5) identifies the condition that renders the phenomenon of irreversibility so dangerous quite eloquently:

> "... the development process is *irreversible*. Whether it proceeds in small steps or in one fell swoop, the result is generally the same: you can't go home again. Irreversibility is not *logically* fatal to the argument; it would not matter that the process were irreversible if individuals were endowed with perfect foresight. However, the inability to foresee all the consequences of the first steps down a path makes irreversibility crucial. Not only can't you go home again, but you can't figure out whether or not you want to until it's too late to change your mind."

Kuhn (1970a, 1970b) proposes that normal scientific exploration occurs within the boundaries of a given paradigm whose fundamentals are not amenable to questioning. According to his thesis it is only when the anomalies and contradictions inherent in any specific paradigm have accumulated beyond some unacceptable level that a scientific revolution occurs and a new paradigm constructed. This shift is predicated on the emergence of a power base that carries authority within the broad scientific field as the launching pad for the revolution. On the basis of this proposition Dosi (1982) distinguishes between research which proceeds

32 See Foucault (1977).

along alternative trajectories within a specific paradigm and breakthroughs which render a paradigm obsolete and require the emergence of a new one. Once a body of knowledge has become established as the orthodox wisdom it would take a revolution to shift to a different paradigm given the absence of a meta-paradigm within which the two can be located. Feyerabend (1975) objects to Kuhn's implicit assumption that paradigm shifts necessarily reflect a progression due to the superiority of one body of established wisdom over another. He contextualises paradigms within a broader setting thus extending the evaluative set of the truth content of paradigms beyond that of "objective" scientific criteria. Foucault (1977) introduced the notion of epistemic discontinuities which, because of the breadth of the concept of an episteme, render even paradigm shifts a localised phenomenon. He defines an episteme as delineating "the conditions of possibility of all knowledge, whether expressed in a theory or silently invested in a practice." (p. 168). The structure of an episteme is dependent on a specific set of historical *a priori* which

> "... is what, in a given period, delimits in the totality of experience a field of knowledge, defines the mode of being of the objects that appear in that field, provides man's everyday perception with theoretical powers, and defines the conditions in which he can sustain a discourse about things that is recognised to be true." (p. 158).[33]

Thus in the case of epistemic shifts Marglin's argument, as quoted above, can be extended to the proposition that it is impossible to assess an alternative knowledge system from within the language, the world view, of the episteme that one is currently located in.

---

33 Foucault (1994: 191) elaborates further on the definition of an episteme as an all embracing system of belief within which diverse knowledge systems are located:

> "... something like a world-view, a slice of history common to all branches of knowledge, which imposes on each one the same norms and postulates, a general state of reason, a certain structure of thought that the men of a particular period cannot escape - a great body of legislation written once and for all by some anonymous hand. ... the total set of relations that unite, at a given period, the discursive practices that give rise to epistemological figures, sciences, and possibly formalized systems ... The *episteme* is not a form of knowledge ... or type of rationality which, crossing the boundaries of the most varied sciences, manifests the sovereign unity of a subject, a spirit, or a period; it is the totality of relations that can be discovered, for a given period, between sciences when one analyses them at the level of discursive regularities."

The main objection to the neoclassical premise that knowledge is perfectly transmittable, and hence universally available, lies in the proposal that knowledge is to a significant degree tacit and grounded in a specific context. Once this objection is accepted, the issue of appropriate technology then arises; empirically, this issue has been evident in the case of numerous imperfect technology transfers in the turn-key projects since the late sixties. Innovations are developed within specific contexts and are partially validated within those contexts; their transfer to other contexts will therefore necessarily often incur transfer costs which will depend on the degree of similarity between contexts. While some of these costs can be approximated by the costs of adapting the innovation to a different environment, there are transfer costs which are not immediately evident and which cannot be accommodated by the price mechanism. The apparent costs of adjustment, which can be priced, would cover different physical environments, differences in physical infrastructure, such as transport systems, different sets of formal institutions, such as legislation, and different factor price ratios. On the other hand those transfer costs which are due to differences in culturally determined practices and routines are less easy to calculate and are therefore excluded from the calculus of orthodox economic theory. The issue of appropriate technology and knowledge can also be significant within national systems of innovation. The degree of significance of this issue depends directly on the degree of cultural and institutional heterogeneity within the nation state. This again is largely determined by the history of the formation of specific nation states. Depending on such histories and the degree of consensus in the process of nation forming, the internal costs of transferring technology and knowledge systems may be higher than that of international transfers.

The issue of appropriateness is also applicable to institutions. In this case, the concepts of cumulative path dependencies and irreversibility are as relevant to the analysis of the evolution of institutions[34] and to the relationship between innovation and institutional change as they are to technology. In this sense the degree of institutional inertia which is required to retain the stability of institutions determines the cost of institutional innovation. This again is specific to the institutional web at varying degrees of aggregation. This in turn determines the incidence of switching costs, due to the accumulation of power over time by agents associated with specific institutional development paths and their ability to resist path switching. In consequence, the assessment of costs now

34 See North (1981) and North and Wallis (1994).

becomes partially mediated through the ongoing conflict between the stakeholders in the *status quo* and the outsiders who have been excluded from its benefits or whose power base within the political economic structure has been adversely affected by the emergence of the current institutional web. Consequently the evaluation switching costs and of institutional evolution paths is itself a political appraisal which is contingent on the relative power bases of the contesting claimants and is the resultant of it.

The essential uncertainty of change and the difficulty of predicting outcomes is the fundamental reason why specific knowledge sets and the related institutional bases may become inappropriate. The divergence between expectations and outcome is positively related to the radicality of innovations and it is most pronounced in the case of techno-economic paradigm shifts (Freeman and Perez, 1988). The degree of unpredictability associated with such shifts may cause them to be seen as inappropriate, *a posteriori*, even by the initial promoters, as well as by those sections of society whose power has been eroded by the change.

The analytical terrain

In this chapter I have mapped the constituents of what has come to be loosely demarcated as a context specific framework within which the technological capabilities of nations are set and develop. I have also examined possible approaches to the understanding of the multiplicity and interrelatedness of factors which cause systems of innovation to develop over time. In the process I have discussed the crucial notion of appropriateness and the criteria against which, in the course of possible evolution paths, these systems can be assessed.

The taxonomic parameters discussed in this chapter offer various measures of the determinants of technology stocks and of the roles played by the various institutional actors within any given national system of innovation. These parameters can be broadly classified into those which indicate: (a) the broad range of innovative activity and technological capabilities within industrial sectors, and (b) the interactions of various institutional players which set the context within which such activities and capabilities are set. The most commonly used indicators which are used for such taxonomies can be conveniently grouped into five broad categories. These are (i) measures which provide some indication of the incidence of innovative activities within sectors, (ii) the nature of inter-relationships of science and technology institutions within and among sectors, (iii) an indication of the degree of concentration of the coordination function both within the national boundaries and with respect to the international economy, (iv) the nature of formal science, technology and innovation policies, and (v) policies, not directly concerned with science and technology, which affect the environment within which technological capabilities develop. On a normative level, one of the goals of a taxonomy of this type is to assess strengths and weaknesses within a given national system. It should be able to identify the presence of bottlenecks to its further development along specific paths and thus provide a valuable tool for science and technology policy formulation.

There are a number of lines along which a historical analysis of the evolution of innovation systems may proceed, keeping in mind that none of them may be followed without controversy, since they represent a choice of the guidelines for the contextualisation of a local "history of innovation" within the broader economic and political history of a nation. Whichever one of these is assumed to dominate the other, whether economic forces shape political history or vice versa, or under the assumption of a mutual inter-determination, the nature of the relationship between the two depends on the schools of thought and the ideologies within which the analyst is located. Then there is the related question of whether discontinuities are to be countenanced or whether the various histories are to be viewed as determined by some set of immanent forces which impart a continuity to the narrative. Even if discontinuities are accepted, their identification depends on the analyst's choice of the criteria which determine the periodisation of the history being considered. The nature of power pertinent to the analyses needs to be explicated and, dependent on this treatment, the control mechanisms can then be identified and addressed.

The very breadth of the concept of national system of innovation can easily become the source of its most damaging critique. The plethora of determinants which are tossed into this cauldron and the definitional elasticity of technological capabilities can cover just about every aspect of the development paths that nations can take. Thus it may be argued that this catch-all term becomes theoretically meaningless and analytically void. The treatment of institutional and organisational change which lies at the heart of this methodology itself becomes subject to definitional ambiguities. If innovation is defined so widely as to include any change in practices and routines which affect the economy, then institutional change can be seen simultaneously as the process which affects innovation and as an innovation in its own rights. In this vein it can be argued that works in this area rapidly tend towards the idiosyncratic, and indeed a perusal of the variety of approaches utilised in the case studies contained in Nelson's

(1993) compilation may be called in as supporting evidence for this charge.[35] This, however, is a charge to which any body of theory that departs from neoclassical orthodoxy becomes liable. The generic field of development economics was, and still is, largely peripheral to mainstream theory largely due to its perceived tendency to violate inter-disciplinary boundary lines. This objection partially originates from an identification of analytical rigour with an extreme degree of abstraction. One of the corollaries of this identification is the ability to delineate unambiguously the inter-disciplinary divides. In this case the issue of this objection boils down to a choice between two mutually exclusive paradigms. The analysis of national systems of innovations lies within the evolutionary approach wherein Occam's Razor no longer constitutes the holy grail. Analyses which commence from within this body of theory do not already hold within the questions that are asked the answers that are sought. In this sense therefore they are truly exploratory and what one language terms "idiosyncratic" another would term "rich".

In general the bulk of the literature on innovation systems has moved away from the original debate *vis-à-vis* neoclassical economics and has focussed on the expansion of the analytical terrain of innovation theory. To some degree, this shift was due to a shift in the legitimacy base of the new approach, with its incorporation into survey methodology and its absorption in the lexicon of politicians and economic planners. However, there is some danger in this shift since the unhappy hybrid of neoclassical and liberal economics that led to neoliberalism still dominates the language of economics and still constitutes the core discourse of economic planning. A bigger danger however may lie in a certain degree of complacency with the original theoretical formulation of the concept of innovation systems. It is important to recall regularly that the motivation underlying the original articulation of the problematic which started the debate was a form of critical practice. It was a deconstructionist approach to the established orthodoxy, a Foucaudian archaeological exploration of the underlying strata of the orthodoxy, enabled by an ongoing questioning of the presumed fundamentals of theory. Its value was to make the

35 In this respect the difficulty of abstracting to derive a general "model" is evident in Nelson's study:

> "The studies reported in Nelson (1993) reveal both the complexity and diversity of national systems of innovation. So overwhelming are these that it is presently difficult, if not impossible, to generalise or even abstract from the effects of national political economies in seeking to specify a model of a generic innovation system at national level." (Cooke et al., 1997: 475)

implicit assumptions of the accepted doctrine explicit, to say what had long remained unsaid. As I have argued in this chapter, the concept of the national system of innovation is contingent on empirical conditions and is thus essentially ephemeral. Its value as an analytical tool depends critically on the specific conditions of time and space and it should therefore be subject to the same sort of questioning that is the hallmark of the innovation systems approach. In the absence of this level of criticality, there is a real danger that the new paradigm may itself become fixed and intransigent as the original questions and the disquiet that led to these questions are forgotten.

The concept of an innovation system has, since the nineties, moved from the fringe of economic theory towards the centre, especially with the introduction of innovation surveys. Innovation surveys, starting with the 1992 *Oslo Manual*, are firmly grounded in an innovation systems framework and subsequent surveys have expanded the definition and application of the concept. These surveys provide a performance monitoring and evaluation tool and have provided the basis for comparisons among different national systems of innovation. There is a possible tension between these two functions. The use of surveys for performance monitoring and evaluation requires the establishment of baseline sets of indicators. The higher the degree of specificity the more useful such surveys can be for national economic planning. On the other hand, a high degree of specificity reduces the value of surveys for inter-country comparisons. All surveys are designed to serve both functions using a combination of a common core indicator base and context specific indicators.

Too easy an assumption of the legitimacy of innovation surveys for inter-country comparisons may however violate one of the more important contributions of evolutionary economics. Dosi (1991: 354) cautions against the assumption of linearity in the evolutionary path of specific systems and the tendency to locate diverse systems within a continuous range. This would obscure systemic differences and implicitly re-introduce the assumption of a necessary convergence of evolutionary paths. This problem may be partially addressed by the specification of sub-sets of systems that strongly share structural similarities with distinct breaks between sub-sets. Again the problem is the choice of the taxonomy that should inform such groupings and the inevitability of degrees of arbitrariness inherent in such choices.

Intermittently throughout this chapter distinctions have been made between developed and developing economies. Since the development of technological capabilities has become a largely accepted requirement for industrialisation and overall economic development, the relevant question then concerns the means required to force the evolution of the national system of innovation of developing economies. From within this approach the required agenda involves the provision of the appropriate institutional setting within which indigenous technological capabilities can be fostered. The specific institutional development path in this venture has to take cognisance of the relevant distinctive features of the political, social and economic context which is being addressed if the appropriate incentive mechanisms for the development of the required innovation system are to be installed. The fact that innovation occurs at different speeds, with the constant possibility of leaps and ruptures, opens up the possibility of "windows of opportunity", which periodically offer developing economies the chance to leapfrog over technology hurdles and to catch up in the process of industrialisation. Perez and Soete (1988) point out the frequency with which this phenomenon has occurred, especially in the case of newly industrialised countries. In fact they propose that the institutional inertia and the sunken costs in industrialised countries which are tied into an existing paradigm may render industrialising economies relatively more flexible in absorbing a new technology, especially in the case of techno-economic paradigm shifts. They caution, however, that the set of internal conditions must be right for the country in question to be able to exploit such ruptures and to leap through the resulting window of opportunity. Thus one perspective on the analysis of the development of specific national systems is an account of the manner in which they have responded to such opportunities.

The wide variety of definitions of national systems of innovation gives rise to different possibilities for the existence of this object of analysis. On the one hand there is the possibility of the non-existence of the national system of innovation. This possibility is premised on a restricted definition of the system of innovation as a sector of the economy and as the catalyst for growth and development. In this case the conditions for the existence of the system of innovation have to be articulated and the critical thresholds of these conditions have to be specified to determine the point at which a specific system of innovation comes into being. Within the context of this definition the fundamental role of state planning is the establishment and the development of the national system of innovation in the pursuit of economic growth and development. On the other hand we can propose the inevitability of the existence of national systems of innovation. This proposition is premised on an expanded definition of innovation to cover all of human activity and on the existence of the (uncontested) nation (or multi- nation) state. Here the role of state planning would be to protect and enhance the viability of the system of innovation. We can therefore conceive of a continuum of definitions of systems of innovation. This would range from national systems of science and technology at the one end, through the incorporation of innovation, expanded to include organisational change and the Schumpeterian inclusiveness of innovation, to an all-inclusive general theory of economics premised on what, for want of a better term, may be called an "innovation theory of value".

A displacement of labour by innovation, and streams of past innovation, as an alternative theory of value would go a long way towards the resolution of the inherent contradictions between production value and exchange value in Marxist theory, since in general innovations are deemed as such if they have been validated by the market. From this perspective all production, and all economic activity, static or dynamic, is premised on accumulated and embodied stocks of knowledge. It is here that technological capabilities become the measure of value, thus rendering the differentiation between static and dynamic analyses invalid. All states would now be seen as being in a permanent state of flux with an ever present tension between the drive to change and the drive to conserve and the static state would simply be a unique case of a rough equalisation of the two forces. We may consider the concept of modes of innovation as a useful analytical tool which may be able to capture the evolution of systems of innovation, provide taxonomy of "development stages" and understand the coexistence of different modes in the same economic space, such as national economies. The modern diffusion patterns of ownership arising from the spread of equity mean that the ownership of the means of production has become less relevant than the control of means of production in our understanding of changes in the political economies of nations and of the global economy. This historical shift in relevance from ownership to control, which could not have been anticipated by classical economists, does not invalidate the analytical prowess of the concept of modes of production; rather, it provides an extension of the concept which captures the role of the modern corporation. The concept of the "modes of innovation" may provide yet a further elaboration of a Marxist approach to the evolution of capitalism and the varieties of capitalism. This approach would be premised on the distillation of the various means of production into the one concept of the means of innovation, both as a stock and as a flow concept.

Within this approach, modes of innovation would be differentiated on the basis of a number of defining criteria. The ownership and control patterns of technological capabilities as the "means of innovation" would be one. Another would be the relationship be within which the various concentrations of the means of innovation are located along with the rate of change within this web. The degree of heterogeneity within a system which would allow the simultaneous coexistence of different modes of innovation also enters as a useful perspective on the nature of the national system of innovation. The main implications for policy would then translate into the drive to shift from one mode of innovation to another on the scale of progression similar to that of modes of production and, in the case of the coexistence of different modes of innovation, to bring about a convergence within the national system of innovation. A tentative classification of modes of innovation would be based primarily on the ownership and control patterns of the means of innovation, ranging from concentrated institutional ownership to broadly spread institutional and individual ownership. The various reproduction mechanisms would also be a differentiation criterion, as would the nature of the relationship between different modes of innovation, locally and globally.

The relevance of the innovation systems approach to the analysis of the economy has largely been posited as a countervailing argument to the failure of the neoclassical model to explain economic change and dynamics in general in an adequate manner. This failure was redressed by placing technical change, technology and eventually innovation at the core of the economic engine. As the rate of change accelerated at unprecedented rates across the globe, this new approach acquired increasing relevance. However, a thorough repudiation of the neoclassical paradigm cannot be based solely on the issue of relevance. Ultimately, it requires an alternative general theory of economics which can provide an explanation of even the most static of economic contexts. It would not be valid to propose that neoclassical economics is more relevant to the analysis of static systems, while innovation theory can explain dynamic contexts better, with the conclusion that since the world has become increasingly more dynamic, innovation theory is in the ascendance while the explanatory power of neoclassical economics is waning. A general economic theory has to be displaced by another general theory, if analysts are not to get into the disastrous quagmire arising from the miscegenation of paradigmatic languages.[36] An alternative general theory should be able

[36] In their ground breaking work, Nelson and Winter (1982) classify theory into "formal" theory that is essentially deductive and "appreciative" theory that is evidence-based and suggest that

> "...economists should be less pessimistic about the prospects of developing a broad-gauge economic theory that encompasses much of

to explain static economic states as well as dynamic ones and it here that a new theory of value may be relevant.

The factors that determine the specifics of the South African context to which an analysis and evaluation of this nature will be applied will be examined in the following chapter. In line with the main arguments presented in this chapter the treatment of the South African case will be historical and the scope of the following chapter is the examination of the highly contentious debates which have rendered the recounting of South African economic history since the sixties the product of overtly ideological battles. The treatment is, however, set within a global context which shifts from colonisation and empire to the post colonial period during the Cold War and finally to the post-Cold War period. These significant shifts in world history are closely associated with the broad periodisation of the history that is recounted here. The adoption of a systems approach to innovation raises the issues of technological determinism and of the hegemony of innovation systems across national borders. These issues are increasingly pertinent within the context of globalisation. Thus, the question which runs through the remainder of this book concerns the extent to which a specifically South African system of innovation emerged as a product of the country's unique and turbulent history.

> what contemporary orthodoxy does but is not subject to its basic difficulties." (p. 48)

They correctly maintain that the two types are, or should be, strongly interrelated. It would, however, be theoretically disastrous to combine the neoclassical economics as the formal theory with evolutionary economics as the appreciative part of the "broad-gauge" theory. As Nelson and Winter point out, the mathematical limitations of neoclassical theory can, and have been, extended but the extensions are still within the confines of the full information constrained optimisation model.

CHAPTER TWO

SOUTH AFRICAN ECONOMIC HISTORIOGRAPHY

One of the main arguments in this book is that the history of any specific national system of innovation cannot be rendered plausibly in isolation from the country's political and economic histories. Indeed in the case of the twentieth century South Africa, with a history marked by one of the more extreme examples of overt social engineering programmes in the post-war era, designed and implemented within a context, both local and international, of increasing hostility, such a segregation of histories would be analytically disastrous. Thus the evolution of South Africa's system of innovation has to be considered as inextricably intertwined with the several other histories of South Africa, and, like them, it is subject to a number of renditions.

One of the apparent paradoxes that arise from a perusal of the history of science and technology policy in the pre-democracy South Africa is that a state which took upon itself the prerogative to define and regulate the minutiae of internal social and economic relations in the service of apartheid ideology declined to develop a coherent national policy framework for the development of the national system of innovation. Thus the manifest contradiction is that of a regime obsessed with control which yet apparently relinquishes control over this crucial component of a nation's growth process. Moreover, as I shall argue in later chapters, this was not merely the result of negligence on the part of the apartheid state. Structures which had been instituted before the establishment of apartheid in 1948 were altered in a manner that effectively divested the relevant state organs of the ability to formulate and implement a science, technology and innovation policy which could be integrated within a national economic planning framework. The various initiatives in this area became progressively fragmentary and, except in specific instances, they failed to establish a sound reproductive base, as measured by levels of R&D activity and the increasing incidence of R&D undertaken by private sector agents. The main thrust of this, and the following chapters, is to explore the reasons, apart from incompetence and mismanagement,[46] for the incompatibility between the political economic requirements of apartheid and the prerequisites for the development of a national system of innovation along the path taken by first world countries and the newly industrialised economies. Therefore, an understanding of the evolution of the state in South Africa and its relation to the economy is central to this analysis.

Following Weber, North (1981:20) defines the state as an "organisation with a comparative advantage in violence ... in the position to specify and enforce property rights." This allows for a wider range of the underlying organising principle than Gellner's (1983:3) more straightforward definition of the state as "that agency within society which possesses the monopoly of legitimate violence". North's definition avoids the notion of legitimacy and thus allows for the possibility of internal resistance which can also employ violence[47]. North identifies two general approaches to the theory of the state. The first is contract theory wherein the state is seen as acting to maximise the welfare of society as a whole. The second is predatory or exploitation theory where the state is considered to be driven by the goal of maximising the welfare of only a section of society at the expense of other groups within that society. He is careful to caution against a simplistic demarcation between the two forms since even the overtly contract state, such as a representative democracy, is still "the ultimate source of coercion" (North, 1981:21) and serves best the interests of the majority group that votes its leadership into power. In this sense the contract state is also a predatory state. Given the blurring of the demarcation lines between the two theoretical approaches, North reduces the criterion of differentiation between them to the specifically overt form of the expression of power, the "distribution of 'violence potential'" (p. 21), across the members of society. According to this criterion the two

46 Posel (1991: 5) argues that

> "...the notion of a single master plan fundamentally misrepresents the political processes whereby Apartheid was built, greatly exaggerating the extent of the continuity, control and long-term planning involved. ... Uncertainties, conflicts, failures, and deviations, although often less visible than the continuities and triumphs of Apartheid, were fundamental to its development."

47 It is pertinent here to note that Gellner (1983:3-4) allows that "there are states which lack either the will or the means to enforce their monopoly of legitimate violence". In this case the use of the term monopoly still remains ambiguous since the basis of legitimacy is defined as pertaining only to the "central political authority" (Gellner, 1983: 3)

accounts differ on the assumptions and measurements of the symmetry quotient of the distribution of "violence potential". Indeed the emerging dominance of a specific ideology, as in the case of the ascendancy of neoliberal economic orthodoxy in western democracies, since the mid-eighties may crowd out any meaningful ideological choice for voters as contending political parties battle on the specifics of forms of articulation rather than on ideological divides. This was the case in post-apartheid South Africa where the differences in economic ideology between the ruling African National Congress (ANC) and the official neoliberal opposition party were negligible. In this case the democratic voting process legitimises and thus deeply entrenches the dominant position of a specific group. When this happens, voters in a liberal democracy are effectively, in terms of the choice sets within which they can exercise their voting power, in a position equivalent to those in a one-party state who vote for specific delegates.[48] Again this was the case in South Africa were ideological battles and choices were removed from the sphere of public choice to the intra party sphere. The first concrete sign of the strong ideological rifts within the African National Congress (ANC) only appeared with the results of the party's 52nd national conference at the end of 2007, where the mostly neoliberal government camp was totally displaced by a left wing coalition with strong lobbying groups from the union sector and the South African Communist party.

The prevalence and range of overtly predatory states diminished rapidly with the collapse of the imperial powers and the process of decolonisation after the Second World War. Of course predatory states still survived and did arise, and have multiplied in number, in the post-war period, but the explicit mandate for exploitation based on an assumed racial and ethnic superiority has virtually disappeared. The deployment of imperialism has mutated into new modes wherein the economic dependency of the emergent peripheral ex-colonies on the industrialised centre has displaced overt political domination from the agenda of the neo-

---

48 Thompson (1995: 251) identifies the causes for the erosion of ideological choice in modern democracies:

> "With the professionalization of politics and the bureaucratization of political parties, active participation in the political process has become increasingly restricted to full-time officials who have turned politics into a career. For the majority of individuals, participation in this process amounts to little more than a choice exercised every four or five years between candidates who appear increasingly indistinguishable in terms of their overall policies and increasingly ineffective in terms of their capacity to alter the course of events."

colonial powers. The legitimisation base of the new imperialism has, in the process of legalistic decolonisation, rapidly transmuted into an ideological one which was no longer race specific. Against this background the case of South Africa since the war and up to the advent of democracy in 1994 stands as a relic of the predatory account of the state associated with colonial/racial domination. It is this fact that progressively made that system "archaic", an appellation whose appositeness I shall explore further on. The parallels between colonialism and apartheid also initiated an analytical approach, that of "internal colonialism", which will also be examined in this chapter.

Once the premise of the apartheid regime as one of the foremost remnants of the overtly predatory state is accepted, the question then revolves around identifying the group whose interests it promoted. In the case of South Africa, the two groups that have been identified as the *protégées* of the predatory state are whites as a unified racial group and capitalists as a class, excluding the possible participation of black capitalists. Since these two sets, while obviously overlapping, are not identical and have often exhibited strongly conflicting interests, the bulk of the writing on twentieth century South African economic history has been dominated by the race-class debate. The basic divergence between the two analytical approaches lies in the relative positions, in terms of domination and subordination, accorded to racist ideology and class relations in the formulation of economic policy, here interpreted in the widest possible terms to include all aspects of property rights, including those over the subjects' own body, i.e. an extensive and overt specification and enforcement of what Foucault (1984) termed "bio-power".[49] In its

---

49 Foucault (1984: 140) defines "bio-power" as the set of "... techniques for achieving the subjugation of bodies and the control of populations ..." and Variava (1989: 264) applies this concept to the specifics of South Africa under apartheid when she says that

> "...(t)he specificity of apartheid lay in its extension of state intervention and race legislation to the microscopic level of relations between black and white. Strategies were constantly formulated and renewed in order to regulate and prevent the minutest possibilities of inter-racial contact. They were accompanied by a series of interventions which were experienced at the level of the body and of everyday conduct and life. Apartheid envisaged an eugenic ordering of South African society which brought with it an extension and intensification of the micro-powers of control by state which was increasingly unfettered in its authority. It was an institutionalized form of state racism which permeated the very body and had an impact over the entire social field. It acted through the smallest

early stages the two sides of the debate were quite exclusive. However, the introduction of the notion of contingency altered both sides of the race/class debate. The class approach came to consider the promotion of capitalist interests, while still paramount in the determination of apartheid policy, as constrained by some of the requisites of racist ideology. The race approach, on the other hand, saw the enactment of a programme of racial domination as constrained by the exigencies of economic viability and survival.

Discourses on the economics of apartheid

The basic tenet of analyses based on race is succinctly summarised by Wolpe, one of the foremost theorists on the class side of the debate, as follows:

> "A few exceptions apart ... the literature - radical, liberal and racist alike ... - analyses and describes the society in terms of racial concepts. Even where the relationship between classes is incorporated into the discussion, race is nevertheless treated as the dominant force. ... The overwhelming importance accorded to race in these approaches is apparent, above all, in their treatment of the relationship between racially oriented action and 'the economy'. ... whether the economy is conceived of in terms of liberal economics ... or in Marxist terms as a capitalist mode of production ... racial beliefs are treated as a force external to, but productive of, distortions in the otherwise rational economic system." (Wolpe, 1980: 292)

One of the foremost early exponents of the race approach is Horwitz (1967), who would these days be classified as belonging to an extreme neoliberal camp. His normative base is firmly grounded in Schumpeter, Hayek and Rostow and holds up the unfettered market as the ideal organising (allocative) principle whose functioning was disrupted by a specifically Afrikaner apartheid ideology. Horwitz (1967:426) sees racist ideology as having overwhelmed the "economic rationality" of capitalism causing "... the self-expression of market forces, of individual capitalist profit-making ... to come to terms with the motivations and ethos of the polity." The early Wolpe (1980:317), on the other hand, categorically states the opposing view, that apartheid "... must be seen as an ideology

---

elements, the family, sexual relations, residential relations and most significantly of all education."

which sustains and reproduces capitalist relations of production." He denies any divergence between race and class interests and argues that:

> "... since the establishment of the Union of South Africa in 1910 (to go back no further), the State has been utilised at all times to secure and develop the capitalist mode of production. Viewed from this standpoint racist ideology and the policy of the State now not only appear as the means for the reproduction of segregation and racial discrimination generally, but also as what they really are, the means for the reproduction of a particular mode of production." (Wolpe, 1980: 293)

The contrast between these two accounts is crucial since it informs the analysis of all the aspects of the relationship between the state and the economy. The treatment of continuities and discontinuities in the histories that are recounted then also differs according to which approach is adopted. Thus, for example, the race approach proposes that the 1924 defeat of the Smuts government and, more decisively, the 1948 victory of the National Party and the establishment of apartheid represent decisive ruptures in the country's history that diverted it from the path of capitalist development occurring internationally within industrialised post-colonial economies. The liberal section of this school saw this rupture as impeding the proper functioning of the invisible hand which would ultimately have resulted in the redressing of inequalities based on race. Some Marxist theorists similarly saw the racial prerogatives of apartheid legislation as inhibiting the development of a fully fledged capitalist mode of production and thus halting the historical path towards the eventual socialist stage. Wolpe, on the other hand, saw no such discontinuity. For him

> "There is undoubtedly a high degree of continuity in the racist ideological foundations of Apartheid and of the policy of Segregation which prevailed in the Union of South Africa prior to the election of the Nationalist Party to power in 1948. It is, perhaps, this continuity which accounts for the widely held view that fundamentally Apartheid is little more than Segregation under a new name." (Wolpe, 1980: 289)

Thus for Wolpe (180: 289) apartheid simply "... entails a considerable increase in White domination through the extension of the repressive powers of the State ...". In this account, therefore, there is not so much a discontinuity as a transformation in the overt legitimising base for the exercise of power. This spans the time from the late segregation period under Smuts for whom a nakedly racist polity had become a serious embarrassment on the international front, and who therefore had to disguise it with the pieties of a cultural missionary, to the National Party for whom such niceties were, at least in the earlier days of apartheid, largely irrelevant. Concurrently the country was moving from a predominantly resource-based economy to a more diversified production base which accelerated with the wave of industrialisation which started on a massive scale in the inter-war period. This industrialisation process was stimulated by strategic state intervention aimed at exploiting industrial linkages that had been ignored by the private sector. Industrialisation generated the necessity of a permanent urbanised black labour force, but associated with this was the potential for trade unionism and for the consequent deleterious effect on profit rates. Apartheid legislation was much more effective in stemming the unionisation tide than the preceding government. In Wolpe's (1980) account, while this secondary industrialisation did cause internal conflicts within the capitalist sector because of the different requirements of the diverse fractions of capital, its most significant effect was the erosion of the pre-capitalist mode of production prevalent within the rural black economy. Wolpe sees the transition from segregation to apartheid as providing a guaranteed supply of cheap labour to the capitalist economy. The liberal race approach, on the other hand, saw the institution of apartheid as providing only a limited benefit to capital, which was more than offset by the costs entailed in abandoning an economic organisation based on unrestricted labour and commodity markets. Wolpe (1980) reinforced his thesis by arguing that the Bantustan policy, which was an integral component of the apartheid blueprint, when combined with the migrant worker system, became the means to increase the surplus value of labour to the capitalist class through the use of the homelands as a subsidising mechanism, for which the capitalist class was not accountable, for the reproduction of the labour force. The pertinent question in this regard concerns the quality of the labour force which was being reproduced. The progressive encroachment on the ability of the rural black population within its designated areas to provide for human capital investment implies the reproduction of an unskilled labour supply. The labour requirements of a growing secondary sector could not possibly be met from this font and it was a recognition of this deficiency during the second world war, more than any other factor, which pushed the Smuts government towards an unprecedented recognition of the rights, a term used cautiously in this context, of urban black workers for education, health and housing.

The interpretation of the imposition of control is also subject to this dichotomy. The race approach would highlight the distinction between the suppression of the white workers' revolts in 1914 and 1922 and those of black workers in 1946 and 1972. The first two are seen as the revolt of white workers whose privileged power base as conferred by the "colour bar" was under attack by employers who wanted to adopt least cost employment practices by eliminating employment discrimination based on race. From this perspective the political discrediting of Smuts who suppressed these revolts is seen as the victory of a racist ideology over the imperatives of economic rationality. The repression of the black workers' strikes is then treated as the articulation of this ideology in protecting the privileged white position which had become irrevocably entrenched. On the other hand, O'Meara (1975) and Wolpe, among others, see both as examples of the suppression of labour power for the benefit of capitalism.[50]

Wolpe emphasises repeatedly that one has to go beyond the racial terminology adopted in most of the laws that regulated the functioning of the labour market and identify what is left unstated, since it is accepted as a given - that their main motivation emerged from the requirements of the capitalist mode of production underlying the economy. In his account the entrenchment of white privilege, given the relative population group numbers, actually served to ensure an everlasting pool of readily available cheap labour, whereas an erosion of privilege based on race would eventually have meant rising overall wages since the political cost of exploiting white as well as black workers would eventually have become untenable. As a mode of analysis, this approach is close to Becker's (1993) application of the extended constrained optimisation approach. Using Becker's language we could render Wolpe's account by saying that the objectives (utility) function of the capitalist class remained unchanged. The only things which changed were some of the components of the constraint, and consequently the ensuing optimisation strategy.

Posel characterises the nature of the early debate as a discourse between two irreconcilable opposed views:

> "... *(E)ither* the design and practice of Apartheid were instrumental in furthering the capitalist cause, *or* they were not. This starkly polarised formulation of the issue inhibited the declaration of a position which was sensitive to both the tensions and the affinities between Apartheid and

---

50 O'Meara (1975: 162, parenthesis added) states that

> "...(t)here are obvious parallels between this (the 1946 black mine workers' strike) and the 1922 general strike of white workers. Both were revolts against the wage policy of the Chamber of Mines which a Smuts government supported. In both Smuts came down on the side of the mine-owners with a ruthless force and was thrown out of office in the following general election as a result of contradictions highlighted by the strike."

> capitalism, and to the fluctuations in this relationship over time and at various points in the political process." (Posel, 1991:11)

The analysis of the "tensions and the affinities between apartheid and capitalism" did however emerge from the debate. Wolpe had argued that the presence of a racist ideology does not explain *per se* the phenomenon of apartheid. He was however aware of the implicit counter-argument that neither did class analysis, on its own, explain apartheid when he concluded that

> "(w)hat is necessary for an adequate explanation is a specification of the historical conjuncture between ideology, political practice and the mode of production." (Wolpe, 1980: 290).

In his later work Wolpe's position changes quite substantially. He cautions against reductionist approaches, whether they are based on class or on race analysis and against an over-emphasis on historical continuity. An account which ignores discontinuities, in his revised assessment, fails to provide an adequate analysis of the causes and effects of structural change and becomes a descriptive account based on an initial premise. The informing theory is then treated implicitly as exogenous to the object of the analysis and, within the context of that analysis, becomes an immutable essentiality. This reaction against a particular type of historical determinism induces the later Wolpe to re-define the relationship between racial domination and capitalist interests as historically contingent rather than necessary. This definition opens up to a rich structural analysis since

> "... that relationship (between apartheid and capitalism) will be both functional and contradictory at the same time - functional for the reproduction of certain relations and class positions and contradictory for others. The contention is that the formation of structures and relations is always the outcome of struggle between contending groups or classes and that this outcome is Janus-faced, being always simultaneously functional and contradictory." (Wolpe, 1989: 8, parentheses added)

Thus the agents of capital could pursue a least cost strategy, but only within an often severely limiting environment, while the architects and implementers of apartheid could never achieve the economic viability on which the permanence of the system they designed ultimately depended. One of the prime characteristics of this tension was the inevitable frustration of both components of the power nucleus of the system. The potential for conflicting interests within the dominant polity was therefore ever present. Its actualisation and the specific form it took, however, was historically contingent and its effects on structure could be either reinforcing or weakening, even, in specific historical instances, to the extent of causing a change in one or more of the fundamental components of the structure. The multiplicity of possible outcomes of these complex relationships then opens up to the possibility, perhaps even the necessity, of ruptures in the evolution of systems.[51]

Proceeding along the lines of the "contingent capitalism" approach, Lipton (1986) refuses to treat capital as uniform and argues that the congruence or dissonance between the requirements of capital and those of apartheid differed according to sector - classified broadly as mining, agriculture and manufacturing - and over time. Complementarity or conflict between the goals of capital and those of apartheid depended primarily on the reliance of a particular sector on skilled labour since the distortions in the labour market introduced by racist legislation and by established labour practices resulted in an endemic shortage of skilled labour and an over-abundance of unskilled workers. The reliance on human capital inputs was least pronounced in agriculture and most pressing in manufacturing industries. A further determinant of the relation between the concerns of specific capitalist categories and racist policy arose from the sources and the type of the demand for a particular sector's output. The growth of the manufacturing sector was constrained by a small internal market where wages, and hence the overall purchasing power of the populace, were kept low. The agricultural sector was also largely dependent on a local market, but faced a relatively income inelastic demand. The output of the mining sector was mainly aimed at the export markets. Thus the manufacturing sector was the one which was most severely constrained by segregation and apartheid policies on both of the components of the profit function. Posel (1991) extends Lipton's disaggregation of capitalist interests to intra-sectoral distinctions between large and small organisations. The former, because of their size and permanence, tend to adopt a long-term planning horizon where the possibility of fundamental changes in the economic environment is taken into account. Small establishments, on the other hand, assume the circumstances within which they operate to be given and therefore try to maximise profitability within the existing context. Within the manufacturing sector, the former type of organisation would be more

---

51 Fine and Rustomjee (1996: 19) set their work within

> "... a theory of the state that locates its policies in terms of the complex outcome of class interests that act upon it and which in turn lead to the strengthening, weakening and even transformation of the underlying class structure."

concerned with the deleterious effects of apartheid labour policy and international isolation than the latter. Indeed, small enterprises, accepting existing factor price ratios, would tend to support any economic regime which guaranteed the containment of the power of organised labour.

A further complication in the identification of the dominant principal behind state policy over time is posed by the shifting ownership patterns of capital. As long as specific sectors were distinct ethnic territories (mining being the domain of foreign or imperial capital, agriculture that of Afrikaner capital, and secondary industry the contested terrain) the relationship between state and capital could be rendered through an account of the nationalist/imperial tension. However, once the ethnic interpenetration of capital started, as it did after the Second World War, this identification became progressively untenable and the analysis of the state as the facilitator and promoter of some specific capitalist group interests to the detriment of others becomes complex and less definite. Thus, one of the many contradictions inherent in the growth of apartheid was that the expansion of the manufacturing sector which was pursued initially as a means to establish a base for a countervailing power against the English owned mining houses also increased the costs incurred by apartheid. However, Fine and Rustomjee (1996) caution against the arbitrary analytical separation of mining and secondary industries, which gives rise to the contradiction. Their argument of the economic interdependence of the mineral-energies complex and secondary industry in South Africa offers a more homogenous representation of capital and a more complex approach to the assessment of the net impact of apartheid on the interests of capital.

Over time, with generally increasing capital-to-output and capital-to-labour ratios, the requirements for skilled labour rose across the economy. Moreover, as capital ownership started to develop across sectors, with the diversification of mining interests into manufacturing and the increasing linkages between agriculture and food processing, the costs of labour market segmentation and low incomes progressively affected a greater proportion of capitalist interests. The increasing international isolation of the country after 1960 further reduced access to export markets, international technology transfers and trans-national investment flows, thus placing severe limits on economic growth.

Against this trend it must be noted that specific sectors of the economy gained considerably from the country's increasing isolation. The establishment and growth of “strategic” industries such as the wide range of sectors that fed into the armaments sector and the synthetic fuels programme were due to the requirements of the “siege” economy engendered under apartheid. The range of industries which benefited from government spending on weaponry extended over the primary and secondary sectors to include electronics, communications, navigation equipment, machine parts and chemicals. Furthermore, geopolitical considerations during the cold war era generated a sound international support base for the economic viability of apartheid, primarily from several European countries and from the United States.

One of the extensions of the race approach was the casting of segregation and apartheid as a special, "internal" type of colonialism. While the term is usually applied to inter-national dominance, the South African situation, where the contours of power, including economic power, were defined along racial lines and where the legislative apparatus had consistently and increasingly placed constraints on the access of a subjugated population to the means of production, including investment in human capital, appears to fit this definition. Thus a stream of analytical work[52] emerged on the foundations of a model which located the form of apartheid domination within a special category of colonial dominance and exploitation. The distancing of the ruling white minority, spatially, economically and culturally, and the imposed hierarchical system were, within this approach, judged as akin to those imposed by a colonising centre over the colonised periphery. The idiosyncrasy of the South African case, of course, lies in the fact that the rulers were themselves natives in the sense that the centre which formed their referent was spatially indigenous. Though both orthodox colonialism and the proposed model of internal colonialism can be defined as overtly predatory states where the *protégée* group is defined racially, it is difficult to find an easy congruence between the changing form of domination within South Africa and that expressed in a colonial relationship. The analogy with colonial subjugation is rendered even more problematic by virtue of the fact that while South Africa was a colony, the internal protégée group that eventually achieved the position of dominance initially defined itself and formulated its ethnic self-image partially as the exploited subject of an imperial power and of foreign capital.

Fine and Davis (1990) and Wolpe (1989) dismiss analyses based on the colonial analogy as analytically facile and prescriptively misleading. Fine and Davis contend that the fact that (overt) imperialism was in its period of demise by the time that apartheid was instituted and that the oppressed belonged primarily to the working class invalidates the analogy between the form of domination in South Africa and that found within colonialism.

---

52 See Fine and Davis (1990: 127, 129-130, 271).

Indeed, if we compare the South African situation under apartheid with Neale's (1989) deconstructive analysis of the evolution of institutions under colonialism, the "colonialism of a special kind" model fares badly. Neale's main thesis is that it is fallacious to conceive of the product of colonialism as the planned outcome of a single monolithic designer. In South Africa, on the other hand, especially with the start of the Verwoerd era, apartheid was a detailed plan of subjugation informed by a coherent and explicit racist ideology. Neale (1989) also identifies two distinct and often contradictory colonising cultures - the metropolitan culture at the centre of the colonising power and the colonial culture of the occupiers in the colony - which determined the specific form that colonial oppression takes. In the case of the situation in South Africa no such distinction existed. Moreover, unlike most other colonial cases, including the late survivors of Rhodesia, Angola and Mozambique, the ruling class in South Africa was far from homogeneous in terms of its cultural referent. While the term "European" was used as synonymous with "white" there was a notable lack of commonality in the core to which allegiance was pledged and therefore the lines of fealty of the ruling class were themselves defined along ethnic definitions which often generally corresponded to class divisions. Neale (1989) uses as a case study that part of the British Empire which eventually became Zimbabwe, Zambia and Malawi. Colonial rule in this area exhibited the same type of racism that obtained in South Africa and yet its expression in terms of the evolution of institutionalised domination was markedly different. This reinforces Wolpe's (1980) argument, noted above, that the premise of racism is, by itself, an insufficient explanation of the apartheid phenomenon. Fine and Davis further argue that an acceptance of a theoretical correspondence between colonialism and apartheid implies a prescription for resistance to apartheid along nationalist lines rather than one which addresses oppression along class divisions. They proposed that in the South African case a resistance movement founded on a programme of nationalist affirmation would, when successful in overthrowing apartheid, run the risk of reproducing the former relations of production. These relations would then be legitimised because of the eradication of their identification of with racial domination.

However, Variava (1989) argues that the articulation of the struggle against apartheid on the basis of identity was the inevitable consequence of the immediate face of apartheid which, regardless of the principal for which it acted as agent, sought to define and construct distinct notions of the self on the basis of racial classifications.[53] In South Africa, especially

53 Variava (1989: 277) states that

under apartheid the correspondence between race and class became too close, with class being subsumed within race as the overriding defining basis of oppression, to have rendered a liberation agenda based on the class struggle anything but futile. This is not to deny the validity of the class-based analysis of South African economic history and if one accepts that the end of apartheid does not signify the end of oppression then there is a basis for arguing that Variava's notion of the "immediacy" of the oppression of the majority can be shifted on to a class basis. The rate at which it shifts would, however, still be determined by the stickiness of class mobility across different racial groupings. It would be reasonable to expect a rapid "democratisation" of poverty as the support structures and effective job reservation, for the white, and specifically Afrikaner, working class were suddenly withdrawn following the collapse of apartheid. This "democratisation" was significantly less rapid in the case higher income professional and monied classes whose power positioning within the South African economy became a virtually indelible structural formation.

Apartheid and modernity

Since the discourse on modernity has dominated most of twentieth century economic history and since the rapidly changing role of science, technology and innovation has become an integral part of this discourse, the analysis of the relationship between apartheid and modernity offers a fruitful departure point and a sounding board for a comprehension of the evolution of South Africa's innovation system. Simpson (1995) locates the origin of the spirit of modernity in the crisis of religious belief and the consequent search for an alternative meta-narrative rooted in a conviction of humanity's control over its own destiny.[54] The specification of the

---

"... the Black Consciousness Movement reacted against the effects of racial oppression, and represented a struggle against apartheid in its immediacy. They did not look for the 'main enemy', the economy, but directed their forces against the immediate adversary, the white South African."

54 In this regard Simpson (1995: 136) states that

"...(m)odernity marks the stage at which totalizing world views rooted in religion and tradition lose their purchase on the European mind. Seized by the anxiety born of fragmentation left in the wake of this loss, there nevertheless remained for some the conviction that some other sort of whole or totality (call it reason) could repair this spiritual wound, and do so

optimal vehicle for the modernist agenda, its prescriptive content, went through dramatic changes during the last century. The main contenders for the role of narrator in this discourse before the Second World War were fascism and communism. In the post-war era the battle for this position was waged between democracy as defined in western industrialised economies on the one hand and communist countries adhering to the Soviet model on the other. In both cases the ultimate non-ideological legitimising base lay in the ability of the respective systems to sustain industrial growth rates with the concomitant reliance on technological progress and efficiency. The dramatic failure of the Soviet economy ushered in the collapse of the Soviet Union in the late eighties and this provided the decisive legitimacy of the Western model and established its universal (global) hegemony.

Luke summarises the generally accepted symptomatic aspects of the specifically post-war western idealised model of modernity as follows:

> "Modernity ... means (a) gaining rational control of the physical and social environment, (b) building a liberal democratic state, (c) participating in world culture, and (d) joining the scientific revolution." (Luke, 1992:212, parentheses added)

From a relativistic perspective, rationality is contingent on the goal set informing the decision maker and therefore, following Stigler and Becker (1977) and Becker (1993), its precepts should be applied exclusively to strategy. Within the context of apartheid therefore, the issue of rationality concerns the choice of strategies adopted in order to achieve the overt goal of a permanent domination of the polity and the economy by whites. It is difficult to arrive at a definitive assessment of the rationality of apartheid strategy in this regard since so many of the *ceteris paribus* conditions under which the apartheid programme was originally formulated changed over time. This difficulty is further compounded by intra-white class and ethnic conflicts which obscure the identification of the specific interests that were served by a racist regime.

Posel (1991) argues against the validity of treating apartheid policies as the consequence of a coherent blueprint and, partially on the basis of this thesis, she discounts most of the literature informing the race-class debate.

> in a way that would not require an impossible return to an earlier innocence."

and Lyotard (1989: xxiii)defined the "...the term modern to designate any science that legitimates itself with reference to a metadiscourse ... making an explicit appeal to some grand narrative ..."

She points to the dissensions within the Afrikaner nationalist coalition, to the frequent redesigning of apartheid policies, to conflicts among the various state organs and finally to the effects of, and the reactions to, the revolts against apartheid as areas of analysis which were marginalised by the mainstream discourse on apartheid. Her argument therefore rests on two distinct contentions - a denial of the consistency and hence the rationality of the apartheid 'blueprint', on the one hand, and of the efficacy of apartheid policies in attaining the avowed goals of the architects of apartheid, on the other.[55] The conflation of these two arguments is, however, misleading. An argument can be made for a rationality in the planning for a long term programme of racial domination, given the initial ideological premise and the internal and external conditions at the time when the structures of grand apartheid were constructed. Evidence of dissension within nationalist ranks at the time of the drafting of the political programme is not conterminous to the premise of rationality. As long as the ideological principles and goals informing decision making are articulated and consistent then the tenet of localised and bounded rationality, as it has been defined here, holds. Dissensions over the means and strategies to achieve the common goal set do not detract from this contention since dissension and conflict over strategy are features of any institutional structure. Posel's other critical platform, concerning the efficacy of apartheid policies, can be related to the argument of the appropriateness of strategic decisions as discussed in the previous chapter, with respect to innovation. Once we depart from the neoclassical conceptualisation of the fully informed decision making environment and accept ignorance as a permanent feature of the planning environment, then unforeseeable eventualities are inevitable. From this perspective, the

---

55 With respect to the rationality of the apartheid programme, Posel (1991: 50-51, parenthesis and italics added) states that

> "... SABRA (the South African Bureau of Racial Affairs) described its project as scrupulously 'scientific', but its deliberations on 'racial policy' were *nevertheless* conducted within the ideological and organizational framework of Afrikaner nationalism, and therefore accepted 'the right to White self-determination' as a fundamental starting point." (Posel, 1991: 50-51, parenthesis and emphasis added)

The wording of this passage indicates that Posel associates rationality (scientific reasoning) with goal sets and hence discounts the internal logic of policies aimed at the fulfilment of a white supremacist programme. Her subsequent elucidation of the explicit rationale underlying SABRA's proposal for total segregation as against the contending version of apartheid which she terms "practical" actually depicts a contention over alternative definitions of what was considered to be the most efficient path towards attaining the undisputed objective of white domination.

revisions of strategic plans that occurred regularly as the result of internal conflict and the unexpected results of policies can be proposed as evidence of the flexibility of the state apparatus in dealing with change.

Given path dependency, as discussed in the previous chapter, institutions themselves can become inappropriate in any of the ways suggested for technology. Unless institutional adjustment is continuous and efficient, evolving structures tend to become self-justifying and thus inevitably depart, to some degree or other, from the initial goal set which informs their establishment. The main source for this *malaise* is, of course, the necessary inherent conservatism of institutions, a conservatism which is justified by the high level of transaction costs associated with continuous adjustment. The more rigid the institutional framework, the greater is the threat posed to the informing rationality of the *status quo* by unpredicted environmental shifts and hence the greater is the resistance to change. Moreover, once the assumption of perfect information about future eventualities is abandoned, the possibility arises that the strategic plan which informs the instrumentality of specific institutions may have been ill-conceived from the start. Thus, an evolving system can be evaluated by an analysis of its appropriateness. This assessment has, of course, to be preceded by a definition of the yardstick against which this concept is to be measured. But, regardless of its verdict, the analysis of appropriateness does not bear on the assessment of rationality at the time that strategy is devised. To mix these two approaches would render the abstraction of the various facets of processes that are to be analysed impossible.

When judged by the other three criteria proposed by Luke, however, the post-1948 apartheid regime departed progressively from the global drive towards modernity. The second condition, the attainment of a liberal democratic culture, obviously disqualifies South Africa from the contenders in the modernisation process since apartheid was, by definition, anathema to the principles of a democratic government. It is, of course true that a number of nations which are not liberal democracies are considered as having embarked on the path to modernity. In fact there often seems to be a correlation though not necessarily a causality between authoritarian regimes and a rapid modernisation process in many of the successful newly industrialised economies. However, what is left unstated in the definition of the condition regarding political organisation is that human capital investment programmes should aim at raising the technological capabilities of the whole population, regardless of whether or not the political vision informing education has been decided along liberal democratic lines. South Africa, both before, but especially after, the establishment of apartheid, failed to satisfy this criterion.

The specifically racist basis of oppression in South Africa after apartheid, along lines too uncomfortably reminiscent of colonialism, led to the progressive isolation of the country from world culture. This quarantine was as much the result of an initial deliberate policy on the part of its planners to isolate the populace from the "pernicious" influence of the global trend towards democracy and racial equality as it was due to its relegation to pariah status by most of the rest of the world. The official resistance to the introduction of television is a particularly grotesque symptom of the well-justified assessment of the impossibility of sustaining the intricate set of social ordering along racial lines in the face of the changing values in the global village. In the process of enforcing this isolation an almost pathological type of parochialism was entrenched and it severely constrained the ability of all but the corporate giants to interact with the global market.

Finally, the country was, through the progressive imposition of economic sanctions, excluded from a free access to an international scientific and technological colloquium. Freeman highlights the growing importance of international networks in technology since the 1980s:

> "In quantitative terms there is abundant evidence of a strong upsurge of various forms of research collaboration, especially in generic technologies (joint ventures, Research Corporations, joint R&D agreements, technology exchange agreements, direct investment [minority holdings motivated by technology factors] and licensing and second-sourcing agreements), involving extensive international collaboration as well as national and regional networks." (Freeman, 1991: 507, parenthesis added from Table 1, p. 502)

In a similar vein, Chesnais (1988) points to the increasing levels of collaboration among transnational corporations, primarily due to the increasing complexity and complementarity of technologies, especially in the case of systemic R&D programmes. South Africa's progressive isolation from international innovation networks became prominent during the apartheid era, starting with its exclusion from the Commonwealth in the early sixties and accelerating as international outrage at the enduring racist regime grew. While a level of technological cooperation was maintained, often covertly, with a number of countries, cooperative relationships were limited to selected industries, usually linked to military programmes, and thus fell short of the broad based international networks of innovators available to modernising economies.

Thus, from the perspective of the global drive towards modernity, the crucial turning point in the history of the country and the development of its innovation system was the National Party election victory of 1948. Up to this point South Africa was, within the context of the empire(s), still abreast with the times. Structurally, it was not markedly different from other parts of the empire. Relatively speaking the country was better endowed, with abundant natural resources, a sound infrastructure and a rapidly growing manufacturing sector, than most other colonised economies. The window of opportunity was wide open and South Africa had a sounder economic base than most of those countries which eventually leapt through towards sustainable growth paths. The division of power along racial lines and the predominance of enclave economies were features shared by most of the colonised countries which were shortly to gain political independence from colonising powers. It was the endurance and legalistic entrenchment of racial oppression after the passing of the empire that shunted the country on to a path which rapidly diverged from that of modernising economies. This is not necessarily an argument for the construction of the 1948 Nationalist electoral victory as a significant discontinuity in South Africa's political economic history. The Smuts government which preceded apartheid had, in spite of its brief flirtation with reforms during the war, exhibited a clear unwillingness to abandon racial segregation. The 1946 suppression of the mine workers' revolt, and the reasons that led to that revolt in the first place, were a clear indication of a reactionary government which could not abandon the *status quo*. Whether the suppression of the claims of black workers had its basis in the adherence to racial domination or in the protection of the interests of employers, it is difficult to construe the National Party's institution of apartheid as anything but a formalisation and an entrenchment of an inherited structure. Thus the argument is that it was the continuity with past policies against a rapidly changing global context that removed South Africa from the ranks of the modern.

Norval recognises the innate divergence between the Afrikaner nationalist upsurge of the thirties and the icons of modernity when she says that

> "(a) set of equivalences were drawn between the city, Englishness, amorality, relativism, artificiality and atheism, while the *platteland* (countryside) was associated with a close communion with nature, God, a rounded humanity, simplicity and the resoluteness characteristic of Afrikaner life." (Norval, 1996:20, parenthesis added)

She concludes, however that "this contrasting of the foreign ... with the own ... did not lead to a rejection of modernity" (Norval, 1996: 20) since

> "...in order to conquer the city and to counter the perceived negative effects of modernity, Afrikanerdom would have to work hard to develop its own positive conception of the city." (ibid.)

She defines the demarcation lines in the battle for the Afrikaner constituency along sets of correspondences attributed to the leaders of the two disparate camps as

> "... a struggle ... between the Boer War generals - Botha, Smuts and Hertzog - who represented the old landed notables prepared to compromise with mining capital, and the new intelligentsia mobilised since the 1920s around the language issue, who wanted to purge Afrikaner identity of its poor and 'coloured' elements, and attempted to reconstitute Afrikaner fiction, language and cultural institutions along exclusionist lines." (Norval, 1996: 36)

There is however a fundamental flaw within this argument that proposes the luminaries of Afrikaner nationalism as the 'young Turks' on a mission to wrest the seat of modernity from the old guard who are affiliated to mining capital, the Empire and, by implication, traditional values. Mining capital and the notion of the 'city' represented the modern sector. The Empire was, at the time of the recounting, already in the throes of the upheavals that would lead to the 'winds of change' in the fifties. The strategy to 'conquer the city' by Afrikaner nationalists was, rather than a process of assimilation of the waves of modernization, an attempt, and ultimately a successful one, to occupy the seat of the nation's economic engine and in the process to erect unassailable bastions against the 'corruptive' effects of the rapidly changing international political order which would have rendered untenable those racial power relations which the Boer Republics had fought for.

Danziger (1971) identifies the shift in the legitimating base of South African racism within the National Party that occurred with the 1948 electoral victory as a more valid case for a modernising compulsion within Afrikanerdom, or at least within its ideologues. This shift is from domination based on "religious parables" to one which "... became secularized and appealed to group norms and cultural relativism" (p. 288). The case for racial discrimination had shifted from one based on the assumption of the intrinsic preordained order of racial hierarchies to an instrumental argument based on economic efficiency and progress. This argument was reinforced by the empirical "evidence" provided by the series of political and economic disaster stories which had started plaguing the rest of the continent in the post-colonial era and by the ratification of the South African political system by the major western powers. Danziger also identifies the limits to this modernisation drive arising from the special case of an overtly coercive state where the majority of the population was excluded from the benefits of a modernising economy. Concurrently the abandonment of an intrinsic legitimating basis rendered the political order subject to attacks on the basis of its effectiveness in delivering the promised economic progress which would improve the life chances of all its constituents. In other words, apartheid had to prove itself as the best possible system for the whole of South Africa's population to a range of interests which included its white electorate, the disenfranchised majority and the whole spectrum of world opinion. As this claim became progressively untenable for the majority of the population, the use of coercion intensified in the attempt to retain the established order. This was complemented by the ultimately futile attempts to co-opt sections of the oppressed populations in an attempt to fragment opposition and to create buffer classes.

The assessment of the performance of the economy under apartheid has been a crucial element of the debate on the identification of the principals of apartheid. Moll states that a "modern economy with great potential which fails to grow rapidly is a curious thing, well worthy of attention" (Moll, 1991:290). Moll uses real GDP growth rates (both official ones and his own recalculated ones) to show that the overall economic growth rate in South Africa was substantially below that of both developed and developing countries after 1950. However, the advent of apartheid shifted South Africa out of the category of modern or modernising countries and the comparison that Moll proposes thus becomes less relevant to the South African case. There is one other, and more crucial, issue which is raised by Moll's assessment of South Africa's economic performance. Overall, the rate of economic growth is a valid indicator of the success or otherwise of an economic system only in the case of contract states where the whole of the population is, at least overtly and constitutionally, considered as the constituent basis of the polity. This was obviously not the case in South Africa. What is relevant therefore is the nature of the correspondence between the failure of real GDP to grow in line with that of other industrial or industrialising economies and the interests of the principal(s) whose goals dominated apartheid policies. Again the assessment of the degree to which the evolution of apartheid institutions was appropriate depends on the identification of the beneficiaries of this system. If overt racist domination were the primary goal, then the system failed, as it was inevitably bound to, given the unavoidable internal revolt set against the context of the various radical changes in the global political power distribution. If, on the other hand, the principal was capital, increasingly homogenous, both ethnically and in terms of the holdings spread across economic sectors, then a more appropriate functionalist assessment of the performance of apartheid would have to consider internationally comparable rates of return on investment, the dynamics of income distribution, the degree of market concentration and finally the endurance of the relations of production established during the period of segregation and apartheid in post-apartheid South Africa. From this perspective a strong *ex post facto* case can be made for class, with capital at the fore, as the prime enduring principal occupying the centre ground of the pre-democratic political economic institutional framework. As we have already stated apartheid could not endure, but this obvious fact does not by itself explain why apartheid ended when it did, nor the manner in which it was terminated. For an adherent to a Marxist account of South African economic history the timing and the manner in which the National Party capitulated to democracy are the conclusive evidence of the primacy of capitalist interests over racist ideology as the driving force behind apartheid. From this perspective the apparent dictates of the global economy, as enunciated by the World Bank and the International Monetary Fund and adopted by the country's first democratic government, slip in smoothly as the substitute legitimising base for the economic relations that obtained under apartheid. Numerous aspects of the development path of the South African political economy in the fourteen years since apartheid tend to support this contention. Macroeconomic indicators, such as GDP growth rates, inflation, fiscal discipline and currency stability have in general been encouraging over this period. However, unemployment levels and the skill base of the general populace remain virtually unchanged and, in the case of income and wealth distribution, have actually deteriorated.

Locating the history of the South African innovation system

The argument advanced in this chapter that the emergence of apartheid implied an abandonment of modernity is not to be associated with a neoliberal, or the less prominent Marxist, version of the race domination account of South African economic history. South Africa did indeed proceed on the path of capitalist development, but it was a path that was marked by capital accumulation with increasing capital/output and capital/labour ratios, along with an increasing physical capital/human capital ratio. This was a path that a number of Latin American countries and India followed through most of their post-war history. The alternative path of capitalist development that was forfeited was the one that is generally evident in the Asian tigers, i.e. heavily reliant on broad based human capital investment. South Africa's pattern of development reinforced the country's competitive advantage with exports of manufactured commodities with high intensities of physical capital and low intensities of skilled labour and a continuing dependence on primary sector inputs while importing commodities intensive in human capital and technology (Moura Roque, 1984; Scerri, 1990, 1995). These trading patterns in manufactured commodities placed South Africa in the category of countries that Wolter (1977), Hulsman-Vejsova and Koekkoek (1980) and Stern (1984) classified as peripheral industrialised economies.

It is difficult to locate definitively an analysis of the history of South Africa's national system of innovation within the dominant debates on its economic historiography since it was essentially a product of the political and economic structures that evolved rather than an overt policy tool used in the construction of that system. The main identifying characteristic of the history of South Africa's system of innovation is that of limited, contingent strategic planning both on the part of capital and on that of the apartheid mandarins. On neither side do we find evidence of a planned coherent national science and technology policy and it is this lack of coordination at a national level that constituted its defining feature. In the case of the state there emerged significant innate unresolvable contradictions between apartheid ideology and the requirements of a national system of innovation suitable for sustainable development. In the case of the private sector, while firms are the primary source of innovations, the forces shaping the evolution of the system within which technology is developed and utilised usually lie outside the ambit of the profit calculus informing private sector decision making processes. Moreover, the contradictions and conflicts inherent in the diversity of agents within the capitalist class would, in the absence of some overriding planning agency which operates outside the market, result in a multi-layered set of motivational forces which will necessarily inhibit the consistency of the direction of the development of the country's innovation system. While the divergence between private and social returns on investment in the 'infrastructure' of innovation are comparable to that obtaining for any public good, this type of investment is rarely tangible in the way that investment in road transport systems and other types of physical infrastructure are. The motivation for it requires a vision of the eventual enhancement of a nation's ability to engage in innovative activity at various levels. This is not a vision that can be expected to emerge from the private sector, except in those cases where an industry is dominated by large conglomerates in a competitive environment. The only industry which has persistently exhibited these characteristics in South Africa has been the mining sector and it is noteworthy that a substantial portion of R&D activity in the earlier part of the twentieth century stemmed from this sector and, according to Fine and Rustomjee (1996), continues to occur in the minerals-energy complex. However, the potential for innovation in a primary sector is, unlike the case for secondary industries, limited. The product is unvarying and the only scope for R&D activity is the development of process innovations to reduce extraction costs. In the case of the mining sector in South Africa the direction of R&D activity was, throughout this century, strongly affected by the presumption of the unique stranglehold of the mining houses on the labour market that assured a continuous supply of cheap labour. This position, as we shall see in subsequent chapters, had significant negative spillover effects on the development of technological capabilities and on the course of industrial development in the rest of the economy.

The debates on South African historiography are pertinent to this study because their prime focus is the identification of the principal on whose behalf the state machinery acted as the agent. This enables us to take positions on the nature of the power base underlying the innovation system that is currently in place and to offer sound theoretical bases for alternative policy proposals. If racial domination were the determining driving force behind the apartheid economy then the collapse of apartheid should, through the liberation of market forces, proceed a long way towards the reconstruction of the economy in line with the requirements for a sustainable development process. This premise would provide the basis for an argument for a reform in inherited state bureaucratic structures and a general policy of neutral intervention in order to correct for inherited market failures without, however, interfering in inter-sectoral relationships. In this case the motivation for targeted intervention would be weak and would only arise in exceptional cases. If, on the other hand, the interests of capital are construed as having been the main driving force in the formulation of economic policy under apartheid, the prescriptive implications are radically different. The industrial structure that emerged from apartheid and the conditions of its survival would then be seen as integrally entwined with the power relations that emerged under the old political regime and as unable to achieve the base for appropriate levels of economic development. In this case policies to increase the racial heterogeneity of equity ownership and of middle and higher management employment compositions would, even if successful, have no spillovers on to the majority of the population. The required strategy in this case would have to be a targeted one driven by the recognised need to alter the present structure and incentives mechanism.

As I have discussed earlier on, one of the main areas of contention in the race-class debate is the construction of continuities and breaks in South Africa's history and this part of the debate extends to the dependent analysis of the development of the country's innovation system. In particular, the development of South Africa's innovation system can be assessed on two levels in the exploration for the possible incidence of ruptures. The first is internal to the system that is being examined while the other locates the local history in relation to changes in the national innovation systems of other countries. The tenet of continuity in the transition from pre-1948 segregation policy to apartheid is most defensible when localised within an isolated local context. When set against the backdrop of global political and economic developments, however, this thesis is much less tenable.

The argument that is advanced throughout the rest of this work is that on the first level there is a substantial amount of evidence of a consistency in the context within which national science and technology planning evolved throughout the history considered in this study. This consistency is anchored in the limitation of this area of planning to the confines of an economic context constrained by the exigencies imposed by segregation and later by apartheid. This assessment goes against the two, semi-official accounts (Kingwill, 1990 and Basson, 1996), of the history of the Council for Scientific and Industrial research (CSIR) both of which identify the same three ruptures. According to these accounts, the first break occurs in 1948 with the National Party's downgrading of the status and independence of the CSIR. The second diversion in the history of this institution is identified in 1987, with the move towards a policy of "market-accountability". The third change in direction is linked to the collapse of apartheid and the establishment of democracy. My position, which will be developed in the following chapters, is that these apparent discontinuities are largely superficial. The heritage of the CSIR was firmly grounded in a science and technology vision which had been articulated shortly after the end of the First World War and in an institutional structure which was established at the end of the second one. The change in direction in 1987, while arising from the realisation of the ineffectuality of national science and technology planning in South Africa, simply marked the final relinquishment on the part of the state of its role as a shaper of the country's innovation system. Moreover, the essential parameter base underlying science and technology planning extended beyond the collapse of apartheid. The shift in the political and economic goal set informing the drafting of the post-apartheid programme in this area (IDRC, 1993; DACST, 1996) overtly marks an obvious fundamental discontinuity in the evolution of the country's innovation system, given the novel democratic context. However, the *modus operandi*, the economic rationale of science and technology planning which is implicitly treated as politically neutral, as divorced from the overtly apartheid objective, remained essentially unchanged.

On the second level, i.e. the study of the evolution of the country's innovation system in relation to the outside world, a case can be made that the 1948 election victory of the National Party did indeed constitute a distinct rupture. For roughly a decade prior to 1948 the conflict between the country's internal politics and its leaders' aspirations for economic growth and international acceptability had generated a wave of internal opposition to discrimination which was becoming increasingly credible and effective in its demands for reform. Had they been pursued, the incipient reforms on several crucial areas of racial discrimination which started during the Second World War would have addressed directly the main bottlenecks to the broad-based development of technological capabilities within the economy. Moreover, during the early half of this century South Africa's innovation system had been developing along a pattern which still exhibited distinct commonalities with an established international norm of successful industrial and economic development. The emergence of grand apartheid from 1948 onwards irrevocably halted this process on both levels. In the first place the new overwhelming political concern with maintaining racial segregation effectively curtailed any possibility of developing a sound technological capabilities base. Secondly, the emergence of a new international technological order after the war, one which placed technological capabilities at the hub of sustainable economic development and international competitiveness, rendered the emerging innovation system in South Africa increasingly obsolete. Subsequent to the argument advanced in the previous chapter that the evolution of a national system of innovation is firmly integrated within the broader economic development process, this shift is symptomatic of the general shunting of the nation's course into a path which became increasingly idiosyncratic and inward-looking as compared to international developments in this area.

The heritage of South Africa's post-war industrial and broader economic history, and the resulting structures, has locked the post-apartheid economy into an innovation system which is incompatible with its development needs. This verdict applies at several layers. At the most immediate level there is a legacy of past specific technology choices, most notably those in the chemicals sector (see Crompton, 1995), which have resulted in industrial linkage matrices that were less than optimal by global standards and were moreover extremely difficult to reverse. In this particular case the choice of a coal based instead of an oil based synthetic fuels industry with its repercussions on the chemicals and the commodity plastics industry was a direct result of the perceived need for self sufficiency on the part of the apartheid regime in the face of escalating international isolation.

Even more pernicious, however, is the determining power of the factor market relations inherited from a history of racial oppression and the consequent endemic shortfall in human capital investment on current technology choices. Lall (1992a, 1992b) and Lundvall (2002), among others, identify education and human capital investment levels as one of the defining determinants of technological capabilities and hence of the national innovation systems of the more successful newly industrialising countries. The composite definition of human capital includes formal education and training, ranging from broad based primary education to technical training, and in-house training by business enterprises. The most rapidly growing newly industrialised economies are those which also provide the better quality of education. Lall (1992a) makes a crucial point about the determinants of human capital development which holds a special relevance to the South African case. This is "the legacy of inherited skills, attitudes, and abilities that aid industrial development" (Lall, 1992a: 170). This is a legacy that engenders a "strong cultural emphasis on education" (Lall, 1992a: 178) which is simultaneously fostered by state and private support mechanisms. He identifies four main aspects of human capital development in which the East Asian Tigers have excelled. These are formal education at secondary and tertiary levels, a high incidence of technical education and vocational training, the high quality of the education that is provided and, finally, the high incidence of in-house training carried out by firms. The impoverishment of human capital in South Africa, as a result of apartheid education policies also prejudices the attainment of one of the features of a labour force which Lall (1992a) identifies as a requirement for efficient industrialisation. This is that the competence gap between the general labour force and engineers has to narrow in order to enable the absorption of technology. The South

African legacy in this respect is such as to pose the cardinal impediment to an industrialisation process marked by increasing competitiveness in product lines containing a high value added component. Again, for a variety of reasons that will be discussed further on, this particular legacy is still binding in the post-apartheid era with industrial planning at state and private levels still occurring under the implicit assumption of an unchanging human capital stock. Writing later, Lundvall (2002) shifts the focus of the analysis of innovation systems from the "knowledge economy" to the "learning economy" in order to emphasise the effects, and the requirements, of the rapidly accelerating rate of technological change. The brunt of the development requirements within this context is borne by human capital, which now is subject to a historically unprecedented high and continuously accelerating rate of obsolescence. This factor renders the damaging effects of the inherited stock of human capital on South Africa's development prospects even more pronounced.

The low absolute and relative R&D expenditure figures and other indicators of innovative activity provide yet another measure which, at the end of the apartheid era, placed South Africa outside the ranking of competitive industrialised economies (FRD, 1993, 1996). These poor performance indicators were themselves symptomatic of an inadequate incentives mechanism which, while a product of history, endured after the demise of apartheid. It is an incentives mechanism whose salient feature is the low, perceived and actual, rates of return on innovative activity. These returns are prejudiced by a poor opportunities base, especially exemplified by low technological capabilities, and by the absence of an official policy which offers, through rewards and sanctions, any clear direction on the pattern of industrial development. A high ownership concentration[56] combined with the limited local markets renders internal competitive pressures negligible as an incentive for firms to innovate for strategic purposes. The inundation of competition from abroad, post apartheid further reinforced the technological lag of local industry.

The binding effects of this inheritance, and the severe limitations that it apparently places on the choice set which the new democratic state faces, were reinforced by the fallout from the collapse of the Soviet bloc. Post-apartheid South Africa was born at the "death of ideology" where the immediate evidence of history is such as to exclude overt state

---

56 Fine and Rustomjee (1996:96) state that

> "...(t)he South African economy has been dominated by six conglomerates which, because of their simultaneous control of mining, manufacturing and financial sectors, are more usefully viewed as 'axes' of capital."

intervention in the market as deluded and even morally culpable. Within this global context, the unique nature of the ANC was the mediating structure through which the race-class debate was translated into policy. A combination of factors had combined to make the ANC quite unique in the history of post liberation movements. It was the longest lived liberation movement which had effectively become the only anti-apartheid movement of note, primarily through the absorption of the intelligentsia of other liberation movements. Its dominant position at the end of apartheid ensured its overwhelming and invulnerable majority in parliament. This invulnerability was primarily due to the nature of the main opposition front which went through waves of fragmentations and coalitions for the first few years of democracy and which could never convincingly shed its identification with white interests. Because of its long history of assimilation and incorporation, the -ANC had no ideological identity but rather encompassed a gamut of political/economic ideologies. Therefore, the ideological struggle which was to mark the first decade or so of the post-apartheid era happened within the -ANC rather than between the -ANC and other political parties. Within the -ANC the main formations were those members who had been in exile and who had organised the world wide ant-apartheid movement and those members who had fought against apartheid from within South Africa. These formations rapidly established the ideological divide. A large portion of those members who had remained in the country came from organised labour and had strong grassroots affiliations, whereas the former exiles were more *au fait* with the world outside South Africa and, since the collapse of the Soviet Union, identified closely with western style liberal economies. The securing of power bases through patronage systems in the post colonial period, as charted by Fieldhouse (1986) among others, did not occur as a contest between competing political parties. Rather the struggle for political ascendancy happened within the legitimate, elected party which was and still is quite invulnerable to any credible challenge to its parliamentary majority.

With no reinforcing ideological base, faced with high unemployment, high public debt, rising inflation and volatile international markets, the democratic government succumbed to the continued exhortation to adopt "pragmatic" economic policies. Within the context of the ruling neoliberal paradigm at the time, this was read as the imperative to liberalise the inherited economic structure in the expectation that with the new political dispensation the growth in business turnover would filter down to benefit the general populace. Implicitly, this was a clear positioning of the post-apartheid economic policy on the liberal side of the race\class debate. The role of the state in the transformation and development process was mainly restricted to the provision of basic needs and the reformation of public finance. This largely neutral approach to development was quite inappropriate for a developing economy like South Africa, with its deep rooted structural deficiencies. The implicit assumption behind this policy stance was that once the precepts of a racist regime and the attendant legislation were removed, market rationality would move to eradicate the systemic distortions created by the political economic evolution of the country over the three hundred odd years of colonial and apartheid administration. The post apartheid growth and development programme seems to have been oblivious to the fact that facilitating market operations would not address such fundamental problems as the dire shortage of human capital, the general absence of incentives to engage in own R&D activity and the existing dependence on packaged foreign technology. Business decisions, whether local or those of foreign investors, would still be basically made on the assumption of a permanence of low skill availability, poor technological capabilities and a limited internal market. Thus, there were a powerful set of forces at work to reinforce the essential features and constraints of the inherited structure.

This continuity of the national system of innovation that had been established under apartheid has proved to be the prime insurmountable obstacle to attempts to translate political freedom into economic liberation. The disillusionment with the performance of the original neoliberal macroeconomic plan has led to a number of attempts to address perceived areas of failure. The ten year review of the performance of the South African economy (RSA, 2003:102) stated that

> "The advances made in the First Decade by far supersede the weaknesses. Yet, if all indicators were to continue along the same trajectory, especially in respect of the dynamic of economic inclusion and exclusion, we could soon reach a point where the negatives start to overwhelm the positives. This could precipitate a vicious cycle of decline in all spheres."

However, in the absence of alternative conceptual planning frameworks these attempts are fragmentary and have proved largely futile in addressing the enduring structural impediments to transformation and growth. The first sentence of the quoted text shows an enduring adherence to the fundamentals of the original macroeconomic plan which saw structural transformation as following liberalisation.

PART 2:

THE HISTORY

CHAPTER THREE

THE PATH TOWARDS MODERNITY

The recounting of the development of South Africa's system of innovation during the first stage of this history runs along two interconnected paths. The first is the development of an institutional framework explicitly charged with the coordination and advancement of science and technology programmes in the country. The other path concerns the changing definition, through policy, of the relationship between state and market. Both paths were affected by events which were external and internal to the development of the South African polity. The most notable of the external events were the two world wars. The First World War provided the stimulus, through policy decisions taken in Britain, for the establishment of the first science and technology planning body. The second war was directly instrumental in the motivation to establish the South African Council for Scientific and Industrial Research (CSIR). The set of internal events is associated with changes in governments over this period.

Initially, governments which saw Smuts in positions of power tended to be, within the conditions peculiar to the South African economy, market friendly, specifically with respect to the mining sector. Those governments which were dominated by nationalist Afrikaner politics, on the other hand, were more interventionist and distrustful of market forces, dominated as these were during most of the period by mining capital. These associations do not necessarily imply a causality. A number of direct state interventions in the market during the Hertzog-Creswell government of 1924-1933 owed their origin in initiatives launched by a Smuts appointee, H.J. van der Bijl. All of these interventions, except the establishment of the Iron and Steel Corporation (ISCOR), were of an infrastructural nature, aimed at providing "public goods". In the case of ISCOR the basis of the studies initiated under Smuts was an exploration of the technological feasibility for such an industry in South Africa. The motivation provided by Creswell, on the other hand, built upon the outcome of the technical reports to make a case for intervention on the basis of a market failure which was not due to externalities or the public good nature of the product but rather to a lack of entrepreneurial capability in the private sector. Eventually, with the accelerating programme of industrial development engineered by van der Bijl, culminating in the immediate post-war period before the National Party victory of 1948, a policy of managed development was firmly entrenched.

If one were to choose a symbol for the tensions and contradictions inherent in the fledgling political construct that was the Union of South Africa, from its inception in 1910 to the irretrievable path choice that it took in 1948, it would be the figure of Jan Smuts. As a Boer war hero, Smuts was an icon of Afrikanerdom. At the same time he was a convinced imperialist who could negotiate with Britain because of his affinity for geopolitik. He was a modernist and an internationalist, who was often ruthless in crushing opposition. As Minister of Mines he became identified as the convinced champion of mining capital, owned by foreign[1] imperialist interests, against his own volk, the white Afrikaner mine labour. He was obsessed with leading the newly formed Union of South Africa into the rank of first world nations. In this pursuit he ultimately seemed willing to sacrifice the privileged status of the white minority in the process, and yet could not take the decisive step in this direction. These contradictions and his ambivalence on the core political issue of his time eventually led to his political demise and the man who drafted the preamble to the United Nations charter, while remaining an apologist for segregation in South Africa, eventually forfeited political power in his own country. This oppositional relationship was set within a range of correspondences. Smuts, the traitor to his own people in the service of the British Empire, was also the supporter of mining capital against the proletariat - white workers in the twenties and black workers in the forties. The Afrikaner nationalist resistance to the political direction represented by Smuts thus became articulated on the basis of both ethnicity and class interests. These correspondences underwent several transformations. Ethnic affirmation became a nationalist movement against foreign capital and progressively the platform for internal racial domination. The white class struggle mutated with shifting political power into an often uneasy conflation of class interests with racial domination. It was this conflation that generated the divergence between the race and the class analyses of apartheid.

1 Terreblanche and Nattrass (1981: 21) point out that in 1918 eighty percent of mining dividends were paid abroad.

Smuts was instrumental in the launching of science and technology initiatives during his terms of office and his involvement was an intimate one. He personally recruited the two leading figures in this process - H.J. van der Bijl, who was to play a crucial role in defining and implementing industrial policy for almost four decades, and Basil Schonland who, together with Smuts, was the architect of the Council for Scientific and Industrial Research and became its first president. The contradictions inherent in the "Smuts phenomenon" were reflected in outlooks of Smuts and van der Bijl and became manifest in the course of national policy on science and technology throughout the country's pre-apartheid history. With Smuts, the political playing field was global and his initiative on defining the role of the state in the development of a national innovation system was outward looking in that it was driven by the objective of leading South Africa into the modern era and placing it among the first rank nations in the emerging international economic order. The one thing that such a policy could not afford was any form of isolation and since the twenties Smuts was well aware that the increasing international disapprobation of segregation policy would eventually exclude South Africa from the company of those nations whom he so admired. Moreover, as I shall discuss further on, the effects of segregation and eventually apartheid on the economy entrenched those bottlenecks, especially in human capital development, which eventually became insuperable obstacles to the evolution of the type of national systems of innovation emerging in first world economies and in the newly industrialising countries. The deleterious effects of these bottlenecks became starkly manifest during the Second World War and it was during this period that the first serious crisis of faith in the long term viability of a modern racially segregated economy emerged. It is therefore difficult to imagine any compatibility between Smuts' political economic agenda and apartheid, not because Smuts was exempt from the contemporary racist belief system[2] or, because, as Horwitz (1967) would have it, he was a

---

2 As premier, Smuts approved the **Native Affairs Act of 1920** which spatially segregated whites from blacks. This was based on the principles recommended by the Lagden Commission Report of 1905, which Smuts himself publicly supported in London in 1917 (Davenport, 1981: 176). The report:

> "... envisaged the territorial separation of black and white, for purposes of residence and ownership, as a permanent mandatory feature of public life. It gave its approval to the establishment of segregated 'locations' for urban Africans ... It also urged the separation of blacks from whites in political life, with Africans represented only by whites in the federal legislature of the future." (Davenport, 1981: 152)

proponent of free market principles, but because the requirements of the development path that he envisaged could not be met within the context eventually generated by apartheid policies.

The antithesis to Smuts was the rising spirit of Afrikaner ethnic affirmation which, despite its minority position, became transformed into an overwhelming nationalist movement. The role assigned to innovation within this political movement was inward looking and reactive, as was appropriate given the tenuous hold on an ethnic identity following defeat in the Anglo-Boer war and the perception of a seemingly permanent subordinate position in the ownership of the primary means of production within the economy. Specific technological advances would eventually

---

The premise behind this policy was explicitly stated by Smuts:

> "... if we are to solve our Native question it is useless to try and govern Black and White in the same system ... They are different not only in colour *but in mind and political capacity* ..." (quoted from Motlhabi, 1984: 7)

The **Natives (Urban Areas) Act of 1923** gave muscle to the enforcement machinery for these recommendations. The bargaining power of black labour was severely restricted by the enforcement of largely inaccessible minimum education requirements for apprenticeship in 1922 and by the exclusion of black workers from the right to engage in collective bargaining by the **Industrial Conciliation Act of 1924**. During the Smuts-Hertzog government strikes by black workers were broken up, usually with violence and loss of life, in 1913, 1918 and 1920. Smuts was, moreover, firmly motivated by his own brand of nationalism. The dismemberment of the Unionist party during the 1921 elections was hailed by him as a great coup along the path to the establishment of Afrikaner dominance. (Davenport, 1981: 188). His advice to the British Secretary of State for the Colonies, in 1924 is indicative of the philosophy informing his vision of the empire in East Africa at the time:

> "All the highlands of Eastern Africa from the Union to Abyssinia are healthy for Europeans and can be made a great European state or system of States ... It is one of the richest parts of the world, and only wants white brains and capital to become enormously productive. ... the Natives by themselves will continue to stagnate as they have stagnated for the last ten thousand years." (quoted in Hancock, 1968: 223)

and his view on the beneficent influence of white settlers was made even clearer in correspondence to a new Secretary in 1929:

> "... without large-scale permanent European settlement on this continent the African mass will not be moved, the sporadic attempts at civilization will pass, Africa may relapse to her historic and prehistoric slumbers, and once more only mining holes and ruined forts may ultimately remain to bear testimony to future ages of what once was. We shall have a repetition of the Zimbabwe, and not an enduring impression on and betterment of the peoples of this continent." (*ibid.*: 225)

become part of the array of instruments employed to entrench the holding position of a people which considered itself constantly embattled, but the development of technology needed to be circumscribed to avoid its potential for eroding the canons of a structure which became progressively archaic against the unfolding backdrop of the second half of the twentieth century.

Although this specific history starts with the first national science and technology policy initiative in 1916, we need to understand the political and economic setting within which it originated. Most twentieth century political histories of South Africa start with the creation of the Union of South Africa in 1910 with Jan Smuts, Louis Botha and J.M.B. Hertzog heading the new government with the South African Party. The rise of Afrikaner nationalism became manifest almost at the inception of the Union, with Hertzog leading the breakaway of cabinet members in 1912 to found the National Party.[3]

It was during this period that a range of extremely repressive laws was implemented, restricting labour and land ownership rights for blacks thus ensuring a pool of cheap powerless labour for the mining sector. Control over the labour market for black mine workers had, however, been in force at least two decades before the establishment of the Union. The Witwatersrand Chamber of Mines had been established in 1889 with the specific purpose of entrenching a monopsonistic position in the black labour market by regulating out of existence any form of intra-industry competition for labour. Along with associated organisations the monopsony position that it established in the recruitment of black labour extended to neighbouring colonies, especially Mozambique. Pass laws had been in existence since 1857, but by the turn of the century they were being written by the mine owners to reinforce their position within this labour market. The first *Native Affairs Commission Report of 1903-1905* specified the two fundamental principles as the basis for policies which treated the country's black population as an essentially non-human resource. In the first place, noting that black farmers were generating sufficient savings to buy land from white farmers, it advocated the

---

3 The spirit informing the founding of the National Party was nationalist based on what today would be termed ethnic lines. Horwitz (1967) quotes Hertzog's words on this occasion:

> "The time has come when South Africa can no longer be ruled by non-Afrikaners ... that I place so much emphasis upon the feeling of nationality of my Dutch-speaking fellow-Afrikaners is because they have a deeper realisation of it, and that is because their ancestors came here two hundred years earlier." (p. 36)

curtailment, through legislation, of the right of black peasantry to purchase land. Secondly, while noting a shortfall in the supply of black labour for industries located in urban centres, it rejected wage increases as a means to increase supply. Subsequent acts which followed were the logical development of these principles. The *Native Labour Regulation Act* of 1911 tied a black labourer to his employer by making it illegal for an employee to break an employment contract and for anyone to entice a labourer from an existing contract by offering better employment conditions, thus eliminating the possibility of wage increases through intra or inter-industry competition for labour. The *Native Lands Act* of 1913 effectively dispossessed a large proportion of the black population from its rural holdings and from 'squatting' rights on white owned land, thus reducing drastically the ability of a large proportion of the black population from earning a sustainable living from farming. Thus, both sides of the labour market were squeezed by legislative means to force black labour from rural to urban employment at wage levels determined by employers.[4]

This recruitment policy could not, of course, be applied to white workers. The one significant measure which was to prove highly detrimental to mining interests was the *Mines and Works Regulation Act* of 1911 which established a statutory colour bar on mines. It specified the allocation of occupations reserved for white workers and the exact terms for each occupation category. Thus a segmented labour supply structure rapidly developed with an over-abundance of applicants for the unskilled labour categories and an endemic shortage of miners who, because of their skin colour, were the sole claimants for skilled jobs. In consequence, during the early days of the Union the mining interests were becoming increasingly opposed to the deleterious effect on profits of the entrenched privileged position of white mine workers. This segmented labour market, entrenched through legislation became the permanent constraint acting on all aspects of economic development.[5] The mining houses were "colour

4 O'Meara (1975: 149) argues that

> "By severely restricting access to the means of production, the Act had the threefold effect of undermining the economic base and independence of the peasantry (effectively destroying a lucrative source of income and subsistence), controlling the growing differentiation within the Reserves (destroying the nascent bourgeoisie), and freeing Africans in large numbers for labour on white farms and in the mines."

5 Horwitz (1976: 29) stated that the pass laws

> "...are so pervading ... as to constitute not only one of the major influences on economic growth but the administrative *deus ex machina* for

blind" in the pursuit of profits, since their disempowerment of black labour had been achieved and the protected position of white labour was the one remaining obstacle to the employers' total control over the supply of labour at all skill levels.[6]

Another crisis for the new government was precipitated by the First World War. The 1910 constitution denied the local government sovereignty over foreign affairs and the British government demanded South Africa's engagement in the war effort, especially with respect to offensives on German South West Africa. This led to the outright revolt of several prominent members of the administration, including various military leaders. This opposition finally led to an overt rebellion in 1914-15 which was suppressed by military force. Thereafter, the Afrikaner nationalist movement coalesced firmly around Hertzog who had from the start refused to recognise South Africa's legal commitment to go to war as Britain's ally.

After the formation of the Union, both Smuts and the subsequent Afrikaner nationalist movement put a high priority on the development of the secondary sector. Smuts was motivated by the requirements of a modern economy while the post-Boer war Afrikaner nationalist/trade unionist coalition saw a burgeoning manufacturing sector as providing a countervailing power base against that of the mining interests. Another impetus to this drive was provided by the need to absorb urban white unemployment and the political need to address the growing "poor white" problem in the twenties. This could not happen without a direct initiative on the part of the state. This policy decision had critical implications for the role of government in the development of the country's technological base since manufacturing held a significantly greater scope for innovation than mining.

Prior to 1916, when the first planning framework for a national science and technology policy was established, state involvement in technology was virtually non-existent. At the time of the formation of the Union the economy was mainly based on agriculture and the mining sector. The former was characterised by large land ownership and antiquated farming

---

the perpetuation of the stratified South African social system under the control of the White polity. They were to become the Frankenstein of political economy."

6 The testimony of mine managers in the report of the **Mining Industry Commission, 1907-8** clearly expressed the mines' views that black workers could easily be introduced into positions reserved for whites and that such a policy, combined with increased mechanisation would lower mining costs. (Horwitz, 1967: 51-55).

methods, a considerable number of poor white tenant farmers[7] and a large population of black squatters. This sector exhibited most of the characteristics of a feudal economy. The mining sector, on the other hand, was the modern component of the economy, characterised by heavy capital investment and an ongoing search for better mining technology. A number of research areas which are nowadays seen as lying within the province and responsibility of public sector provision were initiated because of the requirements of the mining sector. In 1912 the Geological Survey of South Africa led to the establishment of the Government Minerals Laboratory and the Silicosis Medical Bureau. This was followed by the South African Institute of Medical Research (SAIMR) which was established by the mining sector. The Timber Research Laboratory was founded around this time to enhance the beam support structures in mines. Moreover, several private sector initiatives in high technology industry started off as ancillary activities to the mining sector.[8] Thus most R&D activity at this time was financed by private sector funds and driven by specific private sector requirements.

---

7 These were the "bywoner"", the second wave of migrants from the Cape area after all available farming land had been claimed.

8 The largest local group in the chemicals field, the African Explosives and Chemical Industries (AECI), which became a major manufacturer of munitions, owes its origin to the requirements of the mining sector. African Explosives and Industries Limited (AE&I) was formed in 1924 as a joint company between De Beers and Nobel Industries, incorporating the three main explosives factories at Somerset West, Modderfontein and Umbogintwini (Natal). It became a leader in detonator technology in the thirties. In 1932 a major plant was established for the production of synthetic ammonia. This led to diversification into a range of chemical products. In this year South Africa went off the gold standard and the massive increase in mining output provided a major boost in the demand for industrial explosives. A further impetus was provided by World War II. In 1959, a breakthrough was made in developing one of the cheapest explosives in the world, Dynagel. It has regularly come out with major innovations in explosives, fuses and detonators. In 1972, in recognition of the increasing importance of the chemical output of the corporation AE&I became African Explosives and Chemical Industries (AE&CI) and in 1976 became AECI. By 1993 explosives and associated chemicals accounted for only 25% of production. The product diversification of AECI led to a restructuring in 1982 into seven main operating companies covering fertilizers, paints, synthetic fibres, speciality chemicals and factory management. It has shareholdings in Botswana (Soda Ash), and a joint venture with SASOL (originally Suid Afrikaanse Steenkool en Olie - South African Coal and Oil) to produce plastic raw materials. It has entered the biotechnology field with the production of animal supplements.

The periodisation that follows in this chapter corresponds to the country's changes in government. The reason for this is the association between shifts in science and technology policy, and the factors affecting the path of technological development, and the political fortunes of Smuts. The first period deals with Smuts' first term of office. The second sees the country run by a party with an unapologetic white supremacist agenda. The coalition between Smuts and Hertzog over the period 1933-1938 still saw Smuts' political agenda being overshadowed by this political programme. This chapter ends with the dissolution of the Smuts-Hertzog coalition over the issue of South Africa's participation in the Second World War. This ushered in the third period, 1939-1948, which saw Smuts for the first and only time as the country's undisputed political leader.

The launch of national science and technology policy: 1916 - 1924

The first impetus for the formalisation of S&T policies in the post-war period originated from the colonial centre in the form of a 1915 White Paper issued by the Board of Education in Britain[9] which set out the guidelines for a national policy framework on science and technology. The White Paper stated explicitly that the initiative arose from a recognition that Britain had lagged behind Germany in its development of a sound national technology base for its industry with the consequence that numerous severe bottlenecks in production processes could only be solved through imports. This acknowledgement was mainly prompted by the belated acknowledgment that the war that was being fought was one in which production capacity and technology had become crucial factors. An advisory council was set up with the explicit tasks of: (a) proposing specific lines of R&D, (b) proposing the establishment of R&D institutions, (c) establishing research grants, and (d) advising education departments on appropriate measures to improve the supply of R&D personnel. The council was required to cooperate closely with higher education institutions, private sector bodies and government departments (primarily Trade and Industry and Education) in order to implement this new policy. In the same year and early in 1916, shortly after the issue of this White Paper, representations were made to Britain by Australia recommending that the scheme proposed in the White Paper be extended

---

9 *Scheme for the Organisation and Development of Scientific and Industrial Research*, 23rd July 1915. (Cd. 8005).

across the Empire. The rationale for this submission was that the establishment of a cooperative framework which incorporated a wide range of economies had the potential to exploit considerable economies of scale in R&D. Following these initiatives, the Department of Scientific and Industrial Research was established in 1916 in Britain and the system of Research Councils was initiated shortly afterwards, with Australia, Canada, New Zealand and India quickly following suit.

The timing of an equivalent initiative in South Africa indicates that the relevant decision makers in the country were abreast of these developments. In 1916, on the recommendations of a conference of the Councils of Scientific and Technical bodies, the Industries Advisory Board was established under the aegis of the Ministry of Mines and Industry, with the Scientific and Technical Committee as its mainstay. The terms of reference of this committee were to:

> "... advise the Government through the Industries Advisory Board and the Minister on the scientific, technical and industrial aspects of questions which concern the development of the natural resources of the country" [10]

From its initiation the Committee's work addressed the requirements of a national science and technology policy within the context of overall industrial development. In its first report the Committee's recommendations were mainly focussed on the need to draw an inventory of existing information on the country's stock of natural resources,[11] industrial output (including statistics on local sales and exports) and R&D facilities. It commissioned a large number of reports on resources and industrial output and initiated the systematic collection and collation of statistics on agricultural, mining and industrial output. The first measures to ensure a diffusion of scientific and technical information were taken with the establishment of a monthly publication, the South African Journal of Industries. This journal was also to serve the function of providing a medium for the exchange of information with other countries across the empire.

The requirement to liaise with other countries was noted, but, even at this early stage, the committee introduced a cautionary note with respect to

---

10 *Report of the Proceedings of the Industries Advisory Board and of the Scientific and Technical Committee for the nine months ending 31st December, 1917.* (U.G. 21-'18, p. 30).

11 Surveys were immediately requested on geology and minerals, water power, botany and fisheries.

the appropriateness of technology developed abroad for the South African context when it noted that

> "Advantage may be taken of the experience and knowledge already gained in more highly developed countries, but care must be exercised in applying such experience to meet *the special conditions obtaining in this country*."[12] (emphasis added)

The committee did not specify the nature of these *special conditions* and this proviso is significant given the absence of any similar reservation in a memorandum issued in Britain on the guidelines for cooperation in R&D across the empire.[13] Other nations within the empire shared many of the features of the South African economy. Australia, like South Africa, was a mineral resource abundant economy with a strong agricultural sector, as was New Zealand. The shortage of skilled personnel was common throughout the Dominions and a country like India had, as in South Africa, a large proportion of low skilled non-industrialised labour. Given these numerous similarities, it is reasonable to conclude, through elimination, that the *special conditions*, albeit unspecified, referred to the segmented labour market enforced through the "colour bar", which was unique in the empire.

By the last quarter of 1918 the role of the Scientific and Technical Committee had become so pivotal that an amalgamation between it and the Industries Advisory Board was established under the title of the Advisory Board of Industry and Science.[14] This fusion of the two bodies placed national policy on science and technology firmly within an industrial development policy framework and marks the first attempt to establish a *planned* national system of innovation. At this point the principles that were to inform government intervention in the process of industrial development were explicitly specified. The end of the war, however, brought about a dramatic shift in the original vision informing science and technology policy. The new Board explained how a shift in policy in this regard had occurred in the brief period since the establishment of the Scientific and Technical Committee:

---

12 ibid., p. 31.

13 *MEMORANDUM on the Suggestions made by the Governments of Victoria and New South Wales for making the scheme for the organisation and development of Scientific and Industrial Research applicable to the whole Empire.* - Committee of the Privy Council for Scientific and Industrial Research, 2nd March, 1916.

14 Government Notice No. 1384 of 9th October 1918, *Gazette* No. 920 of 11th October 1918.

> "One of the most important questions of the day is the exact relationship of Government to industrial enterprise. ... In view of the success which followed Germany's pre-war efforts to capture the world's trade, which was only rendered possible by direct Government assistance of the most liberal and comprehensive kind, public opinion was at one time inclined to the belief that the future prosperity of a country depended to a great extent on Government participation and control of industrial enterprise. Owing to the marvellous achievements of the industries of Great Britain and America during the war, there is no doubt that public opinion has considerably changed. While ... Government can render substantial assistance in research work, by a system of bonuses or tariffs to such industries as may require it (more particularly key industries) ... the general initiation in industrial affairs should be left to private enterprise."[15]

The original motive for the establishment of national science and technology planning institutions in Britain, and hence in South Africa, was the shock of a new kind of war being waged with Germany, a war where, in a historically unprecedented manner, industrial and technological prowess became a decisive factor in determining the outcome. Pre-war, post-unification economic development in Germany had been remarkable both by virtue of its rapidity and by the direct participation of government in technical education and in the funding of R&D programmes. During the nineteenth century the state, especially in Prussia, had set out systematically to establish technical teaching institutes and polytechnical schools to address specifically the bottleneck in the training of engineers. Moreover, unlike the histories of other industrialised countries, the general availability of primary education in Germany preceded industrialisation. By the time the war broke out

> ... Germany had established a sophisticated system for education in scientific, technical, and commercial matters, reaching from elementary school to the doctoral level. (Keck, 1993: 122).

Germany had also established a large number of field specific research institutes, most of which were jointly financed by state and industry. The result of this policy was that Germany attained world leadership positions as a manufacturing and exporting nation in pharmaceuticals, chemicals and electrical products. It was, moreover, rapidly moving to a leading

---

15 *Report of the Proceedings of the Industries Advisory Board and of the Scientific and Technical Committee for the period 1st January to 30th September, 1918 and of the Advisory Board of Industry and Science for the Quarter ended 31st December, 1918.* [U.G. 33 - '19], Cape Town. (p. 5).

position in mining and metal processing, machine construction and motor vehicles. The only industry where Britain had maintained a clear and enduring technological lead throughout the nineteenth century was in iron and steel production.[16] This remarkable achievement had occurred only because of the establishment of

> "... new institutional forms that enabled German firms to move quickly as new product areas and new processes were opened up by inventions and advances in scientific knowledge." (Keck, 1993: 130).

The German model anticipated in many respects those followed by Japan and the South East Asian Tigers in the post war (II) period, but while the early military successes of Germany in the war stimulated the British drive to emulate its programme of economic development, its defeat, through a non-logical association, caused the abandonment of the relationship between state and industry required by this science and technology programme. The move was from a model of strategic intervention with the state articulating a vision of the desired structural transformation and then drawing in private sector agents in an alliance to achieve the vision, to one of neutral engagement where the role of the state was to facilitate the functioning of the market as guided by its incumbent agents. South African policy in this area followed suit.

The 1924 retrospective survey of the work of the Industries Advisory Board over its duration from 1916 to 1923[17] sums up its contribution to addressing information bottlenecks with a view to stimulate the development of manufacturing industries which could exploit comparative advantage based on the country's resource endowments. The main achievements were in the areas of the compiling and diffusion of knowledge and in this endeavour the *South African Journal of Industries* was commended as an important means for the dissemination of information. However, this publication was discontinued a year later, in 1925. The Board had successfully motivated for the compilation of statistics on production and trade. It had also started the first data base on scientific publications in the country. It had commissioned a number of surveys on specific natural resources with a view of exploring the possibilities for downstream expansion into manufacturing. Where the potential for expansion was assessed to be viable, recommendations were usually on the state's role in the facilitation of private sector initiative. The

---

16 See Keck (1993: 116-133).

17 *Report of the Advisory Board of Science and Industry, 1924.* Cape Town, p. 139-154.

board also commissioned and published a large number of reports on specific product lines. One of these, on iron and steel industries, was to have significant repercussions a few years later in the state's first major direct involvement in a line of production other than those associated with the development of infrastructure. The revision of tariff policy initially amounted to little more than a recommendation for the elimination of tariffs on imported raw materials which could not be produced locally. However, in 1923, with the dissolution of the Advisory Board for Industry and Science, the Industries Department included the Board of Trade and Industries, to which tariff policy was entrusted. Under the new auspices policy on tariffs gradually began to move towards a protectionist stance *vis-à-vis* emerging industrial sectors. The Industries Division took on most of the other functions of the defunct Scientific and Technical Committee, except for the administration of research grants which function was now entrusted to a separate board.

The 1921 election saw the dissolution of the Unionist Party and the incorporation of most of its members into the victorious South African Party. The committed and successful involvement of South African troops in the war had helped to entrench a solid power base for one of the more fractious parts of the British Empire. It was during the war that Smuts obtained his platform in international politics when his recommendations for the drafting of the League of Nations were accepted and adopted by the American president, Wilson. It was during this period that Smuts' expansionist aspirations became manifest. In the aftermath of the war Smuts and Botha negotiated strenuously with Britain for the incorporation of Swaziland, Bechuanaland, Southern Rhodesia and Southern Mozambique within the South Africa political sphere of interest. The motivation behind this policy was essentially security for a white dominated South Africa, the same motivation that later informed apartheid policy to establish a *cordon sanitaire* around South Africa. Initially there were indications that his programme for an integrated region comprising most of sub-Saharan Africa under South African administration might become a reality. The factor that ultimately defeated these ambitions, even at this early stage, was the reluctance of Britain to proceed with annexations under the tutelage of a white dominated South Africa in the face of the expected protest by the black populations in the diverse colonies that were considered. The heavy-handed manner in which an uprising in South West Africa, which had been drawn into the South African administration umbrella after the war, was suppressed in 1921 elicited strong signs of disapproval from other Commonwealth members. India was the first to lead international condemnation of South Africa's racist policies when Smuts refused to ratify a motion for a more equitable treatment of Indians in Commonwealth countries. This recalls Neale's (1989) analysis of the manner in which the considerations of colonial administrators at the metropolitan centre could differ from those of the colonists in the occupied countries. In the case of South Africa, however, there was a further consideration and this was Britain's reluctance to allow an extension of influence to a colony whose loyalty to the crown had always been unpredictable.

The world depression of the twenties hit South Africa badly, perhaps harder than industrialised economies with a diversified production base. The two mainstays of the South African economy, agriculture and mining, came under review and the imperative to shift the bias of the economy towards manufacturing activity acquired a renewed urgency. The two main bottlenecks to economic development which were repeatedly identified at this early stage were inappropriate technology and the distortions in the labour market. However, both arguments were set within the context of the discourse on race at the time and were thus bedevilled by ineradicable contradictions.

These contradictions became starkly manifest during the crisis which hit the mining sector in the early twenties. The rapid drops in the gold price, combined with rising costs, were forcing widespread closures of marginal mines. The *Report of the Low Grade Mines Commission* in 1920[18] pointed out that one obvious counter measure was to increase substantially the proportion of black employees by redefining the "colour bar" to admit black workers into some of the employment categories previously retained for whites.[19] This, however, led to a fierce resistance from white miners who were adamant about the enforcing of the policy of job reservation as it stood. The resistance escalated after the drop in the gold price in 1921 led the mines to increasingly adopt employment strategies which progressively undermined job reservation for whites. It was fuelled by attempts by employers in coal mining and engineering sectors to lower wages and the intransigence of the main electric power producers in the face of demands for wage increases. Resistance to similar previous attempts by the mines to erode the "colour bar" had already

18 Union of South Africa, *Report of the Low Grade Mines Commission*, Government Printer, Pretoria, 1920, U.G. 34/1920. The extracts which are used here are from Houghton and Dagut (1973).

19 The Commission attempted to bolster its argument for dispensing with the "colour bar" by pointing to the contradiction between the assumption of an innate racial superiority and the practice of job reservation: "To stand entrenched behind artificial barriers may appear to be an admission of weakness ..." (para. 188).

erupted in the strike of 1914[20] which Smuts suppressed by imposing martial law and deporting strike leaders.[21] The miners' strike of 1922 was much more widespread and the violence which erupted justly earned the episode the label of a "civil war" even though it was limited to the Rand. The Smuts government certainly dealt with it as an armed uprising and fatalities were high. It was this, combined with resentment at South Africa siding with the Afrikaners' "enemies", the British, against their traditional "allies", the Germans, that led to the defeat of the Botha-Smuts government and the election of a coalition party between the nationalist Hertzog and the Labour Party leader Creswell in 1924. The miners' revolt also opened a rift between black and white workers. Some union leaders tried to justify the starkly racist demands of the white miners by arguing that the initial contest had to be waged against capitalists and that only when this was won could the issue of discriminatory employment practices be addressed. This claim did not wash with black workers and a series of confrontations occurred in which a number of black mine workers lost their lives.

As mentioned above, the economy at the time was based on mining and agriculture and whatever sporadic technological activity there was originated in the requirements of these two sectors.[22] Agriculture, however, was seriously inefficient by the standards in other parts of the empire. De Kiewiet (1967) points to the technological gap between the South African farming sector vis-à-vis those of New Zealand and Canada as an explanation of the low productivity endemic in the rural communities in this country and as a major contributing factor for the devastation wrought by the droughts of 1914 and 1918.[23] The 1923 *Final*

---

20 The strike referred to here happened early in 1914. The other which took place in September was in protest at South Africa entering the war against Germany.

21 Horwitz (1967: 91).

22 Meiring Naudé and Brown (1977).:

> "In general a study of the development of the development of scientific research in South Africa reveals that research in the various disciplines was usually conducted on an *ad hoc* basis to overcome problems of immediate practical importance. Our scientific institutions have frequently tended to grow out of such research."

23 De Kiewiet (1968: 251, emphasis added) points out that

> "...(t)he construction of scrupulously up-to-date dairies, and the application of motor power to tractors and combines gave New Zealand and Canadian farmers a great advantage over the unskilled labour and poor organisation of South African farming. Of all the dominions none seem to have had more climatic difficulties to overcome, *or more antiquated methods to combat.*"

Report of the Drought Investigation Commission focussed on the rapid degradation of agricultural land. Its conclusion was that this impoverishment was not due to altered rainfall patterns but to the inappropriate techniques adopted by white farmers who seemed oblivious to the dangers of over farming and who declined to use agricultural land as an exhaustible resource. This report concluded by recommending strong government intervention to remedy this market failure. The low yields on farming - by international standards - were noted in the *Report of the Economic and Wage Commission* in 1925. The agricultural problem was revisited in greater detail almost ten years later in the report of the Carnegie Corporation Commission.[24] Land impoverishment was attributed specifically to Afrikaner farmers who were still operating as "pioneer farmers". This meant intensive farming until yields dropped below some viability limit and then migration to fresh pastures. With the rapid diminution of new land the agricultural sector as a whole was now suffering the consequences of over-farming. English-speaking farmers on the other hand, and this applied to second- and third generation farmers as well as recent immigrants, were seen as the innovators who adopted farming techniques that were more appropriate to the local context. The Commission proposed education as one of the long term measure to alleviate the "poor white" problem but the immediate solution to the problem, fuelled by fears of racial demarcation lines, was to commence on the introduction, albeit informally, of the colour bar in secondary industry.

In 1919, the year that Smuts became the prime minister, following Botha's death, H.J. van der Bijl was appointed as Scientific and Technical Advisor to Government and commenced duties in this capacity in 1920. This appointment was to partially reverse the change in the nature of state involvement in the country's industrial development. Van der Bijl, who was Smuts' personal appointment,[25] stated his appraisal of the task he was

---

24 Carnegie Corporation Commission: The Poor White Problem in South Africa - Part I, 1932, *Rural Impoverishment and Rural Exodus*.

25 Smuts was a close friend of the van der Bijl family and he and he approached H.J. van der Bijl's father to persuade his son, who at the time was firmly established in academia in the USA and who had attained world renown in thermionics, to return to South Africa to take up the post of Scientific and Technical Advisor to the government (see Jacobs, 1948: 73-74). Apart from his scientific accomplishments, van der Bijl's track record until his recruitment by Smuts had fitted him well for his post in South Africa. He obtained a doctorate in physics at the University of Leipzig and went on to a lecturing post at the Royal College of Technology in Dresden. Shortly afterward he was effectively recruited by a notable academic from Chicago University to work as a research scientist for AT&T for seven years before accepting Smuts' invitation. Apart from an

facing early in his career when he deplored the country's continued economic dependence on the extraction of exhaustible resources and deprecated the contemporary secondary industries which he considered as having been viable only because the war and the depression following it had for a period of time dampened international competition. His agenda therefore was to turn South Africa into a "veritable workshop" (Jacobs, 1948: 118). He drafted the country's first science and technology policy framework, as the term is understood today, and submitted it to the Smuts government in 1921. The motivating arguments that were used were based on (a) economies of scale in R&D, (b) the public good nature of R&D, (c) the need to increase the value-added component of the country's natural resources, and (d) the requirement to acquire a competitive edge in the international markets for manufactured commodities.[26] This was designed along the lines adopted at the time by the more industrial Commonwealth countries. However, the van der Bijl proposals came too late and during too turbulent a period for the Smuts government to command the required attention and thus reverse the demise of the Advisory Board for Industry and Science in 1923. The defeat of Smuts in the 1924 elections meant that Van der Bijl's recommendations, specifically on science and technology policy, were sidelined indefinitely. Van der Bijl's role did not end here, however. He was instrumental in the planning and establishment, in 1923, of the Electricity Supply Commission (ESCOM) and in commissioning the reports which led to the creation of (ISCOR) in 1927. During the Second World War he was put in charge of war supplies, answerable directly to Smuts.

Van der Bijl was truly a man at the forefront of the modern age. Science and engineering were, for him, the repository of the solution to the ills of humanity and, in an era which saw the emerging prominence of American technology and the vast revolutionary New Economic Plans in the Soviet Union, he had no objection to being labelled a socialist (Jacobs, 1948: 220-224). He was the motive force behind the launch of programmes of state organisation of public utilities and what he saw as strategic product lines, such as steel. He envisaged the agricultural sector

---

impressive record of research output, he also became well versed in patent laws and litigation procedures. Even more pertinent to his qualifications for his forthcoming appointment was his publication of a paper on R&D, shortly before his departure from America, in which he demonstrated his understanding of the relationship between the various stages of research and development, and the various structures required to translate ideas into economically viable innovations. (*ibid.*: Ch. 3)

26 See Kingwill (1990: 5).

managed as one state enterprise with individual farmers as shareholders. He conceived and created a new industrial city, Vanderbijl Park, whose every aspect was planned to the last detail. He initiated successful experiments in workers' nutrition, reformed pension schemes and launched medical aid schemes. Yet, like Smuts, this personage who was literally the engineer of South Africa's rapid and successful modernisation process operated unquestioningly within the segregation paradigm. His plans for the residential and health conditions for black workers in Vanderbijl Park were motivated by the same reformist principles that informed Smuts and Hofmeyr, reinforced in his case by an intolerance for waste and inefficiency which covered any aspect of the human condition. There is never, however, any indication that this engineer whose vision on the requisites of a modern economy was complex and revolutionary within the South African context and who had the courage and stamina to carry through his plans often against formidable opposition ever considered the segregated labour market as a main impediment to successful industrialisation. This dilemma is evident in van der Bijl's treatment of the issue of housing for black employees in ISCOR. While the existing system of accommodation in compounds offended his sensibilities, the labour costs of skilled builders imposed by the colour bar rendered the notion of building adequate housing on the basis of contemporary technology for black labour unacceptable to the engineer's notions of efficiency - "It is a crime to pay a man four shillings an hour to build a house for a man who earns four shillings a day ..." (quoted in Jacobs, 1948: 147). The obvious solution, i.e. to eliminate the colour bar was, however, an option that could not be contemplated because of the political implications which he so explicitly stated:

> "... I doubt the wisdom of the idea of attempting to train Natives in the art and skill of building houses by the ordinary established methods, unless we are willing to prepare for relegating eventually practically the whole of the building trade to non-Europeans." (*ibid.*: 147)

The solution to this dilemma was typical. He invented a new type of low cost housing whose construction required minimal labour skills. In van der Bijl we see incarnated simultaneously the confines of a specific paradigm, i.e. the system of racial segregation, and inventiveness within the confines of that paradigm which in turn serves its reinforcement.

As noted above, most of the economic functions normally associated with public sector provision were initially undertaken by the private sector, specifically mining. A typical case is the development of power supply systems where initiatives were originally driven by the requirements of the mining sector. The first significant supplier of electricity, the Victoria Falls Power Company Limited (VFP), was established in 1906 specifically to supply electricity to the mines. For quite a while it was the largest electrical power supply in the British Empire. It also established a world precedent by building power stations on coal fields, thus significantly reducing transport costs and hence power delivery costs. It also operated a power station which was equipped with the world's largest air compressors for use by the mining sector and operated the largest steam generating station in the empire. At an early date the state had expressed concern at a private monopoly controlling this utility and the report of a commission of enquiry had resulted in the *Transvaal Power Act* (20 May 1910) which formed the Power Undertaking Board as the executive agency ruled that the state had the right to expropriate any electricity power supplier 37 years after the issue of a licence to operate. Thus, VFP was terminated by 1948. The rapid expansion of the mining sector into the interior of the country also stimulated a huge increase in demand for railways and, given that the electrification of railways was being considered at the time, this increased the demand for electrical power.

When van der Bijl was appointed as scientific advisor to the Department of Mines and Industries in 1920 he determined that a cheap source of power was an essential component of the infrastructure required for industrialisation. On the basis of the recommendations of the report of Charles Merz the *Electricity Act* of 1922 was passed which saw the establishment of ESCOM in 1923 and the commencement of production in 1925. ESCOM, which set the model for future parastatal enterprises, was significant as the first major state controlled enterprise which was run on a non-profit basis in collaboration with private enterprise. At the time of its establishment the supply of electric power was still the virtual monopoly of the VFP and until the expiry of this company's licence in 1948 there was a close partnership in a number of power supply ventures between ESCOM and VFP. With the launch of the new corporation the per unit cost of electricity was almost halved, thus stimulating a rapid transformation of the power base of most industrial production processes. By 1936 van der Bijl was able to claim that "... South Africa is one of the most electrically-minded countries in the world" (Jacobs, 1948: 91-92). In 1948 ESCOM took over and the accumulated scientific, technical and managerial expertise finally became public property. The first focus of the new corporation was the electrification of railways. In planning the Congella power station, van der Bijl adopted (against the advice of consultants) boiler technology (using pulverised fuel) which was still in the experimental stages. The solution of the technology problems associated with this type of boiler took 27 years.[27]

Shifting policies on state and market: 1924-1938

This period epitomises the innate contradiction of South African political history which renders the class/race debate so contentious. In a uniquely qualified manner the election of the Hertzog-Creswell Pact coalition to power was a victory of the proletariat over big capital. It was, at the same time, a victory which entrenched in the statute an order of privilege within the labour market defined on racial lines, thus limiting the definition of the proletariat to a minority within the labour force.[28] Variava (1989: 234) lists the methods used by the Pact government to enforce the informal colour bar within the secondary sector. These included the granting of public contracts to companies guaranteeing an all-white workforce and the threat of lifting protective tariffs in industries which did not satisfy an employment quota of white workers. Moreover, employment practices within government departments and municipalities rapidly changed to substitute white employees for black employees, at higher wages. The 1925 *Economic and Wage Commission* discussed at length the costs incurred by the colour bar for South African economic development. With the drive towards industrialisation the bottleneck posed by an uneducated black labour force (the 1921 census had shown that almost ninety percent of black children were illiterate) had become apparent and the effects on productivity and competitiveness of the reliance on low paid, low skilled labour were discussed specifically. Combined with this there was a demand constraint due to the low wages

---

27 D.B. Ready, President of the SAIE was a major innovator on the economical uses of coal in the supply of electricity. See 1940. "Power Supply for Central Station Auxiliaries", paper presented to SAIE. 1947 (13 February). "Some Economic Factors in the Planning, Operation and Maintenance of Steam Power Stations".

28 The class analysis of the shifting political bases saw no contradiction in this alliance. As O'Meara (1975) puts it:

> "The white labour aristocracy initiated by the Nationalist/Labour Party `Pact' government of 1924-1929 was largely completed, and white working class opposition and pressure on the government substantially relieved. The much-feared threat to Afrikaner nationalism posed by potential class mobilisation was largely removed, freeing a future Nationalist government to consolidate Afrikaner capitalism provided it defended the position of privilege it had created for white labour." (p. 150)

and the consequent low purchasing power of the majority of the population. There was therefore a dire need to embark on investment in broad-based education since industrialisation required the absorption of the greater part of the black majority into the "European" economic institutions. The "costs" of such a policy were also spelled out. These were the expected rising aspirations of black workers as they were integrated into an industrial economy, especially one where, unlike the mining sector, the colour bar did not officially exist, towards a further integration and the assumption of an equal status with white workers. This would increase the competition which a white worker would face in the labour markets.

However, the initiatives led by the Labour side of the coalition established a set of "safety nets" for white workers, covering housing, health and employment conditions. The privileged position of white workers at all skill levels in the labour market was entrenched by the *Wage Act* of 1925 and the *Mine and Works Amendment Act* of 1926. Eventually the "socialist" element of the Pact government withered away with nationalist ideology emerging as the pre-eminent informing *raison d'être*. The essential ephemeral nature of the class component of the new government's political agenda quickly became evident in the political fortunes of the Labour Party as Hertzog progressively marginalised Labour Party members of parliament in the allocation of cabinet posts. Ultimately white workers, especially Afrikaners, identified their agenda with that of the Nationalists with the result that the Labour Party fared very poorly in the subsequent election and virtually disappeared from the political scene. The leader of the Labour Party, Creswell, had irretrievably forfeited rural and proletarian Afrikaner backing in 1914, when he steered his party away from a boycott of South Africa's participation in the First World War against Germany. Horwitz (1967: 103) highlights the increasing parochialism of white voters around the 1929 election. He mentions an election speech given by Smuts in Ermelo where he proposed a future where the Union of South Africa would form a part of a federation of African states, a speech which was instrumental in his ignominious defeat at the polls.

The science and technology policy which Smuts had initiated may in its vision be linked to Smuts the internationalist, a politician eager to integrate South Africa into the emerging modern global economy. If this association is correct then it is logical that the initiative should have died with his political demise. However, there was a contrary, albeit indirect, motivation for the advance of the national technology base. This was the result of the push for secondary industrialisation initiated by the

Hertzog/Creswell government. The immediately obvious motivation for this policy was the dire need to solve the "poor white" problem caused by an escalating rural-urban migration which was itself fuelled by increasing poverty on the farms. The push for industrialisation was reinforced by two policy initiatives. One was the institution of a protectionist trade regime. The other was the initiation of direct participation by the state in specific sectors.

In 1924 the case for protection was argued along Listian, infant industry lines.[29] The argument for protection by local manufacturers rested on the inevitably high cost structure caused by the effective, though unofficial, colour bar within the manufacturing sector. The adoption of protective tariffs in the face of impassioned objections at the time would therefore also have been due to the acceptance of the "price" that had to be paid for the maintenance of white worker privilege. The proposal for protection ratified earlier recommendations that imported raw materials for industrial use should be exempt from import taxes. It also proposed that rail transport for industrial goods should be subsidised. The specific protectionist proposal rested on a combination of a tariff barrier policy and on a local sourcing government procurement policy forcing government departments to rely as far as possible on local suppliers. Moreover, it was also recommended that the mining sector should be urged to follow suit in its procurement policy.

The most notable example of the protectionist policy based on local sourcing was the creation of ISCOR in 1927. The public sector had already undertaken an interventionist role in the provision of a national rail transport system with the formation of the Union and the establishment of ESCOM, but these initiatives were still well within the accepted definition of public utilities. ISCOR was unique in that it represented the first major instance where the state took on the role of a private enterprise. The

---

29 The infant industry rationale for protection was stated explicitly in the House of Assembly debate:

> "... if you are going to establish factories you can only do so successfully by giving them adequate protection until such a time as they are strong enough to compete successfully with the imported article. Why can't we take a lesson from other countries, Australia, for instance, which not only affords every one of her industries a high protection but goes further and supports them in the most practical manner by a standing order to every one of her public spending departments that before they spend a shilling overseas they must thoroughly exhaust the local market." (House of Assembly, *Debates 1924*, quoted from Houghton and Dagut, 1973:90-91)

rationale for an indigenous iron and steel industry had been officially recognised as early as 1920.[30] The recommendations at that time were for the facilitation of a market response through guaranteed prices and orders for iron and steel products, but against state investment.[31] When the Bill was proposed[32] it drew the furious charge of socialism (Bolshevism), perhaps partly because it was launched by Creswell, as Minister of Defence. The case for this unprecedented type of government intervention was argued on a number of fronts. The crux of the issue was, of course, the abundance of mineral resources in South Africa. One argument was that the strategic issue of national security was being prejudiced by a dependency on foreign suppliers for steel and iron requirements, a curious harbinger of similar arguments defending the establishment of parastatal enterprises in the apartheid era. Creswell's main thrust was on the extent of the indigenous research and development capability and he listed numerous beneficiation processes developed locally. He quoted studies done by the Union Geological Department and the report commissioned by the Advisory Board of Industry and Science on iron and steel

---

30 The rationale for the establishment of ISCOR was stated in the following terms:

> "Having regard to the facts that an iron and steel industry is essential to the economic independence of the Union, that the demand for Governmental railway purposes alone assures a considerable and continuous market, and that agricultural, mining, factory and all other machinery manufacture depends upon a supply of cast iron and steel, there must be a general agreement as to the desirability in principle of such an industry being established." (*Report of the Advisory Board of Industry and Science for the year 1919.* Cape Town, 1920. [U.G. 43-'20]: 13)

31 The nature of state support and protection for the was explicitly stated:

> "It was recommended that at the present time Government could render practical assistance by causing full investigations and reports to be made ... since the industry would necessarily have to be worked on a considerable scale to compete with imports from overseas and would demand a large provision of capital, *some measure of security and reasonable prospects of obtaining profits are essential.* The Board, therefore, suggested that Government should advertise their guarantee for a term of years of on or other of the following:-(a) A minimum price ... (b) A Bounty ... (c) The purchase at a given price of a minimum tonnage ... *It was reluctant to advise the government to contribute to the capital expenditure* since the methods detailed above have been successfully practised elsewhere and involve no risk of loss of State capital." (*ibid*: 13, parentheses added)

32 House of Assembly Debates, 1927.

industries, in 1919.[33] He quoted, furthermore, a feasibility study carried out by a combined team of German, British and Dutch experts, which attested to the viability of a local iron and steel industry, given sound management and sufficient funding. He mentioned a number of failed private sector initiatives which attempted to set up beneficiation enterprises and which had asked for, but been refused, government assistance for their continuance. His definitive statement for direct government intervention, as opposed to facilitation policies dependent on private sector response was unequivocal:

> "... if the establishment of such a works was not going to be postponed into the indefinite future, if we were not going to be content with simply making steel out of scrap or with tentative experiments in making pig iron, ... you must have ample capital resources, and the history of the matter showed that it would only be by the Government themselves stepping in and cutting this Gordian Knot and providing the security of Government interest and a substantial amount of financial responsibility. ... you would not get further than making steel out of scrap, or ill-considered schemes, unless the Government came in and took an active and definite part in the providing of sufficient capital to establish a really well-thought out steel works. ... There are ... good reasons and very good reasons indeed, that in an industry like this, just as in the case of electricity, that you should take it entirely out of the hands of the private entrepreneur ... " (quoted from Houghton and Dagut, 1973: 96-99)

Apart from the bills introduced to improve productivity in farming, this was the first instance where the government of the day based an argument for direct intervention in the market on the grounds of the contribution of technological advances to the increase of the value-added component of the final product. The main objection to the feasibility of such an enterprise in South Africa, and the main reason for a lack of private initiative in this sector, was the paucity of the current internal market for steel products and of projections based on extrapolations of current consumption levels. By ignoring these projections, the state, with van der Bijl as its main advisor, adopted "big push" strategy on a sector which was considered as constituting one of the pre-requisites of industrialisation, and whose social returns were judged to be considerably in excess of the private ones. In this respect van der Bijl, the strongest motivator for the establishment of ISCOR, focussed on industrial spillovers and multiplier

33 *Report of the Advisory Board of Industry and Science for the year 1919.* [U.G. 43-'20] - Cape Town. p. 24.

effects, actual and potential, as the prime criterion for the choice of industrial growth sectors.[34]

ISCOR operated under numerous constraints. At its inception it faced a depressed world market for steel and one which was moreover controlled by the international steel cartel of which it had to become a part. Initially it also faced dumping by foreign producers. Government controlled the price of iron and steel until 1985. However, in the long run it had a number of impressive cost advantages. It benefited from the low cost of initial share capital. It reaped benefits from vertical integration since ISCOR operated its own mines. Finally, given that it was a parastatal corporation, it enjoyed a subsidised electricity supply from ESCOM. The ISCOR operation also managed to solve, in its early days, technological problems which initially threatened the feasibility of steel production in South Africa. Coke ovens were developed which could use Transvaal coal in spite of the fact that it was initially declared uncokeable. Similarly iron deposits which were initially deemed unfit for beneficiation were, through investment in R&D, rendered exploitable. These developments were initially constrained by a scarcity of engineers with the required degree of specialisation but this bottleneck was eased by sending promising candidates for training abroad and by compelling contractors to ISCOR to train engineers.

This was an indication of the shift in the direction of a science and technology policy for the country. The early attempt to establish an institutional basis for the formulation of a comprehensive policy framework in this area had started off as an emulation of the British response to the German threat and had died with the perceived recession of the war crisis, resulting in the avowal of a liberal, market friendly, position on the part of the state. The 1924 government did not resuscitate the official science and technology planning organ, but, capitalising on the initial spirit motivating the Science and Technical Committee, and

---

34 Van der Bijl's emphasis on industrial linkages seems to have been one of the main criteria underlying his industrialisation plans. Thus, in 1941 he urged the development of large scale housing programmes on the basis of the backward linkages that they offered:

> "I can think of no scheme that will give such a fillip to industry as a bold housing scheme ... This is a most important outlet for post-war investment and employment. If one starts analysing all the constituents that go to the construction and furnishing of a house, including kitchen and pantry utensils, there is almost no limit to the industrial expansion necessary to meet the requirements of such a scheme." (quoted in Jacobs, 1948: 131)

informed by a socialist agenda for its white constituents, it proceeded to enact interventionist policies which established localised strategic technology growth points. It is significant that van der Bijl, who had been commissioned by Smuts to formulate the (aborted) first science and technology policy framework, was the leading figure under the new government in the establishment of ESCOM, ISCOR and, in 1940, the Industrial Development Corporation (IDC).

On the technology front, some of the programmes which had been launched by the Advisory Board of Industry and Science were firmly established. In 1925 a research centre on sugar was established entirely by private funding. In 1930 the Department of Trade and Commerce established a Fuel Research Institute and in 1932 initiated research in marine biology within the Division of Sea Fisheries.

There is a distinct difference in emphasis between the science and technology policy drafted under Smuts and the one implemented under Hertzog. Smuts, himself a scientist, was concerned with establishing formal institutions specifically designed to deepen the country's scientific base. His priority stemmed from the perceived need for a national scientific research base. van der Bijl was the technologist who would provide the link to applications to industrial development. Under Hertzog the focus was on industrial development and, again with van der Bijl at the fore, R&D activity was strictly the handmaiden of specific industrial initiatives. The integration of specific S&T initiatives within a broader industrial development policy framework provides an early example of planning from a national system of innovation perspective. During this period the only one of Smuts' initiatives, as far as basic scientific research was concerned, which endured was the Research Grant Board was established in 1918 with the express purpose of funding university research.

In 1933, following four years of depression and a steadily declining GDP, Hertzog and Smuts formed the United Party which effectively was a coalition government. Nattrass and Ardington (1990: 10) see this coalition as a marriage of convenience between the two politicians with Hertzog aiming at removing the last remnants of black voters from the roll and Smuts intent on protecting mining interests from any increases in taxation. The dilution of the original agenda of the National Party caused D.F. Malan to split from Hertzog and, retaining the National Party name, to form an opposition based on hard line Afrikaner interests.

The dramatic rise in the gold price shortly after the formation of the new government spurred a surge in economic activity which was further fuelled by the commencement of ISCOR's massive production programme.

Towards the end of this period there was a resurgence of broader based science and technology initiatives. In 1938 the Research Grant Board was reconstituted into two bodies under the Ministry of Education - the National Research Council and the National Research Board. The former was concerned with formulating national policy on science and technology priorities while the latter was the executive body. Van der Bijl's 1921 proposals were taken up formally and would, in all probability, have been implemented but for the outbreak of the war. Politically the arrival of the war sundered the fragile alliance of interests between Hertzog and Smuts, with the former refusing to go to war against Germany on behalf of Britain and the latter consequently taking up the premiership.[35]

The Smuts premiership: 1939-1948

This period saw a convergence of events which created the conditions for a feasible process of the dismantling of a segregated polity and the entry of South Africa into the post-war community of democratic, industrialised economies. It was a period marked by dramatic structural upheavals at several levels. The catalyst for the relatively sudden acceleration of processes which brought the "South African way of life" to an unprecedented crisis was the war. The war brought Smuts back into power and it also infused the political and economic costs of segregation policies with an immediate urgency in the eyes of the decision makers. In the process the struggle against segregation acquired an articulation, intensity and focus which it had largely lacked before. The ANC emerged firmly as a representative of all the disenfranchised sections of the population while the organisation of the black trade union movement attained an effective coordination of both the urban proletariat and, because of the links resulting from the migrant labour system, of the rural population. From within the structure of the government the Natives Representative Council, a body with a dubious heritage, became an increasingly vocal and lucid critic of the Smuts/Hofmeyr government. In

---

35 Davenport (1981) explains the division lines on policy regarding South Africa's commitment to the war effort quite simply"

> "Both men (Smuts and Hertzog) probably realised the dangers to white South African unity involved in making war against Germany for the second time in less than twenty five years, when the unpleasant memories of the first occasion were still green; but for Smuts the international dangers (of an Axis power German victory) out-weighed the domestic, whereas for Hertzog it was the other way around." (p. 231, parentheses added)

isolation none of these forces would have posed any threat to the existing structure that had not already been experienced since the formation of the Union, but in conjunction they opened up the possibility of an irreversible rupture in the history of white domination. It was during this period that the CSIR was established and it is indicative of the interrelatedness of the factors which were at play in the disruption of the established order that the only sound critique of the CSIR bill came from one of the luminaries of the Natives Representative Council.

The advent of the Second World War had a number of interlinked effects on the South African political economy all of which created the conditions for an integrated and sustained opposition to segregation. The economic conditions for this effect were the combination of the increased demand for manufactured commodities and the skills bottleneck. Thus, it increased substantially the political bargaining position of the black proletariat. On the technology front the war provided a major stimulus to an industrialisation drive and indigenous innovative activity. Finally, it paved the way to the establishment of the CSIR.

The war stimulated an economic boom through a massive defence budget and South Africa geared up its production structure to supply a wide range of inputs into the war effort, especially in mining, steel, textiles and clothing. In the process it shifted the economy's output mix towards manufacturing, which by 1943 exceeded mining as a proportion of national output. By the end of the war industrial employment had increased by more than sixty percent with the bulk of the increase occurring in metals and engineering products (Jones and Müller, 1992: Table 12.3). At the same time the base for the long-term viability of the manufacturing sector remained highly volatile and dependent on the markets created by explicit policies, in contrast to that of the mining sector. While the stimulus provided by the war on industry was equivalent to an export drive, the post war maintenance of the expansion became dependent on import substitution, encouraged by protectionist measures established in 1948, and an expanding local market. At the same time this expansion itself required an increase in imports of intermediary goods due to local bottlenecks in the chains of production and the restrictions of the local market.

The most significant bottleneck which was brought to the fore by the increased demand for manufactured commodities was the one imposed by segregation policy within the labour market and this is where Smuts' pragmatic side emerged predominant over his concerns about the political "sensitivities" of white voters. The shortage of skilled labour resulted in the setting in motion of reforms which, if they had come to fruition, would have largely eliminated labour market discrimination.

The transformation of the liberation movement

The war caused Smuts to reaffirm his commitment to the country's role in global politics thus retarding the process of introversion of the country's political development. The war had contradictory effects on South Africa's placing in global politics. Hancock (1968: 412) points out that in the early years of the conflict the Cape route, and hence South Africa, was crucial to the Allied cause but that this positioning evaporated with Allied victories in North Africa and the opening up of the Mediterranean to Allied shipping. This was a harbinger of the post-war future wherein the vagaries of the international tensions among super-powers had a direct influence on South Africa's position in international political fora. It was a clear signal to Smuts that segregation politics would become rapidly untenable in the near future if his aspiration to place South Africa within the community of those nations that he idealised was to be achieved. The urgency of his perceived role in international politics was reinforced by his growing fears of Russian territorial gains in post-war Europe (Hancock, 1968: 418-420).

The war years saw a coalescence of what previously had been largely fragmented and often conflicting tendrils of black resistance to segregation policy. In the early days of the Union the South African Native National Congress, the principal platform of protest against segregation, essentially represented the interests of the proportionately minuscule petty bourgeoisie component of the black population. Its programme was a conservative one, aimed at persuading the government to co-opt within the ranks of the enfranchised part of the population those blacks who saw themselves as distinct from the mass of the "... rawest blanketed heathen(s) ..." (D.D.T. Jabavu, quoted in Lodge, 1983: 2-3). The government's intransigence and the emergence of the Industrial and Commercial Workers' Union in the early twenties were instrumental factors in broadening the constituent base of the organisation, which changed its name to the ANC, to represent the entirety of the disenfranchised. The Communist Party of South Africa, which emerged as the other major player in the labour market, initially forfeited its appeal to black workers through its alliance with white workers in the conviction that a victory over capital would necessarily eradicate discrimination within the working class. But by the late twenties the failure of this policy led to a change in strategy and to an alliance between the two movements. By the beginning of the thirties, however, divergent strategies between the CPSA on the one hand and the ANC and the ICU on the other led to a split in the two movements and contributed to the diminution of the CPSA's role as a representative of black labour. The combination of effective measures adopted by the government to trammel workers' resistance and the political voice of the increasingly reactionary white unions had largely disabled the black workers' movement through most of the thirties.

The war brought out in a stark depiction the contradiction between the ideals of freedom and democracy which Smuts had publicly touted as the motive behind South Africa's commitment to the war effort and the effective repudiation of these very values within South Africa. The Atlantic charter, drawn by the allies in 1942, explicitly extolling these ideals as the reason for the war against the Axis powers led to an immediate and urgent demand for South Africa to deploy the very same democratic principles.[36] The ANC led by A.B. Xuma focussed its claim for universal suffrage in the Bill of Rights which it presented to the Smuts government in 1943. This Bill represented a major transformation in the articulation of an alternative to the *status quo*. For the first time the claim of the oppressed was for a unified country in which the whole of its population was to be accorded equal rights within the burgeoning welfare state which the white government had constructed for its white voters. Thus it represented a break from the demand for a gradual co-option of a trickle of blacks into a state of equality with whites on the basis of an arbitrarily defined merit as well as from an Africanist claim for self determination which seemed to echo in essence the government's programme of "parallel development". Smuts and Hofmeyr, with their repeated emphasis on gradual reforms, unequivocally rejected this Bill and in the process any possibility of shifting the political economy of the country out of the paradigm whose costs and contradictions had now become starker than ever but whose bonds seemed unbreakable.

---

36 The rage and frustration at the enduring incongruity between the government's foreign and domestic policies were forcefully expressed in 1946 by P. Mosaka, a member of the Natives' Representative Council:

> "This Council ... deprecates the Government's post-war continuation of a policy of Fascism which is the antithesis and negation of the letter and the spirit of the Atlantic Charter and the United Nations Charter. The Council therefore, in protest against this breach of faith towards the African people in particular and world freedom in general, ... calls upon the Government forthwith to abolish all discriminatory legislation affecting non-Europeans in this country." (quoted in Ballinger, 1969: 193).

In the case of the labour movement, the sudden shortage of labour at all skill levels had shifted bargaining power in favour of the masses and the various strands of the black union movement rapidly coalesced to exploit it effectively. The incipient movement for reforms during the early part of the war elicited the expected reactions from hardliner conservatives, leading to an indecisive situation which in turn rapidly precipitated a series of crises and confrontations with black liberation movements and organised black labour. Collective bargaining rights for black labour were initially contemplated and effectively recognised when the Minister of Labour officially approved the launching of the Congress of Non-European Trade Unions in 1941[37] but this recognition was short-lived. Strikes by black workers were proclaimed illegal due to war conditions[38] while no such ban was imposed on white unions. Initially this measure was justified on the grounds of war exigencies but eventually it became a permanent proscription. In spite of this there was a spate of strikes, due to dropping living standards and atrocious working conditions, including low wages, culminating in the widespread black mine workers' strike of 1946. The government reacted harshly and the strike was put down forcefully at the cost of a number of lives.

It is reasonable to propose that the government's resistance to the two distinct lines of rebellion, though related, emerged from two separate motivational platforms. The demands of the ANC attacked the foundations of the South African political system and the privileged status of whites in the country. As such they implied a direct cost, in terms of votes, to any party which subscribed to their merit. The demands of organised black labour, on the other hand, did not directly impinge on the provisions of job reservation for white workers. Their claims amounted to a demand for increased bargaining power in respect of wages and employment conditions. The immediate negative response to this side of the struggle would therefore have originated from the concerns of employers regarding the impact of a broad based organised industrial labour force on the wage bill.

The Natives Representative Council, "... a body called upon to co-operate in the application of a policy it had never accepted ..." (Ballinger, 1969: 157), was established in 1936 as the *quid pro quo*, in terms of black representation, for removing the last of black voters from the common roll in the Cape and the final total elimination of individual black voting rights. Given its provenance, it was established in the face of black opposition

37 See Davenport (1981: 239-240).

38 War Measure 145 (1942) and War Measure 1425 (1945).

which was expressed under the aegis of the 1935 "All-African Convention" held in Bloemfontein. However, this instrument of segregationist politics[39] rapidly transmuted into a locus of a coherent radical assault on the foundations of the political credo which had spawned it. The changing composition of the black representatives on the council is one indicator of how this body was effectively appropriated by the liberation movement. In the first council, apart from J. Dube, the first president of the ANC and journalists, the black representatives' forum consisted of teachers and small farmers. In contrast, the 1943 council contained Z.K. Matthews, a professor of Law and Native Administration, P. Mosaka, a prominent businessman and an outstanding graduate from Fort Hare, A.W.G. Champion and S. Msimang, both eminent trade unionists, and A. Luthuli, the only chief ever to be elected to his post rather than being nominated by government and who later went on to become a president of the ANC. From 1938 until its dissolution in 1952 it became a consistent source of critique of segregation informed by the explicit objective of shifting "... the debate over native policy *from a discussion of control techniques ..to a discussion of immediate and long-term welfare.*" (Davenport, 1981: 239, emphasis added). Margaret Ballinger, its representative in the House of Assembly and an economist by training (Hancock, 1968: 477), focussed on the failure of the Smuts government to commit itself to a renunciation of the principles and implementation of segregation. Her attacks, which reflected the council's approach, were constructed along two related but separate arguments, an ethical one and a 'pragmatic' critique which highlighted the incompatibility between segregation and economic growth.[40]

---

39 At the launch of the Council the Minister of Native Affairs was explicit in defining the limitations on the effectiveness of the new body when he cautioned it members to "... be moderate and reasonable in your resolutions, for the more reasonable your requests, the greater the possibility that the Government will meet your wishes." (Ballinger, 1969: 144).

40 The ethical objection was formulated as follows:

> "Behind our whole policy of social improvement and of social uplift lies the basic denial of human rights which destroys politically the whole virtue of that position." (M. Ballinger, *House of Assembly Debates*, 1947, col 11071).

while the economic flaw was pointed out in the following manner:

> "How could South Africa hope ... to find jobs for a growing White population except on the increasing effectiveness of the non-Whites both as producers and consumers ... Was not the greatest danger to Whites and White standards in South Africa the very cheapness of Black labour?" (Ballinger, 1969: 61-62)

The effects of this pressure group on official policy were numerous and notable. By 1942 the acceptance of a permanent urban black population was rapidly displacing the definition of urban black labour as migrant labour[41] and, in principle at least, it was acknowledged that the urban black population should be eligible for the basic provisions of a national welfare system, always with the implicit proviso of an enduring differential *vis-à-vis* whites. These provisions covered health, education,[42] unemployment benefits and pension schemes.[43] In the case of housing the state simply proved unable to break the constraints on its ability to provide for the rapidly increasing requirements of black workers and their families.[44] The manner in which these reforms were initially enacted

---

41 The 1942 report of an Inter-departmental Committee under the chairmanship of the Secretary of the Department of Native Affairs urged for the abolition of pass laws with the immediate effect of an almost total curb on the demand for passes by the police and the consequent virtual elimination of arrests for pass law infringements.

42 Black education had always been suppressed. In 1921 it was estimated that as much as ninety percent of black children were illiterate and that only 3.5 percent of the black urban work force could be considered educated. The 1925 Native Taxation and Development Act tied the financing of black education to tax revenue, primarily from the notorious poll tax, extracted from the black population and by 1932 the Native Economic Commission estimated that 75 percent of black children still had no access to education. (De Kiewiet: 1957: 233-234) In 1945 a major policy change in the direction of addressing this deficiency was made when the provision for black education was separated from the black poll tax, thus ending, in this regard, the engineered poverty trap wherein "... the most backward part of the community was made responsible for its own development ..." (De Kiewiet: 1957: 234). Government expenditure on black education consequently increased substantially and the one tertiary education institution reserved for black (the Native College at Fort Hare) became eligible to government funding on the same criteria as applied to other colleges and universities in the country. (Hancock, 1968: 480-481)

43 Hancock (1968: 480, emphasis added) writes that

> "Hofmeyr's budgets of 1944 and 1945 extended social security beyond the barriers of the colour bar by making old age and invalidity pensions the right of every South African, *albeit at different levels of payment in accordance with different social standards associated with race and colour.*"

44 The rapidly increasing urban black population in the war years brought the shortfall in the provision of housing to crisis proportions. A report of the Social and Economic Planning Council in 1943 estimated this shortfall to amount to 125000 houses. By 1947, according to the estimates of the Native Affairs Department this had risen to 159000 houses for established families and required housing space for 106900 unmarried mothers. (Hancock, 1968: 477) The

indicates that they were planned as a permanent feature of post-war South Africa and not merely as a war expediency provision.

These reforms, however revolutionary they may have been for their proponents as well as their opponents within government, were still defined within the existing segregation paradigm. The essential irreconcilability of the vision informing the reformers within government and that underlying the demands of the representatives of the black population is exemplified in the exchange on the future of black education between Hofmeyr and Matthews during a council session in 1943 (Ballinger, 1969: 171-172). Hofmeyr, a more convinced liberal than Smuts, proposed reforms on education policy which were grounded in a philosophy of "separate but equal" development paths for different races. While eloquently apologising for the unequal budget allocation for separate educational programmes, he proposed that unless black education was based on "indigenous culture" it would result in the production of the black student "... as an inferior type of European". Matthews responded that different cultural heritages did not imply the necessity for a different education and that "... he had yet to discover what aim and method African education required as distinct from that of any other group; even for rural Africans, whose need is surely that of any other rural group, namely becoming good farmers." He maintained that the result of separate education would be that the black population would be excluded from the modernisation process by "... going off into this blind alley of African civilisation and not marching together with the rest of the peoples of the world towards a world civilisation ...". His explicit objective for black education was the acquisition of "... knowledge, skill and the techniques necessary for their application ...", i.e. technological capabilities. Though successive governments had, over the period considered in this chapter, established the basis for an industrialisation process and the related technology initiatives, this exchange between Matthews and Hofmeyr helps to define the impasse that the development of the national system of innovation had reached. Hofmeyr was simply reiterating the commitment to separate development which had been announced by Smuts more than twenty five years before (see endnote 2). It is now the liberation movement, articulated through Matthews, that enunciates the modernist agenda while the Smuts government remains captive of a language that

---

provision shortfall was due to shortages of building materials and skilled labour, which itself arose from the colour bar operating in the building industry. This period saw the start of the substantial organised squatter movements. (Davenport, 1977: 241).

was already becoming archaic within the emerging international technological order.

Smuts (and Hofmeyr) constantly vacillated between a weak acceptance, on vaguely articulated humanitarian grounds, of the need for the enfranchisement of the black population and the inability to commit himself to it, due to his trepidation of the reaction of his constituents.[45] The end result was that Smuts reacted in what became a typical recurrent response to the demands of the Natives Representative Council by accepting the need for reforms but qualifying it by a consideration for white fears. The rift between Smuts and the Natives Representative Council was best articulated by Ballinger who denounced a gradual reform programme as still operating within a racist paradigm and consequently clamoured for "... a policy which recognized that Africans are citizens of this country and not things apart" (Ballinger, 1969: 200). Smuts' arguments for gradualism, coming as they did from the man who had shown little regard for local white sentiment when he put down the revolts of 1914 and 1922 and when he had committed his country to the war effort in 1939,[46] rang false and did nothing to ease the surge of black resentment at the widening gap between the government's promises and its record of delivery on reforms.[47]

---

45 Hancock (Ch. 27) tentatively proposes that the schism in Smuts' stance on the abolition of segregation was both personal and political.

> "... the Natives want *rights* and not improvements. There we bump up against the claim for equality which is most difficult to satisfy except in very small doses which will not satisfy the leaders. I have so far done my best to follow the other line (of improvements) as less open to white prejudice and opposition." (Smuts' correspondence to M.C. Gillett, quoted in Hancock [1968: 481]).

46 Jan Smuts' attack on Hertzog's proposal that South Africa should remain neutral in parliament on 4 September 1939 was as follows:

> "I have always been prepared to give way, to hold the peace and to see that the young life of this nation is given a chance, and for the people to have the opportunity to grow together. Today we have come to the point where I have to call a halt and I have to adopt a different attitude; and I do so because I am in my very soul convinced that we are up against most vital issues for the present and the future of this country." (quoted from Ballinger, 1969: 98)

47 Ballinger (1969: 117-118) succinctly sums up how the aspirations for the easing of segregation which had been raised during the war years were thwarted:

> "... we came out of the war ... with the area of African freedom not widened but signally contracted. ... all strikes of all Africans in all circumstances had become and remained illegal ... while no machinery for negotiation and conciliation was provided ... all effective bargaining power

In 1943, in response to a bill proposed by government to devolve the power to release areas for urban black domicile rights to local authorities, the Council brought out a document[48] addressing the shortcomings of the *Native Urban Areas Act* of 1923 which was still in effect. The Council's argument was that a permanent urban black population had become an irreversible phenomenon and that the existing act which had been drafted on the assumption that the "... African was ... a temporary sojourner in the urban areas whose permanent interests lay elsewhere, namely in the Reserves" (Ballinger, 1969: 177) had become obsolete because of the rapid industrialisation over the intervening couple of decades. In its customary manner the Council based its argument for reforms on the dual principles of justice and pragmatism. Its plea was for a six point reform plan which would grant urban blacks representation in local authorities, urban land ownership rights and a guarantee of the permanence of those rights, the abolition of influx control, the right to self-expression, which covered freedom of speech, assembly and action, and freedom to negotiate the price of their labour. These demands were viewed as carrying too high a political risk by government and the bill of amendment to the act was passed in 1944. The permanence of an urban black population had, however, become an accepted reality and it formed the premise on which the recommendations of the report of the Fagan Commission, which was published early in 1948, were based. The conflicting proposals of this report on influx control and pass laws reflected the endemic conundrum of the Smuts government. The hesitant moves to ease controls over the movement of labour that were adopted by Smuts were intended as a strategy to placate the demands of Ballinger (Davenport, 1981: 244) and the Natives Representative Council and thus allow for a period of time during which white voters could be persuaded of the desirability of the transition towards full enfranchisement for blacks. However, the Fagan report came out too late to have any influence on policy. Smuts paid the

---

was denied to the rapidly expanding African labour force. ... new demands for housing ... became increasingly difficult to meet, so that slums erupted in or around every urban area, large and small. ... a system of influx control was established and encouraged ... This system involved a wide extension of the already bitterly resented pass system ... In spite of a great deal of lip service to new ideas and ideals, and to the need to meet modern problems with modern methods, South Africa ... was not only carrying on the methods of the eighteenth century but extending their operation to new fields ..."

48 See Ballinger (1969: 176-179) for a full rendition of the preamble of the document.

ultimate price for his long procrastination on reform and the electoral victory of the National party brought an alternative programme, articulated in the Sauer report, which rendered the hesitant reforms proposed by the Fagan commission immediately obsolete.

The establishment of the CSIR

The emergency conditions of the war provided van der Bijl, in his position as Director-General of War Supplies, with the opportunity to actuate his programme of industrialisation without any of the constraints imposed by market rationalists in peace time. In van der Bijl's assessment the war provided a unique opportunity to explore the limits of indigenous innovative and organisational capabilities and the incentive to extend these limits, thus establishing new structures, based on revealed and enhanced technological capabilities, which would irretrievably alter the country's industrial development path.[49] Indeed the war elicited a veritable revolution in South Africa's industrial structure pushing the country into areas of production hitherto untouched and stimulating a quantum leap in innovative activity and human capital investment. The immediate impact was on ISCOR in terms of output and, more significantly in terms of the suddenly increased range of products required for the war effort. Another sector which grew rapidly, was the motor vehicles industry which by 1941 was combining imported engines and chassis with locally produced components to assemble sixty-five types of army vehicles of which 30000 were supplied for the Abyssinian campaign (Jacobs, 1948: 161). More significantly, South Africa became adept at repairing damaged war

---

49 Van der Bijl identifies the paramount effect of the war effort on the future course of South African industrial development as

> "... the insight into our great industrial potential - a potential which, if suitably guided, can be used as a powerful driving force in the period of economic reconstruction which must follow the war. No investigation of our industries, no national industrial survey by commissions or individuals, no conferences of experts could reveal what has been revealed by this great collective effort, namely, the cleverness of our engineering designers, the resourcefulness and high standard of proficiency of South African engineers, the adaptability of our artisans and mechanics and the high standard of their workmanship ... given proper organization, South Africa can, with its own brains and materials, embark upon a new era of industrial development that will have a profound effect in increasing the affluence of our people and raising the standard of living of the poorer sections of the community." (speech delivered during a tour at a munitions factory in October, 1940, quoted in Jacobs, 1948: 172-173).

equipment, with the consequent expansion of the machine parts industry catering for land vehicles, aircraft, shipping and weaponry. The war also saw the emergence of a prototype for short-term technical training under the Central Organization for Technical Training Scheme which provided three to six-month training programmes to provide work shop skills. As early as 1934, van der Bijl had bemoaned the lack of a financing institution for industry, equivalent to the facilities available for the mining sector. In 1940 this shortcoming was rectified and van der Bijl was appointed as chairman of the IDC, which was established as the facilitating agency for industrial development and provided aid on the technical level, as well as managerial and financial aid, to industry. The launch of the IDC was pivotal in respect to the development of the institutional base for the country's technology base. Its terms of reference provided for a project appraisal procedure which assessed proposals within the context of long term viability.[50]

The Second World War brought concern with technology to the fore, culminating with the concern with "big science" following the development and deployment of the atom bomb. Henceforth science and its applications were irreversibly intertwined in the eyes of state planners, and South Africa was no exception. Van der Bijl, who had been the architect of South Africa's first Science and Technology policy framework, became the Director General of War Supplies and in this capacity was responsible for the coordination of the country's industrial resources for the war effort and for coordinating South African war supply structures with those of Australia, New Zealand and India for the Middle East theatre. The war had also had spillovers on the development of new products in the South African engineering sector in such diverse areas as machine tools, electrical motors and transformers, radar equipment, radio and ship repair and construction (Jones and Müller, 1992: 174).

While Smuts was in London as a member of the British wartime cabinet he was planning for the creation of national science and technology planning body with Basil Schonland. The end result was the establishment of CSIR in 1945 (Gazette No 3553, 5/10/45). The initiative was being implemented almost twenty-five years after Van der Bijl had formulated the first blueprint and this time lag introduced a new factor in

50 Van der Bijl cautioned that

> "It is not the intention that this (Industrial Development) Corporation (of South Africa, Limited) should provide cheap money for the indiscriminate establishment of industrial concerns, which may lead to mushroom developments and undesirable and inefficient production methods." (quoted in Jacobs, 1948: 130).

the motivation for a national policy in this area. This time there was a note of urgency due to the growing conviction that, in this essential component of the industrialisation process, South Africa was lagging behind other industrialised countries, especially within the Commonwealth.[51] In the second reading of the Bill (16th May 1945) the motivation for the establishment of the CSIR in terms of addressing the organisational bottlenecks of a national science and technology policy, as articulated by the Acting Prime Minister, Hofmeyr, was explicit:

> "... there is no reason to decry our scientific achievements. We have, however, fallen short in one respect in comparison with other countries, and that is in the general organisation of our research activities and their co-ordination. We have our research work in the Union in universities, in Government and in semi-Government institutions, in laboratories and in the studies of individual workers; *but we have not done enough to bring them together, to secure the better organisation of research activities and to stimulate new workers and new lines of investigation.*" (*House of Assembly Debates*, 1945, col. 7378, emphasis added), and "The organisation which this bill proposes to set up will have two main functions, a stimulating function and a co-ordinating function." (*ibid.*, col. 7380)

The co-ordinating role had the two main objectives of reducing overlapping and duplication of research efforts and of exploiting potential research complementarities through the elimination of isolated research activities. The R&D institutions that were identified as meriting attention were the universities, national research laboratories and industrial research institutes.[52] The concern for a national co-ordinating function was timely. By the year that the Bill was being tabled various specific areas of R&D activities were well established under a wide range of largely independent authorities. The original geological survey under the Department of Mines in 1912 had led to the establishment of the Minerals Laboratory which converted to the Government Minerals Laboratory in 1944. The South African Medical Research Institute had also been in existence since 1912.

---

51 The National Research Council in Canada was formed in 1916 and had continued with its role as the national coordinator of the public sector role in S&T. In Australia the Commonwealth Council for Scientific and Industrial Research was formed in 1926. Even in India, the Council for Scientific and Industrial Research was established in 1942. South Africa was thus lagging behind the main members of the Commonwealth. It had lost this initiative when it dissolved the Advisory Board for Industry and Science in 1923.

52 *House of Assembly Debates*, 1945, col. 7381.

The Department of Agriculture had nine research institutes running, covering veterinary research, citrus and sub-tropical fruits, afforestation and forest products. Under the authority of the Department of Commerce and Industry, the Fuel Research Institute had been established since 1930 and the Division of Sea Fisheries, entrusted with research in marine biology, was established in 1932. The main parastatal corporations - ESCOM, ISCOR and the IDC had also been conducting R&D in various relevant fields. The Sugar Milling Research Institute, financed entirely by industry, had been in operation since 1925 and the Leather Industries Research Institute had been established at Rhodes University College in 1941. The need for a co-ordinating role was therefore obvious enough. The CSIR was, however, also charged to engage in its own R&D in order to address areas of research which were neglected through market failure.

The new body was to be directly responsible to the prime minister, aided by a committee of ministers. The ministries that participated included the ministry of education, the ministry of economic development, the ministry of agriculture and ministry of mines. Emphasis was placed on its independent status as far as policy formulation and implementation were concerned. Funding would be controlled by parliament and its budget would be audited by the auditor- general. It was also proposed that the body should seek contract work to be funded by private enterprises.[53]

The terms of reference of the CSIR were as follows:

1. The coordination of R&D in (a) government institutions,[54] (b) tertiary education institutions,[55] and (c) state-aided bodies.[56]
2. The application of pure and applied research to the development of natural resources and industry. To this end it would engage in basic research, assist, through sponsoring and technical assistance, R&D sponsored by other agents and

53 ibid., col. 7382-3.

54 This included Agriculture and Forestry, where involvement was limited to industrial processing of agricultural products, Health and Housing, where the CSIR took on the responsibility for all R&D with respect to building technology, Health and Nutrition, Commerce and Industry, where the main function concerned standardisation and international liaison (involvement on standardisation was reduced with the eventual split-off of the South African Board of Standards).

55 This concerned the administration of research grants to universities.

56 This was limited to formal representation on the Fuel Research Institute, the Government Metallurgical Institute, the SAIMR and all government-aided research institutes and associations outside the public service.

establish industrial research units (the development of co-operative research institutes in conjunction with associations of firms) and national research institutes.[57] Private sector R&D would be encouraged through the remission of income tax on R&D, direct financial assistance and the provision of research facilities.

3. The training of scientific and technical personnel, directly and through sponsoring schemes and the enabling of university research through grants and bursaries as well as the creation of employment for graduating researchers.
4. The CSIR was to act as a national agency for the collection and diffusion of information on the latest technology in the international front through the creation of a central library and information service.
5. The CSIR was entrusted with the liaison in collaborative R&D programmes with other countries through the establishment of scientific missions abroad.
6. Human sciences and agricultural research were explicitly excluded from the charter of the CSIR.

Initially the CSIR was established outside the main body of the public service. It was accountable directly to the Office of the Prime Minister and the salary scales for its personnel were negotiated separately from those applicable in the public service. Given the dearth of existing researchers, the first bottleneck which the CSIR faced was in the recruitment field. Recruitment operated through personal networks and invitation and the initial drive was on training overseas and general investment in specific types of human capital. During its initial two years the CSIR rapidly established the basis of a wide research institutional network.[58]

---

57 National Physical Laboratory (1946), National Chemical Research Laboratory (1947), National Building Research Institute (1946), Telecommunications Research Laboratory (1946) and National Institute for Personnel Research (1948).

58 In the years 1946 and 1947 alone the following institutions were founded:
National Physical Laboratory
National Building Research Institute
Telecommunications Research Laboratory
National Bureau for Personnel Research
Library and Information Division
Scientific Liaison Offices (London and Washington)
Leather Industries Research Institute

The blueprint for the CSIR was based on models adopted in Canada and Australia at the time and there seems to have been no acknowledgement of the inherent structural differences between South Africa and these model countries which exhibited none of the market distortions specifically arising from the exigencies of a racist ideology. However, the role of human capital (apart from that embodied in scientists and engineers) in the effective implementation of a science and technology policy and in economic development in general had not as yet entered the mainstream of economic theory at the time. This was the time of capital accumulation growth models. As mentioned above, the low levels of skills among the majority of the black labour force, and hence the majority of workers, had already been articulated as a matter of concern in the twenties and, in spite of a clear acknowledgement of the potential danger posed to white supremacy, the government of the day had, because of the war crisis, opted for a broad-based push on the educational front, in the interests of industrialising the nation.[59] In spite of this recognition there was no reference to the pressing need to ease this bottleneck in the CSIR proposal.

Nothing that was proposed in the new Bill was, in itself directly contentious and this is evident in its virtually unanimous approbation in the House of Assembly debates. Its deficiency, and a crucial one, was in what it omitted and hence in the manner in which it circumscribed in perpetuity science and technology policy for the country. The specifically articulated omission came from Hofmeyr when he said that "What is meant by a stimulating function in relation to research will ... be obvious enough." (ibid. col. 7380). No further direct reference was made to this "obvious" aspect and therefore the assumption is that there was a concurrence that the stimulating function referred to existing practices of research grants and technical aid provided by the IDC, excluding consideration of fiscal incentives and trade and industrial policies specifically aimed at the deepening of the technology base of industry.

The main objection to the bill, and a devastating one, came from Margaret Ballinger and it concerned the explicit exclusion of "social and

---

Fishing Industry Research Institute
South African Paint Research Institute
National Chemical Research Laboratory
The University Research Grant Scheme was launched in 1946. (Kingwill, 1990: 291-292).

59 These arose from the recommendations of the Social and Economic Planning Council and an Inter-Departmental Committee under the chairmanship of the Secretary for the Department of Native Affairs in 1942.

economic research" from the terms of reference of the new body. In her submission Ballinger eloquently articulated the fundamental shortcoming of the new agency and since her critique identified the *malaise* which was to bedevil science and technology policy in South Africa for the next five decades, it bears to be quoted extensively:

> In so far as the object of a scientific research institute is in essence social, I cannot understand why ... it was decided to separate the control of scientific and technological research from social research. The intention of this research is to develop our natural resources with a view to the building up of the standard of living of our own people ... I do not know how we can approach an objective of that kind when we know as little as we do ... about the character of the people whom we hope to serve. At present we are trying in South Africa to build a new society ... with the most lamentably inadequate knowledge of the type of society for which we have to plan. ... the most urgent need at the present time in this country is to find out what the social and economic conditions of the whole of our population are. ... In recent years, we have had the report of the Agricultural and Industrial Requirements Commission and the reports of the Social and Economic Planning Council. I suggest ... that all those reports which have been indications of the lines upon which certain people have thought that we ought to proceed with our planning, are based on the widest generalisations. ... all our scientific and technological investigation is going to lead us nowhere unless it is linked up with a careful analysis of the character of the people, their conditions and their potentialities. (*ibid.*, col. 7396-8)

Ballinger thus debunked the much touted significance of the CSIR proposal through her argument that its activities would proceed in an information vacuum with respect to the economic structure that it was ostensibly designed to affect. She went on to specify the type of information that she considered essential for the formulation of a sound science and technology policy:

> "We are told by the Agricultural and the Industrial Requirements Commission ... that we have labour resources that are eminently adapted to mass production methods. This ... is a generalisation. I want to know on what it is based. I want to know (1) about the standards of efficiency of the population and the basis on which they are measured. (2) ... how the labour conditions of this country compare with the labour conditions of other countries. (3) ... how our industrial organisations have been influenced by the type of labour force available in this country. (4) ... how the character of that labour force has encouraged or retarded the reclassification of occupations in industry. (5) ... how the building industry has developed in this country as compared with the building industry in

> America or England, how the organisation of the shoe making industry compares with the shoe making industry in other countries (6) ... whether our labour resources allow us to import the sort of machinery other countries use and to use it in the same ... way as they use it. (7) ... whether we can apply the enormous developments in mass production methods ... whether ... methods can be adjusted to the needs and conditions of this country ..." (ibid., p. 7398, enumeration added)

As can be seen from this quotation, Ballinger's concern was at the omission of any consideration of the role that human capital, other than that of scientists and engineers, was to play in the development of the country's technological capabilities (point 1). She was also aware of the prime determinant of competitive advantage in the emerging global markets (points 2 and 5). Her objections show an incisive awareness of how the effects of segregation had limited labour productivity (point 4), absorptive capacity for new technology (points 6 and 7), management cultures and industrial organisation (point 3), and, in consequence, competitive ability in the international markets. Ballinger's assessment was remarkable in its incisiveness not only within the South African context but also against the backdrop of the state of theory at the time.

Her cogent submission effectively placed the scope of the CSIR as proposed in the bill at the level of an exercise in the rationalisation of various research activities within an existing context, a proposal which eschewed any possibility of fundamentally altering the economic context within which technological capabilities were determined. The foremost implication of her critique was that the new body would not, in any significant manner, enhance the country's technological capabilities. The other significant, but, within the South African context, a relatively minor area of omission in the new bill was the integration of policy on technology with industrial and trade policy. This too would have fallen within the sphere of economic research which the bill specifically excluded.

It is significant that Ballinger was very much a voice in the wilderness. The lengthy debate which extended over three sessions contains no response of any consequence, either positive or negative to her critique. The other submissions during the debates show a complacency and a self-congratulatory attitude about local inventiveness and resourcefulness in a wearisome listing of local innovations, tempered by a xenophobic note,[60]

---

60 The ethnic drive was explicitly and officially stated:

> "... this bureau should in the first place be an Afrikaans national bureau in the broadest sense of the word. Its purpose is to contribute to the

and only slightly ruffled by quibbling over the past fates of individual researchers.[61] The tone of the exchanges was extremely parochial and it is evident that the consensus was that the institution launched by this Bill would be the final administrative step in bringing the country into the rank of the scientifically advanced nations. It is significant that no mention was made of the implications of technological advance to the country's competitive positioning in the global markets. The only reference to the international context was in terms of vague pronouncements on the necessity to protect internal markets and an aspiration to attain the position of a technological benefactor to other countries. This was to a large extent the spirit which had informed protectionist policy. While the classical infant industry argument envisages the ability to compete on world markets as the validation of the costs of protection, the petitioning for protectionist measures in South Africa was almost uniformly couched within the context of survival within the local market. This absence of a debate over fundamentals as opened up by Ballinger was perhaps inevitable given the paradigmatic incompatibility between her position and that of the drafters of the bill, as well as the audience it was intended for. One can go even further and propose that her concept of the proper role and requirements of a science and technology policy anticipated theoretical developments in this field by a number of years.

In a way, the positioning of the CSIR by the Smuts government outside the structure of the public service served to circumscribe its policy making domain with respect to science and technology. The old Advisory Board of Industry and Science had been fully integrated within the policy formulating structures on industry and trade policy. The CSIR, on the other hand, had no specific charter to advise on industrial development and selective tariff policies. In the light of Ballinger's critique the action taken by the National Party after 1948 to incorporate the CSIR within the main body of the public administration structure represents a clear understanding of the limited sphere of influence of this body as it was constituted by the bill, rather than an arbitrary diminution of its status. The rapid decline of the role played by the CSIR in the development of the country's innovation system over the following decades was a direct consequence of the limitations inherent in its original terms of reference.

---

knowledge, the capacity and the prosperity of the Afrikaner nation. ... the members of the council of the bureau must be Afrikaans citizens." (House of Assembly Debates, 1945, col. 7388)

In fact, all the presidents of the CSIR until 1990 were Afrikaners.

61 ibid., col. 7403-7406.

An assessment

Smuts' indecisiveness on the question of the extension of equal political rights to the general populace led to his defeat in the 1948 elections. The combination of insufficient conviction on the need for reforms and lack of will to act upon the recommendations of the Natives Representative Council, on the one side, and half-hearted statements about the need for reform, on the other, increased the visible forms of resistance on the part of the black population while making him vulnerable to the charge of being a traitor by the National Party. In retrospect the close election results of 1948, with Smuts actually winning a numerical majority of votes and a Nationalist victory significantly enabled by a superior organisation of its electoral campaign,[62] can be used to argue that Smuts' defeat was largely attributable to a combination of a faltering vision and an insufficient focus on internal political affairs. Smuts was caught in another contradiction which intersected with the nationalistic conundrum - his inability to detach himself from the labour market legislation initiated by the mining sector, in spite of the sharp lesson that the war had delivered on its crippling effect on economic growth and development. Smuts' inability to extricate himself from this bind, and his consequent defeat in the polls, irrevocably locked the economy into a particular development path tied to the primary sector. The development of the secondary sector was constrained thereafter on several levels - through lack of human capital investment and an increasing reliance on a small internal market. The implications for the development of the country's innovation system were equally dispiriting. The scope for innovation in mining is specific and has a limited spillover potential for the rest of the economy. Moreover, the reliance of this sector in South Africa on extremely low labour costs necessitated a policy of increasing suppression of any possibility for upward mobility for labour which spilled over to the rest of the economy and severely limited the pool of skills available for other industries. Not only was productivity growth hamstrung by this syndrome, but so was the capacity to absorb new technology other than that which was labour displacing and made limited demand on the skills component of the labour force. Smuts the modernist had mistakenly hitched his cart to a sector which, in spite of being the most modern in the economy at the time, was essentially based on production relations which were, even then, already archaic within the context of the global economic modernization process.

62 See Davenport (1981: 251).

While it is often futile to engage in retrospective hypothetical scenario building, in this case it may be worthwhile to project a possible course of political and economic development had he won the 1948 election, on the basis of the one constancy that had become manifest in Smuts' political career. This was his overriding obsession with the placement of South Africa firmly at the forefront of international politics. The failure of his efforts to extend South Africa's hegemony over a wider Southern African region, combined with the increasing international outrage at South Africa's internal politics, would have provided a strong incentive for reform. The brief war experience of the labour market bottleneck had already elicited a reformatory response from Smuts. The requirements of post-war industrial expansion, combined with increasing claims for higher wages would have amplified the need for reform. Finally, although it was early days in the general understanding of the broad human capital requirements of a sound science and technology policy, van der Bijl's strong initiative in this area would soon have highlighted the severe constraint imposed by the contemporary segregationist labour and educational policies.

The introduction of innovation in the recounting of South African economic history blurs beyond recognition the easy association introduced by liberal economists between Smuts as the proponent of a freely functioning market on the one hand and the National Party as the interventionist regime on the other. The argument used by Smuts and his advisors in respect of science and technology policy was based on an acknowledgement that in this sphere market failure was inevitable and demanded corrective action by the state. In the case of the nationalists these arguments were ignored and the initiative was neglected. As shall be seen further on, in the case of the early history of Council for Scientific and Industrial Research, this neglect was not a chance one but was symptomatic of a distinct divergence in vision. The structures initiated by van der Bijl, designed to force the country into a modern competitive industrial age, were either pressed into the service of grand apartheid policy or became ineffectual. In either case they developed into sources of distortion of the development process, reinforcing the very inhibitors to the advancement of the country's technological capabilities that they were originally designed to erode.

CHAPTER FOUR

SCIENCE AND TECHNOLOGY POLICY UNDER APARTHEID

The assessment of the 1948 elections either as constituting a break in the country's political economic history or as the evolution of established structures depends on the particular stratum of historical recounting that is considered. The move away from reductionist renditions of either side of the race-class debate has allowed the acceptance of several strata as relevant to the recounting of the apartheid years, but it is their ordering, the relative depths that are assigned to them, that now constitutes the contested analytical terrain for historians. Such strata are far from impermeable. Political positions on race, the resistance to racist politics, class interests and conflict, economic constraints, the fluctuations and changes in the global economy, and the changing shape of the national system of innovation are all amenable to both distinct and interrelated analyses. Such analyses are, however, dependent on the appraisal of which stratum underlies other strata. Permeability implies some acceptance of causality and hence a position on relative layering can be translated into the assessment of prime determining forces as distinct from secondary feed-back effects. The implications for current economic policy in the post-apartheid era follow from alternative positions since the assessment of the requirements for a break from the apartheid heritage depends on the assessor's choice of a specific stratum as constitutive of the bedrock of the apartheid phenomenon.

The immediately defining characteristic of apartheid was that from 1948 until the country's first democratic election in 1994 the political system, while officially based on a parliamentary model (for white voters), effectively became a totalitarian regime within the lexicon of post-war politics.[1] The evaluation of degree to which the establishment of apartheid

1 Though elections were contested by various parties, the control of parliament by the National Party for more than forty years conforms to Morin's (1992) necessary condition for totalitarian rule:

constituted a break with a process of political development that, in the account of liberal economic historians, would have eliminated segregation because of the increasing demands of economic rationality, instead of being a continuation of the established sets of power relations depends, as I have discussed previously, on which side of the race-class debate the analyst comes from. What is indisputable, however, is that apartheid constituted a clear and unambiguous signal that the principle of racial segregation (and domination) was beyond debate. The contested area for apartheid politicians now became the issue of which policy option would best serve to ensure the viability and long term sustainability of apartheid. The language of contestation for the main competing policy agendas transmuted into a discourse on economic viability and it was the shifting assessment(s) of this viability that came to determine the fortunes of apartheid. The first twelve years saw the resolution of the fundamental question of the participation of black labour in the economy and the clear articulation of the apartheid model as enunciated by Verwoerd. The sixties, which saw the start of South Africa's formal international isolation, turned into the boom years for the apartheid economy. However, the advent of the oil crisis in the early seventies, combined with a resurgence of widespread mass protest and the increasing effectiveness of the international anti-apartheid movement, marked the start of a crisis, economic as well as political, which was to become endemic to the polity. The eighties saw the escalating crisis of faith in the sustainability of apartheid within the ruling establishment itself, with often erratic and inevitably doomed attempts to reform some part or other of an apartheid machinery that was increasingly being seen as obsolete. The eighties

---

> "The state is completely dominated by the party apparatus and hence becomes an instrument for the enslavement of all society. The state is not omnipotent but is subjected to the omnipotence of the party while at the same time enhancing it. That is why one of the main aspects of the anti-totalitarian revolution is the revival of the autonomy of the state and the corresponding withering away of the party's domination, right up to the point where it loses the political monopoly which guaranteed its totalitarian power." (p. 89)

However, Adam (1972) points out the crucial difference between apartheid and other totalitarian regimes, specifically Stalinist Russia and Nazi Germany, is the fact that totalitarian regimes in general depend on a mass movement, a forced eradication of differences among the populace through the overriding definition of its constituents as equal citizens of the state. In South Africa on the contrary apartheid depended on an enforced fragmentation of the populace and a denial of common citizenry.

came to an end with the capitulation of the apartheid government with the unbanning of the ANC.

The saga of the rise and eventual fall of apartheid, as distinct from the previous segregation model, was a complex product of contesting forces in two distinct, albeit related, arenas - the internal and the external contexts. In the case of the former, a number of conflicts were concurrently determining the manner in which the regime adapted in order to survive. With respect to the internal liberation movement, the earlier reaction on the part of the apartheid structure was one of repression and separation. Simultaneously, attempts were constantly under way to co-opt collaborators from within the various disenfranchised communities. The first manifestation of this strategy was in the form of the homelands policy which depended for its success on the collaboration of the administrators of these "independent" *bantustans*. Eventually it became evident that the economic viability and the self-sustainability of the homelands were impossible. The eventual acceptance of a permanent large black urban labour force and resident population elicited efforts to foster the development of a black bourgeoisie to act as a buffer between an increasingly militant black labour force and the white owners of the means of production.

The other source of internal conflict arose between the interests of the different fractions of capital and specific apartheid policies. The relationship between the apartheid state and the private sector shifted towards congruence with the result that the interests of capital became central to the country's political and economic course. The relationship between state and market was also being affected by changes in the nature of the opposition to apartheid, both internally and internationally, and by the changing input requirements ensuing from global techno-economic paradigm shifts.[2] These shifting conditions in turn affected the

2 Adam (1972: 154) pointed out the essential incongruity between apartheid and the requirements of the modern economy:

> "... an expanding economy built essentially on migratory labour, as the grand Apartheid envisages, is not compatible with this stage of technological development. ... Even with a high degree of mechanization ... South Africa's growing economy would still call for the transference of an increasing number of contract workers into skilled producers. This new type of qualified ... worker will be hard pressed for high individual productivity ... Individual productivity cannot in turn be easily commandeered. It is grounded in a mentality, basically not at odds with the surrounding social system. Individual productivity presupposes psychological incentives in terms of a more or less satisfied labour force, and it is difficult to see how the present system of white-controlled

congruence of the two broad goal set categories, and hence in the nature of the collaboration between state and capital. As the country's economic base shifted towards secondary industries, the detrimental effects of apartheid policies on industrial relations, skills availability, and the constraints on the growth of the internal market became increasingly costly to employers within the manufacturing sector. These costs were exacerbated by the effects of sanctions on the access to international markets, to capital, to skills and to technology.

There were, however, several related processes occurring on the two sides of the labour market during the apartheid era that imparted a high degree of stability to the economic environment. On the side of capital there were two main developments which imparted cohesion. The first was the interpenetration of English and Afrikaner capital through establishments, mergers and acquisitions, as documented in detail in Fine and Rustomjee (1996, Ch. 7). This process of interpenetration was the outcome of state policy specifically aimed at the advancement of Afrikaner capital. This reduced significantly the intra-white ethnicity of capital and hence the type of state/market conflict which had been consistently evident during the segregationist period. The second was the integration of capital across mining, manufacturing and financial sectors. This served to internalise the contradictory effects of apartheid economic policy on the different sectors, thus significantly reducing the potential opposition to apartheid arising from diverse capitalist interests. A coinciding process of amalgamation was occurring within labour. An immediate source of political stability for the apartheid government was obtained by the co-option of white labour, through virtually assured lifetime employment, as, in the rendition of a class analysis of apartheid, a sub-category of the *protégée* group. Thus, from the perspective of a history of class formation and class conflict, the apartheid era is distinct in that it established the conditions, through state policy, for the coalescence of specific polarised groupings of white-owned capital,[3] with the state as

---

residential and political mobility can achieve basic contentment among those on whom it increasingly depends."

3 As recorded by Fine and Rustomjee (1996), the process of the consolidation of capital over the post-war period was slow and subject to intermittent conflicts, but

> "... the 1980s witnessed the emergence of five interpenetrated `axes' of capital straddling the mining, manufacturing and financial sectors. Their origins differed ethnically and sectorally. (Anglo American Corporation) had moved from gold and diamond mining into domestic manufacturing, domestic finance and regional and international mining. Sanlam had pooled Afrikaner financial resources to break into mining and

its agent on the one side, and labour, black and uniformly disenfranchised on the other.

The global context within which apartheid existed was fundamentally different from the one during the pre-apartheid segregationist period. In the twilight of the colonial era after the war South Africa was still an accepted member of the world community. International protests arose from within the Commonwealth but, though they were a cause for concern to Smuts, were still largely ineffectual in affecting the course of the country's internal political development. In the post-colonial era, with the rise of nationalist movements throughout the various empires, South Africa's racist regime, especially after its formalisation under apartheid became the international *cause celebre*. The country's exit from the Commonwealth in 1961, followed by its expulsion from the UN, marked the onset of increasing international isolation. The main brake on this process of international isolation emerged from the new post-colonial imperialist dictates of the cold war, since the apartheid regime incessantly and successfully allied itself with the anti-communist powers. Eventually, the combination of the increasingly visible repression, highlighted by the Sharpeville massacre in the early sixties and the Soweto uprising in 1976, and the cessation of the cold war eroded and finally eliminated apartheid's support base in the international political arena.

The period 1948-1961 saw the rise to pre-eminence of H.F. Verwoerd, apartheid's foremost ideologue, who became Minister of Native Affairs in 1950[4] and Prime Minister in 1958. It was this period that marked the articulation and entrenchment of the basis of apartheid and it was an articulation that evolved out of a maelstrom of strongly opposed views on what the apartheid ideal required for its achievement as well as from the conflict with forces on the ground which were opposed to this political programme. This period, which commences with the electoral victory of

---

manufacturing. Rembrandt had grown domestically and internationally, retaining a focus on cigarettes, tobacco and liquor production but also diversifying its investment portfolio. Anglovaal, the smallest group, had retained a historical base in manufacturing. Thomas Barlow had developed its manufacturing interests, diversified into mining through the acquisition of Rand Mines in 1971 and had retained the financial backing of SA Mutual, mainly to prevent itself from being taken over by other conglomerates. Only Liberty/Standard remained purely financial, as it had been originally." (Fine and Rustomjee, 1996: 173)

4 E.G. Jensen, the Minister in place when the National party came into power was a remnant of the previous government and was the target of an intensive campaign for his removal to this cornerstone of apartheid policy by W.W.M. Eiselen who was instrumental in getting Verwoerd appointed to the post.

the National Party and the formal institutionalisation of apartheid and ends with the departure of South Africa from the Commonwealth just after the Sharpeville massacre, was, from the perspective of this particular history, formative of the national system of innovation which was to dominate for the rest of the century in a number of ways. The specific features of the apartheid economy which would have a direct effect on the shape of the country's innovation system were numerous, covering the obvious areas of the labour market, formal science and technology initiatives and the related trade and industrial policies, and they were all comprehensible within the overall language structure of apartheid. It is implausible to attribute the consolidation of the emerging shape of the industrial base of the economy, and its consequent technological profile, to anything but apartheid. Other processes, mainly the system of accumulation, are necessarily contingent on the specifics of the requirements of the apartheid agenda. At the same time it is analytically fruitless to engage in alternative scenario building exercises in the manner of some liberal historians in order to assess the "opportunity costs" to business of the restrictions of apartheid. Any political economic setting poses restrictions on business practices and if the skills shortages and constrained markets were the results of apartheid these could be more than compensated by the eradication of effectively organised labour which allowed employers the power to dictate employment conditions with a degree of freedom unparalleled in any industrialised economy.

Through the systematic eradication of the various articulations of countervailing forces and the erosion of the probabilities of attainment of alternative outcomes the new regime locked the economy, and its national system of innovation, into a structure whose basis had been established during the previous regime but which had hitherto been under a sustained and increasingly concerted attack on its claim to immutability. By the end of this period intra-parliamentary debate on the morality and viability of separate development had been effectively eliminated, organised extra-parliamentary liberation movements had been routed and the country's rulers had clearly signalled their willingness to pay the price of increasing international isolation for the continuance of apartheid. It was during this period that the policies designed for the advancement of Afrikaner capital and the consequent process of the integration of capital irrevocably bound the economy, and the ensuing patterns of industrial growth, to that constellation of sectors defined as the minerals-energy complex by Fine and Rustomjee (1996).

On its election to power the Malan government was beset by a tension between a number of contradictory motivations. Its main concern was to consolidate and strengthen the tenuous political victory that it had achieved on the basis of its commitment to the segregationist political agenda on which it had built its electoral campaign. In this pursuit it needed to formulate policy in a manner that would maximise the growth of its white constituent base during its first term of office. Thus, the shape of the emerging era was a resultant of a debate on the nature of the agenda for an enduring and viable apartheid polity. The primary point of internal contention that arose was between the two competing policy programmes which Posel (1991) respectively identifies as the "purist" one calling for total segregation and "practical" apartheid and it essentially hinged on the role allotted to black labour in the economy.

The advocates of total segregation saw the elimination of economic dependence on black labour as essential to the attainment of the ideal of long-term, sustainable racial segregation. While forced to accept the existing reliance on black labour in secondary industry, this position also stressed the costs to the white dominated economic system of low labour productivity among black workers and the implications for the wage bill of increasing unionisation. According to the proponents of this strategy the easing of the skills bottlenecks on further industrial development could be brought about through labour-substituting capital investment and technological change and through the immigration of skilled whites to swell the ranks of workers in those high skill categories reserved for that population group.

The competing policy agenda was motivated by the fears of industrialists and farmers of the cost implications of foregoing the existing supply of abundant cheap labour. Moreover, in the case of the farming sector, the purists' agenda would have required a considerable increase in the land area allotted to the black rural sector for the viability of their vision of a total programme of separate development along racial lines and this would have entailed considerable land redistribution away from white farmers. For industrialists the main concern was the continuing availability of cheap labour and the main policy initiative that they required was the reversal of the power gained by organised black labour under the previous government. For both sectors the establishment of a permanent controlled urban black population was thus seen as the ideal means to achieve a stable self-reproducing semi-skilled labour force for industry while reducing the exodus from the farming areas. Verwoerd's plan of grand apartheid marked the victory of the pragmatists. Although the skills bottleneck was never sufficiently eased,[5] the diverse skills requirements of the private sector were covertly factored into the implementation of pragmatic apartheid. Within secondary industry, job reservation was never as rigid as in the mining sector and it "floated" across time and across industries. Thus, in this important respect the overarching racist "ideology" proved sufficiently flexible to accommodate the input requirements of the various fractions of capital.

The immediate political programme of the National Party had two major objectives - the virtually complete exclusion of blacks from spheres of political and economic power and the solution of the poverty syndrome among poor Afrikaners. The first was achieved through the introduction of a profusion of laws defining and entrenching racial segregation in a wide range of areas. The freedom of association between members of different racial groupings was severely restricted,[6] as was the freedom of (spatial) movement for blacks. The position of black workers was progressively defined as that of sojourners in urban areas,[7] education at

---

5 One of the many contradictions arising from the new political concerns affected the importation of white skilled labour on which both sides of the debate laid some stress, albeit to different degrees. One of the first moves to entrench the integrity of what Norval (1996: 105) terms the new "imaginary surface of inscription which purported to provide an ordering system of the whole of South African society" based on the precepts of the myth of Afrikanerdom was enacted through the 1949 South African Citizenship Bill which simultaneously rendered it more difficult for immigrants to acquire citizenship and virtually eliminated the privileged position which Commonwealth subjects had enjoyed over other immigrants (Davenport, 1977: 257).

6 The *1950 Population Registration Act* required identification on the basis of racial grouping which became the paramount defining parameter of the citizen's position in South Africa. The *1949 Prohibition of Mixed Marriages Act* and the *1950 Immorality Amendment Act* defined marriage and sexual relations across the "colour line". as illegal. The *1953 Reservation of Separate Amenities Act* required the separation of contact between whites and blacks at most public facilities.

7 The 1950 *Group Areas Act* restricted residential rights to specifically defined areas according to racial grouping. In this case the distinction was finer than "White/Non-white" and provided separate rights for Blacks, Coloured, Indians and White. The 1952 *Native Laws Amendment Act* restricted urban residential rights for blacks on the basis of place of birth and lengthy residence and employment histories. The main instrument of control was the pass book whose requirement was introduced by the 1952 Black (Abolition of Passes and Co-ordination of Documents) Act. Other landmarks were the 1954 *Black Resettlement Act* and the 1959 *Promotion of Bantu Self Government Act.*

every level for blacks was separated from that for whites,[8] and a number of acts progressively entrenched the colour bar across the economy and effectively halted the growing trade union movement.[9] The second goal, that of guaranteeing a sinecure employment for Afrikaners, was attained through an extension of effective job reservation practice throughout a rapidly growing public sector.

The blueprint of apartheid, its economic feasibility study, came out in the report of the Tomlinson commission (Union of South Africa, 1955, 1956) whose methodology, in spite of the subsequent evidence of the wide inaccuracy of the projections of the demographic trends on which its recommendations had been based, was to fundamentally determine the economic structure thereafter, even though Verwoerd rejected most of the recommendations of the report regarding the feasibility requirements for *bantustans*. This study worked backward from the basic requirement of apartheid (which was being renamed Separate Development) that the black section of the population should as far as possible be removed from the designated central areas of white dominance. The policy of establishing *bantustans*, as self-sufficient homelands, was to be the foundation stone of this programme. However, the major constraint, an insurmountable one, on the fulfilment of this policy was the area of land required for allocation to rural blacks as compared to existing allocations and the impoverished state of these areas. On paper, the solution to this constraint required that the estimated minimum income requisite for the sustainability of a rural family be adjusted downwards and that structural changes in production and distribution should be recommended in order to raise income from

---

8 The report of the *Bantu Education Commission* of 1951 proposed a separate educational system for blacks, controlled by central government (rather than by provincial government and missions) with syllabi which relied on colloquial languages and on manual training. Separate education along racial lines along the recommendations of this report were made law through the 1953 *Bantu Education Act*. Racial separation was imposed in tertiary education by the 1957 *Extension of University Education Act*.

9 1953 Criminal Law Amendment Act.
1956 Riotous Assemblies Act.
1956 Industrial Conciliation Act
1953 Native Settlement of Disputes Act.
1950 Suppression of Communism Act.

The Suppression of Communism Act was amenable to a wide enough interpretation as to enable the Minister of Justice to move against virtually any organised challenge to the established political order. This caused a rapid disintegration of organised labour on the left which was further exacerbated by the emergence of right-wing white trade unions.

agricultural land in order to make the figures of the attainable tally with the requirements of the envisaged programme of separate development. In the case of the industrial nucleus of the Vaal triangle, where there was no possibility of establishing a "homeland", black residential areas spatially separated from the urban centres were established. Ultimately four "independent" *bantustans* were created along ethnic lines. These were Transkei (Xhosa), which was declared independent on the 26th October 1976, Bophuthatswana (Tswana), which was declared independent on the 6th December 1977, Venda (Venda), declared independent on the 13th September 1979, and Ciskei (also Xhosa), declared independent on the 4th December 1981. The other six homelands - Gazankulu (Tsonga [Shangaan]), KaNgwane (Swazi), KwaNdebele (Ndebele), KwaZulu (Zulu), Lebowa (Northern Sotho or Pedi) and QwaQwa (Southern Sotho) - were assigned partial administrative autonomy. These spatial economic constructs could never be viable systems of innovation given the land resource constraints imposed by the apartheid model. Indeed their implicit *raison d'être* was to bolster the illusion of a viable model of separate development. In this pursuit, artificial economies were gradually set up with varying levels of success which through fiscal means generated local employment bases within these constructs. A more lasting effect was the establishment of new systems of patronage leading to new local administrations which were friendly to the apartheid regime. Efficient administration was low on the agenda of homeland administration and the central government was willing to bear the costs of corruption and inefficiency in order to maintain the illusion of a working model. The enduring effects of these power structures helped determine the provincial re-configuration of the post-apartheid economy and continue to haunt the spatial economies of South Africa to this day (Scerri, 2008).

The new political ordering affected the shape of the national system of innovation through its impact on the growth path of technological capabilities on a number of levels. The immediate change in the institutional base for science and technology policy was in the structures which had been established previously during the Smuts regime. This, however, was symptomatic of the wider sea change affecting the political economic destiny of the country and thus has to be placed within the broader context of effects on other determinants of technological capabilities as reflected in the effects of the new policies on the context within which industrial development would occur. The prime area of relevance in this case is the impact of apartheid labour and education policies on human capital growth and the consequent availability of skilled labour for the industrialisation process. A less tangible, but more enveloping, set of determinants lies in the changing culture within which economic decisions at every level of aggregation would be taken in the future. Nelson (1990b) argues for an "optimal" setting for innovative activity in a system which achieves some balance, a tension whose specifics are contextually determined, between a national planning schema and bounded market rationality. This balance varies across a spectrum whose limits at one end are set by the public good nature of innovation and at the other end by the essential unpredictability of future systems of knowledge which cannot be identified from the basis of current systems and thus require the play of markets to summon forth their emerging shapes. The comprehensive and totalising plan, on which apartheid policy formulation was predicated, especially within the framework of dominance that it presupposed, sacrificed the role of both elements of this tenuous combination. In the process of the refinement of the apartheid blueprint the setting within which a viable innovation system could develop was impoverished while the strategy options set for private enterprises motivated by the drive for maximising economic surplus generally reduced the requirement to innovate.

By the end of this period internal opposition to apartheid had been effectively quelled. The black labour union movement had been put into disarray and intra-parliamentary opposition had been rendered ineffectual. The National Party felt secure enough in its position of power to pull the country out of the Commonwealth just ahead of its forced expulsion and to bear the costs of the apparent inevitability of increasing international isolation. The basic legal underpinnings of grand apartheid had been laid down and the compliance of the main effective players in the new script had been obtained. The nuisance caused by influx control policy to the labour recruitment practices of industrialists had largely been eliminated through implicit arrangements that would bypass the officiousness of bureaucrats in this regard and the economic system settled down to the long term programme of industrialisation within the parameters of the new programme.

Within the set of exigencies of apartheid the process of industrialisation was to rely on increasing mechanisation and the consequent diminution in the reliance on a broad-based skill component in the labour force. Science and technology policy in turn followed the requirements of this vision, reinforcing these trends by fragmentary programmes which were led both by the requirements of the current industrial structure and those of the new political economic structure facing the real and growing prospect of international isolation. International isolation provided the impetus for acquiring self-sufficiency in armaments and energy with the consequent implications for research in the relevant fields. The focus on these areas did not, however, provide the appropriate context for a consistent and coherent policy programme which could establish a sound and wide technological capabilities base. The eventual fossilisation of the main R&D coordination organ, the CSIR, which is charted below, can be seen as a symptom, an inevitable consequence, of this endemic malaise within apartheid economic planning. The origins of this malaise of course pre-date apartheid and in the case of the CSIR it was its initial terms of reference which had from the start denied it the power and space to conceive and enact a national science and technology policy.

The entrenchment of the National Party's political position enabled the uninhibited implementation of the Verwoerdian programme. Effective parliamentary opposition to apartheid virtually disappeared as poll after poll reinforced the conviction that the National Party had become the country's government and the permanent protector of white dominance. Indeed, the only serious parliamentary crises that the National Party faced were precipitated by the extreme right wing of the party which regularly revolted from the late sixties onwards and eventually formed the *Konservatiewe Party* and the *Herstigte Nasionale Party*. However, after the major setbacks of the fifties, the liberation movements on the ground rapidly gained momentum leading to an intensification of the revolutionary movement and consequently of the forces of repression against it. Internationally the country became a pariah, but as long as Africa was deemed a cold war theatre, South Africa enjoyed the barely covert patronage of the foremost industrialised economies in the west.

The rapidly increasing repression since 1948 had elicited an equally rapid resurgence in popular resistance. This culminated in the Sharpeville massacre of March 1960, followed by the declaration of the ANC and the Pan African Congress as illegal organisations, massive countrywide arrests and the imposition of a state of emergency. The effects on the economy were contradictory. The progressive economic and political isolation of South Africa started in earnest at around this time as the country withdrew from the Commonwealth in 1961 and pressure increased from a wide range of countries to have South Africa expelled from the United Nations. Initially, after Sharpeville, there was a large increase in capital outflows and a deepening balance of payments crisis, and the state reacted to this by raising tariff barriers and imposing stringent exchange controls. Eventually, however, the increasingly repressive policies adopted by the state, which effectively crushed political opposition, signalled stability to investors, both local and foreign. Investment funds began to flow into the country and the sixties turned into a boom period for the economy. The increasing government revenues facilitated the implementation of the *bantustan* policy with substantial transfers of government funds used to establish these semi-independent governance systems. Tax and other fiscal incentives were widely used to encourage the location of industries to the borders of these homelands in order to increase employment opportunities away from the industrial centres.

The international oil crisis in the early seventies and the abandonment of the gold standard marked the start of the end of the economic boom for South Africa. These external factors were compounded by the massive resurgence of the liberation struggle which had been generally suppressed in the previous decade. This reached unprecedented levels both in terms of the base of the revolts and in the levels of militancy. The culmination was the student revolt in Soweto in 1976 to which the government reacted with a highly visible brutality. This time around, in spite of extremely repressive counter-revolutionary measures, including the murder of Steve Biko and countless others, the revolts were not suppressed but rather increased in intensity and in their disruptive effect on both the economy and the country's governance. Most of the relevant economic indicators show a similar pattern over the seventies and the eighties, with a modest upward trend, marked by fluctuations until the early eighties and a generally downward trend toward the end of the decade. The same general pattern applies to GNP per capita, manufacturing output, manufactured exports, the capacity to import, investment and productivity indices (see Joffe et al., 1995).

Towards the end of the seventies an number of legislative changes were introduced to reduce the constraints imposed on employers by job reservation. Davies (1979b) attributes this to three linked factors. The first was the growing skills shortage. Davies quotes studies which showed that the shortage of labour at the higher end of the skills spectrum had been growing in South Africa since the late sixties, especially in comparison to countries at similar levels of industrialisation. These studies predicted an increasing skills gap for the future. A second factor was the decline in foreign long term investment in South Africa which was at least partially attributable to the increased perception of political instability by foreign capital following the 1976 revolts. The third factor was the combination of rapidly accelerating black militancy and the increasingly apparent identification of the apartheid government with white business. This last factor prompted the call for policies aimed at promoting the emergence of a black bourgeoisie and a class of skilled black labour with a view of co-opting it within the existing white (capitalist) power echelons. As will be discussed further on, this was combined with the start of education initiatives to draw in black participants in the market economy on a more equitable basis with equivalent white labour. These efforts were to a large extent motivated and spearheaded by the private sector which now frequently attempted to distance itself from overtly racist policies of apartheid.[10] It is ironic that the attempt to co-opt a privileged section of the black population at this point in the country's history would have answered the earliest demands of the South African Native National Congress before it became, as the ANC, the broad based voice of revolt, largely because of the intransigence the government of the day.

The eighties marked the start of the crisis of faith within the National Party. A serious of reports commissioned by the government testified to the parlous and worsening state of the economy (briefly eased by the gold price boom in the early eighties). This rising awareness of the growing untenability of the economic system generated by apartheid, combined with increasing pressure from the liberation movements which were rapidly rendering the townships ungovernable and an intensification of the international anti-apartheid movement, prompted the Botha government to launch some reform initiatives. Botha, however, exhibited the same vacillation that had characterised Smuts' attempts at political reform forty years earlier. This hesitation was exacerbated by the 1987 election which brought in the Conservative Party as the official opposition. This time, however, the extra-parliamentary liberation movement was much stronger, as was international opposition to apartheid, especially since the cessation of the cold war following the disintegration of the Soviet Union had eradicated South Africa's strategic significance to the west. The regime's increasingly brutal attempts at suppressing widespread revolt fuelled its flames until the National Party pragmatists under the leadership of De Klerk staged a palace coup and shortly afterwards unbanned the ANC and all other political organisations previously considered illegal in 1991. From 1991 until the democratic elections of 1994 economic planning was in a hiatus while the terms for the negotiation on the process to democracy were under way against a background of increasing violence, most of which were covertly sponsored by government agencies. The Government of National Unity in a democratised South Africa submitted the country's first White Paper on Science and Technology in 1996.

---

10 Most of the quoted calls for the easing of the colour bar in Davies (1979b) arise from the business personalities, representative institutions and political allies.

Science and technology policy

Superficially, 1948 appears as the year which marked a radical shift in the state's formal science and technology policy through a redefinition of the status of the CSIR. However, as I argued towards the end of the previous chapter, the limitations of the original science and technology vision which had determined the perimeters of the CSIR's operational concerns had engendered an institution which lacked the basis for a fundamental critique of the main constituents of the national system of innovation. The structural design of the CSIR was essentially that of a functionary organ with the task of rationalising science and technology programmes across the country and to engage directly in specified areas of research. Its capacity to advice on policy in the visionary manner of a van der Bijl had been left out of its formal charter, rendering the allocation of this function subject to the overall programme of its political masters of the day. The "van der Bijl function" was directly due to Smuts' aspirations for the country's international status. This space had, however, never been formally articulated within the CSIR charter (vide Ballinger's critique) and the ease with which the new regime downgraded its position within the state's policy formulating structure was the result.

Thus the apparent ruptures, represented by two historical breaks in 1948 and 1987, in the role that the state assumed towards science and technology, were both due to the inability of both Smuts and van der Bijl to accept that their modernist aspirations for the country's national system of innovation required a radically different ideological underpinning. The evanescence of the drives that the two men had initiated thus had its roots in their inability to accept this causality. The shelving of van der Bijl's 1921 recommendations when Smuts lost the 1924 election can perhaps be seen as a passive act of neglect. The downgrading of the status of the CSIR, a powerful institution with a high profile, by the National Party was an active act, not a mere disregard for the need to set up an institution of this sort. The control exerted by central government over the CSIR led to an amplification of bureaucratic norms and strictures which progressively restrained the public planning and advisory role of the institution and transformed it into an executor of a largely pre-ordained and fragmented state policy.

With the election of the Reformed Nationalist Party in 1948 the CSIR almost immediately suffered a dramatic demotion and the encroachment on its mode of operation occurred at every level. Its accountability was relegated to the Ministry of Economic Affairs (even the term Science and Technology was omitted from the nomenclature of any ministry) and it was drawn into the bureaucratic environs of the public service, with control established over appointments and research directions. Even salary scales were set up in line with civil service rates, thus causing a constant haemorrhage of scientists, either to the private sector or to overseas employment. Basson (1996) points out the degree of direct control over the nature of the institution that was exercised through a selective employment policy:

> "Some political appointments followed, many of them in leadership positions, and *the incumbents in turn tended to employ staff of the same political persuasion*." (p. 22, emphasis added).

It was not that the issue of appointments had not hitherto been implemented on ethnic lines since the CSIR was already the preserve of Afrikaners.[11] With the advent of the National Party, however, control was now extended to decisions as to *which* Afrikaners were preferable as executors of national policy. This selective employment strategy further established the dominance of a single common institutional language, thus limiting the potential for the CSIR to develop a critical voice. The lineage of presidents established during its initial heyday was carried forward in the appointment of S. Meiring Naudé (1952-1971) who strived to overcome the constraints on the institution's growth - a 7% limit was placed on the annual growth of the budget of the CSIR in 1957 (Basson, 1996: 24) - by eliciting joint financing for R&D programmes from industry. This tactic reinforced the growth of specific market-led programmes and during the term of office of Meiring Naudé the relative share of private sector funding for R&D projects increased almost nine fold. In the process the capacity of the CSIR to provide an extra-market and extra-public service critical faculty was further restricted.

One possible explanation for this shift would counterpoise Smuts, the economic rationalist abreast with the latest developments in the Commonwealth during the post-war era, against the inward looking isolationist policy of apartheid, obsessed with control at the cost of relinquishing the means to establish the science and technology base of a

---

11 In 1945

> "Schonland sought out a fellow physicist, Professor Stefan Meiring Naudé, head of the Physics Department at the University of Stellenbosch, to lead the National Physical Laboratory at the CSIR. ... Schonland is reported to have jokingly threatened him that if he did not take the job, he would appoint an Englishman instead. Naude' needed no further persuasion." (Basson, 1996: 19).

rapidly industrialising economy. The explanation for the move would then hinge on the specifics of control adopted by the National Party. Apartheid was the reflection of a state obsessed with control and engaged in one of the most thorough experiments in social and economic engineering (state enterprises, price controls, labour market controls, tariff protection) in the twentieth century. An institution like the CSIR, as established by the Smuts government, would, within this account, be seen as too much of a wild card and had to be redefined within the bureaucratic strictures of the central administration. The alternative account would see no fundamental rupture. The alteration of control mechanisms with the change in the controlling party would be seen as one of degree. The marginalisation of the advocates of total segregation and the establishment of "practical" apartheid emphasises that the old concerns still ruled and that all that had really changed in 1948 was the political will with which these concerns were now to be addressed. From this perspective the genealogy of the limitations on the science and technology policy informing the country's national system of innovation is linear and uncomplicated and ruptures can only be posited on the basis of potential development paths conjectured on the extrapolation of forces whose effects had yet to become manifest.

The flurry of institutional network building which the CSIR had embarked on in its first two years subsided dramatically during the following twelve.[12] The institution had effectively exhausted the potentiality of its limited role within the area of national planning and the logic of its definition as an institution launching body implied a progressive divesting of power. The case of the nuclear research programme was symptomatic of this syndrome. In 1948 the Atomic Energy Board (AEB) was established with the CSIR responsible for basic research on nuclear energy. It eventually assumed the name of the Nuclear Development Corporation of South Africa (NUCOR). In 1955

---

12 During the period 1948-1959 the following initiatives were implemented:

1948	Scheme for medical research units.
1949	Sugar Milling Research Institute
1950	Scientific Council for Africa South of the Sahara.
	South African Wool Textile Research Institute.
	Bitumous Binder Research Unit.
1954	National Nutrition Research Institute.
1955	National Institute for Road Research.
	National Mechanical Engineering Research Institute.
1957	Scientific Liaison Office (Cologne).
1958	National Institute for Water Research.

(Kingwill, 1990: 292-294).

CSIR research into nuclear physics and the radioactivity group in the NPL led to major technological breakthroughs but by 1959 saw the separation of nuclear research and the AEB from the CSIR. In 1962 the Scientific Advisory Council was established as a mechanism through which contributions could be made by various research institutions towards the formulation of a national science and technology policy. It was responsible to the Department of National Education. These processes narrowed considerably the domain and the areas of effectiveness of the CSIR, consequently further diminishing the standing of the institution within the bureaucratic power hierarchy.

The country's increasing international isolation, especially after the Sharpeville massacre constituted another significant determinant of the emerging innovation system. Until South Africa's resignation from the Commonwealth the CSIR had set up offices in Britain, the USA, and West Germany. The CSIR moreover was part of a Commonwealth-wide network of science and technology institutes, under the aegis of the British Commonwealth Scientific Offices. Although, as Kingwill (1990: 56) points out, contact at an informal level did survive South Africa's departure from the Commonwealth its exclusion at a formal institutional level could not but have significantly reduced its access to foreign technology, rendering this source more expensive.

At an institutional level the apartheid years saw the rapid decline of coherent science and technology programmes and the CSIR not only became ineffectual but eventually came to be seen as such, leading to the reforms of the late eighties. However, these reforms were not sufficient to address the fundamental flaws in the national science and technology planning model. The development of the country's innovation system during the period of segregation prior to 1948 had been informed by a largely integrated planning framework on industrial development. Alternate governments had, because of their political prerogatives, focussed on one or another of the aspects of science and technology. However, this coherence was flawed by its neglect of the human capital bottleneck, and necessarily so since the required set of policy measures on this front were inconsistent with the prevailing racist ideology. The disappearance of comprehensive science and technology planning with the onset of apartheid and the end of fundamental debate was inevitable. Under apartheid the fragmentation of a policy framework geared to the development of a sound science and technology base extended to ancillary areas. Other aspects of development planning which bore a direct influence on the national system of innovation also manifested a rationale which could not be in any manner construed as conducive to the promotion of technological capabilities. Thus, for example, the complete appropriation by the state of black education led from the late sixties onwards to an accelerating process of revolt by black students, culminating in the 1976 riots and the virtually complete disintegration of pre-tertiary schooling systems. Trade policy was primarily driven by employment creation requirements and tied to the principle of comparative advantage which retained the emphasis on the country's natural resources. Industrial development remained informed by the exigencies of Verwoerd's plan for a viable system of separate development.

By 1986 the performance of the CSIR as constituted by the National Party in 1948 had disappointed most of the diverse expectations regarding its function. It had become generally accepted that the institution had generally failed to act as the promoter and facilitator of the development of a sound economy wide technology base and 1987 saw a major redefinition of the institution's terms of reference and a consequent fundamental restructuring. Basson (1996) identifies the absorption of the CSIR into the mainstream of the public sector as the primary cause of its decline. This had two distinct effects on the internal incentive structure. On the one hand the job security implicit in a sinecure employment drew in a number of scientists who found a haven for research, usually preferable to that offered by universities since no teaching was required. In the initial decades the prestige associated with the CSIR and the ideal conditions for basic and applied research did elicit an amount of research output which attained levels of excellence as defined by academic criteria. This culture however eventually became an elitist one in the sense that the objective of R&D within a broad economic context became cloudy and a number of research programmes developed their own *raison d'être* outside of any consideration of their applicability to the country's needs. Incentives for performance blurred as civil service salary schemes were introduced with increments dependent on length of service and security of employment led to a high degree of sheltered employment. The construction of a management structure on the standard lines of public service administration, combined with a reluctance on the part of active scientists to perform administrative duties gradually divorced the fragmented research programmes from the managerial structure of the CSIR. Basson identifies defence research as the institution's main claim to prestige with a political administration which had become obsessed with the needs of a siege economy. Consequently other research avenues were relatively under funded. Defence R&D gradually became the only type which was consistently driven by specific needs and the CSIR lost credibility as an institution which could contribute anything worthwhile to the promotion of technology initiatives for the private sector or for the public good.

The neglect of policies aimed at the stimulation of R&D within the private sector is evident in the fact that no special incentives were ever offered for this type of investment. R&D expenditure by firms enjoyed the same tax status as any other type. However, R&D expenditure is not comparable to investment on capital equipment. Investment in factories and machines is a relatively riskless investment in that it is characterised by fully known specifications. The magnitude of the risk involved in R&D is different from that of investments in other resources due to the attendant uncertainty regarding the output of innovations and the virtually total inability to recoup any of the resources expended on research in the eventuality of failure to attain the research goal. Freeman (1982) decomposes the uncertainty factor into a technical one and a marketing one. The former pertains to the probability of R&D activity resulting in an innovation. The latter refers to the translation of the innovation into a market success. Freeman's review of empirical studies indicates that the uncertainty associated with marketing usually exceeds technical uncertainty. The role of R&D incentives schemes is specifically to reduce this uncertainty through a variety of measures in order to stimulate private sector R&D in those areas which are deemed as fruitful for the wider development process. Moreover, the magnitudes of the externalities content accompanying the generation of technology introduce a gap, often a wide one, between social and private returns to R&D because of the inherent inability of the R&D performer to appropriate all, and sometimes most, of the returns on investment in innovative activity. Again the role of the state is to narrow this gap in selected areas. In the case of South Africa the absence of such schemes, combined with assured markets in areas of production specifically linked to military strategic requirements resulted in a general failure to establish the incentives mechanisms for the promotion of private sector R&D outside the contemporary core industrial base of the economy. Even within this core, it was public sector R&D activity which led. Apart from the mining sector, private R&D was consistently low. Given the specific risk profile of R&D investment it is often assumed, along neo-Schumpeterian lines, that in the absence of incentives it is only large firms which enjoy a degree of monopoly power that will undertake R&D. Kamien and Schwartz (1978: 252) discussed the financial constraint on R&D investment and its implications for market structure in terms of

> "the virtual necessity for it to be financed internally from a firm's current profits and accumulated funds. This feature of R&D underlies the

view that a firm must possess some monopoly power, along with the associated monopoly profits, for it to carry on R&D."

The private sector in South Africa has always been marked by extremely high degrees of concentration of ownership and control but this has not resulted in high levels of private R&D spending, except in mining. This deficiency was the consequence of the incentives structure that developed within the apartheid economy.

The indictment of the CSIR (the Reikert 1979 commission, the Wiehahn 1982 commission, J. de Wet's 1983 recommendations, the Kleu 1983 report and the White Paper on Industrial Strategy, 1985) was, or rather should have been, an indictment of the state's policy on science and technology. The failure to comprehend the proper role of the public sector in the evolution of a national system of innovation and a myopic focus on the most evident symptom of the CSIR's malady, its "divorce from reality", resulted in a reformation which was entirely reactive. Basson (1996) documents the turbulence that the CSIR, and by implication the entirety of the public sector's science and technology policy, was undergoing over the years 1985-86. The long stagnation of the institution had reached a head and internal dissatisfaction on a number of issues was articulated formally to consultants engaged with an assessment of the state of the organisation. These included resentment against salary levels, a bureaucratic management structure, insufficient funds for basic research, the lack of goal-driven research, the duplication of research efforts and the inefficient running of R&D programmes.

Some of the recommended changes did indeed lead to a more coherent coordination role for the CSIR. The foremost among these, following the de Wet (1983) report was to combine the Main Research Support Programme and the Co-operative Scientific Programmes under a new institution, which was to be attached to the CSIR, in 1984. This was the Federation for Research Development (FRD). The FRD eventually became independent of the CSIR in 1990. The Kleu (1983) report emphasised the need to shift the bias of the public sector research effort towards programmes which were more applied to perceived national requirements. The White Paper on Industrial Development Policy (1983) charged the CSIR specifically with the role of enabling technology diffusion throughout the economy.

However, the primary reaction, both from within and from outside the institution, to the CSIR as it had become, an institution which was overly managed from the centre of the public service and which had grown into a bureaucracy without a goal, led the drive towards a higher degree of accountability to market agents. This was the origin of the notion of framework autonomy which granted the organisation the independence which it had striven for since the late forties. It was, however, an independence which required the CSIR to prove itself in the market by providing services which were tailored to clients' needs from within the private sector. This move led, in effect, to a curtailment of the institution's independence. The new policy stance was symptomatic of the drive for deregulation occurring in the USA and Britain at the time and which South Africa emulated.[13] The other institutions which achieved this type of independence under framework autonomy were the Human Sciences Research Council (HSRC), the Federation for Research Development (FRD), the Council for Mineral Technology (MINTEK), the South African Bureau of Standards (SABS), the Medical Research Council (MRC) and the Agricultural Research Council.

At this time the CSIR performed four distinct roles - direct R&D activity, management of national research facilities, research funding and a patenting and licensing authority. The research institutes and facilities under the auspices of the CSIR were classified into five categories - sector-oriented research institutes,[14] discipline-oriented research institutes,[15] profession-oriented research institutes,[16] national research

---

13 Saul (1991) offers a class-based suggestion for the rapid embracing of a neoliberal policy stance in the eighties. As the interpenetration of Afrikaner and English capital progressed, the shift from an ethnic to a class division among the white population became marked. Afrikaner capitalists and professionals eventually had more in common with the equivalent classes among English-speaking South Africans than with working class Afrikaners. This newly unified class adopted fervently the neoliberal agenda of privatisation and deregulation and more concerned about its future in the global economy than with the institutionalised adherence to racist ideology. It was also this factor that largely contributed to the eventual political capitulation of the apartheid regime. Class tensions within the Afrikaner populations grew markedly in the immediate post-apartheid period, with the working class feeling that they had been betrayed in the negotiations with the ANC.

14 Applied Chemistry Unit, National Building Research Institute, National Food Research Institute, National Institute for Aeronautics and Systems Technology, National Institute for Coal Research, National Institute for Materials Research, National institute for Telecommunications Research, National Institute for Oceanology, National Timber Research Institute, National Institute for Transport and Road Research, National Institute for Water Research and the South African Wool and Textile Research Institute..

15 National Research Institute for Mathematical Sciences, Laboratory for Molecular Cell Biology, National Chemical Research Laboratory and the National Physical Research Laboratory.

facilities[17] and industrial research institutes[18] (Basson, 1996: 55). From 1988 the rationalisation programme and the new market oriented policy started to show its effects in the divestment of the CSIR of a number of these functions. In 1988 the National Institute for Telecommunications Research, the Cyclotron at Pretoria and the Shark Deterrent Project were closed down. The Molecular Cell Laboratory was taken over by industry and the Applied Chemistry Unit, the Mechanical Design Office and Transport Services were privatised (Basson, 1996: 182-183).

In effect the CSIR moved from being a subject of the dictates of central government to those of the private sector. Basson (1996) sums up the results of this policy shift as follows:

> "Although the system (framework autonomy) freed the research councils from much of the restrictive civil services practices, it failed to provide a strategic framework of national priorities. In the process of allocating resources, the organisation, with the Board's guidance, was left to set its own priorities. These decisions ... were made in the absence of an encompassing national strategic framework." (p. 60, parenthesis added).

The adoption of framework autonomy was construed as the substitution of one deterministic model of efficient allocation, based on a populist internationally fashionable vision of market functioning for an old and disappointing one of state intervention. This was, of course, a mis-specification of the options since state intervention in South Africa, even though it operated on a scale unparalleled outside regimes deemed totalitarian by the western industrialised economies, was not manifest in a coherent science and technology plan. Initiatives in this area were either market-led by the incumbent owners of the means of production or motivated by security and military imperatives. The fallacy in the apparent swing from the one extreme of an interventionist policy to an overtly market friendly one lay in the inability and unwillingness to recognise that the impediments to the development of technological capabilities were virtually indissoluble from the political underpinning of the South African economic ordering. The shift to a reliance on market

---

16 Chemical Engineering Research Group, National Institute for Mechanical Engineering, and the National Electrical Engineering Research Institute.

17 Hermanus Magnetic Observatory, National Accelerator Centre, Radio Astronomy Observatory, Satellite Remote Sensing Centre and the South African Astronomical Observatory.

18 Fishing Industry Research Institute, Leather Industries Research Institute and the Sugar Milling Research Institute. These institutes were jointly financed by the private sector.

exigencies within the contemporary context could only reinforce the prevalent structure through the assumption of a modicum of legitimacy based on the claimed "neutrality" of impersonal and apolitical markets. In the process the state relinquished its power to alter the structure within which firms operated.

Industrial and trade policy

The ruling debate over trade policy during this century has been between import-substitution and export-promotion policy agendas. Both, however, have been bedevilled by constraints directly attributable to apartheid economics. Import-substitution programmes faced the economies-of-scale impediment in a country were the majority of the population was consigned to low income categories. The consequence of protection would therefore imply the emergence of inefficient enterprises. At the same time the same phenomenon, primarily in the case of the general low levels of human capital rendered South Africa internationally uncompetitive, except in the case of the primary sector. A further exacerbating factor that had to be contended with was the growing international campaign for sanctions against trade with South Africa.

Lall (1993) points out that trade policy under apartheid had resulted in a regime which offered the highest protection for mature, labour-intensive industries while exposing technology-intensive industries with high growth potential, such as electronics, to international competition. The trade regime was geared to protecting employment in established low growth sectors which offered little scope for the development of technological capabilities, at the expense of infant industries with high growth potential, exhibiting high technological spillovers. At the same time industrial policy was mainly directed at offering incentives for investment in and around the "homelands" (Transkei, Bophuthatswana, Venda and Ciskei) created by apartheid, with employment as the only qualifying criterion. As discussed above, apartheid required for its long term viability a decentralisation of economic activity towards the rural areas, especially in and around the homelands (which came to be called "national states" in a bid to achieve legitimacy) to attain the goal of a stable distribution of the black labour force between the rural and the urban sectors. Until the homelands became self-sustaining and fiscally independent of Pretoria the foundation stone of Verwoerd's model of "separate development" would remain flawed.

After more than three decades since the institutionalisation of the "separate development" model, employment creating industrial development in the homelands was still in a parlous state. Initially, apart from the disincentive to investment posed by the lack of infrastructure in the peripheral areas, one of the main blocks to industrial development was the prohibition against the entry of "white capital" in these areas. However, the continuing poverty and the ensuing migration of black labour to the centre forced the government to abandon this important precept of the original model. Even so capital refused to flow in the direction of the homelands and the government went so far as to put legal blocks on investment in the centre in order to force the desired relocation of industry. Even this policy failed and in 1982 a new programme of regional industrial development was launched. The sheer magnitude of the funding that was allocated to this effort[19] indicates the increased desperation which years of failure on this crucial front of apartheid strategy had engendered. Progressively, apartheid became a captive of the contradictions forced on it by the requirements of the emerging shape of post-war industrial development which demanded broad based human capital investment as a prerequisite for the leap into the new technologies which started proliferating at an unprecedented rate and which rendered the orthodoxy of capital-biased, labour-saving technological change obsolete.

The main thrust of the new strategy was a revision of incentive schemes in order to direct new investment towards these peripheral areas. The old system of tax concessions, which essentially rewarded commercial success, was replaced by direct cash subsidies, linked to employment levels, designed as a permanent prop to the cost structure of private enterprise. Moreover, in 1983 the Development Bank of Southern Africa was launched with the express purpose of acting as the bank to the "national states" for the development of infrastructure.

Human resource development

The pivotal goal of the programme of grand apartheid was the management of regional labour flows across the country in such a manner as to assure equilibrium between the supply and demand sides of the

---

19 Hirsch (1991: 145) points out that

> "The funds devoted to direct industrial decentralization incentives alone currently swallow about one-half of the budget of the Department of Industry and Commerce. If other budgetary allocations to decentralization are included, such as those allocated to the financing of the Development Bank of Southern Africa and other funds devoted to infrastructural development that makes the programme possible, decentralization takes a large bite out of the South African government's budget."

labour market in both the urban and the rural sectors. The indicator of success of this policy from the perspective of the exigencies of grand apartheid would have been the long term absence of either surpluses or shortages of labour in either sector. By this measure, apartheid labour policy implemented through influx control was a lasting failure. Posel (1991) points out the enduring feature of chronic simultaneous surpluses and shortages of labour in secondary industry and proposes as one of the causes the crudeness of the aggregate definition of black labour adopted by the implementers of influx control policy. This was a definition that failed to differentiate between various categories of skills available and the existing requirements by a heterogeneous industrial sector. It was consequently even less capable of estimating the requirements for growth industries within the secondary sector. Aside from its moral implications, grand apartheid was a singularly incomplete plan for the economic development on which its long term survival depended. Posel (1991: 257) notes that larger enterprises whose experience in the labour market had enabled them to recruit the skills quotient which they required were now forced to apply to the labour bureaux for their labour requirements and, because of an influx control policy which treated black labour as homogenous, consequently suffered a lowering in the skills component of their labour force. The colour bar contributed significantly to labour shortages in the skilled categories reserved for whites, while the appalling wage and other work conditions at the lower end of the job category spectrum resulted in shortages for the more menial work.

Influx control, however, had a multiplicity of objectives, some of which encroached on its capacity to suit the requirements of employers, whether in the urban or the rural areas. It was an instrument of punishment for individuals and communities which manifested signs of protest against the new regime and in the process it cut across class lines in a manner which differed from the old pass law system which had allocated a privileged status to blacks who were educated, wealthy or held important administrative positions within their communities. In the process it had the unintended effect of unifying resistance to apartheid.

Influx control policy was constantly subject to a tension between its commitments to the labour requirements of industrialists and white farmers, respectively. This tension was manifest primarily in the case of low skill intensive industries where urban employers preferred migrant workers who, because of their unfamiliarity with the urban labour market and due to their conditioning by the semi-feudal working conditions on farms, were less likely to object to poor working conditions. Larger enterprises in the secondary sector, on the other hand, tended to favour a more permanent black labour pool within which the reproduction rate of a level of skills, usually through informal methods or through in-house training, was more assured.

In the end the lasting repressiveness of influx control implementation was a testimony to the failure of the objectives of separate development since the industrial decentralisation and rural upliftment on which this programme depended should have reduced to a minimum the need to exercise overtly authoritarian control over the exodus of labour towards the cities. Unemployment levels for blacks in urban areas continued increasing, especially among the youth and, in spite of increasing proscriptions, so did the flow of migrant job seekers from the rural areas to the cities.

The skills bottleneck applied at every level and the one most immediately pertinent to the new administration with its burgeoning bureaucracy was the inability to recruit skilled Afrikaners. Posel (1991: 118) reports on the low literacy levels among the Afrikaner population during the fifties and the limits that this placed on the growth of the employment base of the state apparatus. However, the most binding skills bottleneck applied with regard to the black population and the dictates of separate development necessarily required policies that would render this constraint a permanent feature of the country's innovation system. The effective long term enforcement of white dominance required a permanent erosion of the basis for revolt and one of the foremost tools in this regard was through the appropriation by the state of the right to determine the type of education available to blacks. The *Bantu Education Act* of 1953 and the *Extension of University Education Bill* of 1957 were explicit in this regard. Curricula for blacks at every level of education were to be designed to emphasise ethnic identity and to minimise the aspirations and the ability of the oppressed majority to conceive of the possibility of reaping the fruits of any possible universal enfranchisement. Following the *Bantu Education Act* of 1953 a series of other acts[20] established an educational system which was fragmented, and differentiated, in terms of syllabi, examinations, hiring practices and administrative and financial control,[21] along racial demarcation lines. A further depressing effect on

---

20 Amendments to the Bantu Education Act in 1954, 1956, 1959 and 1961; the Coloured Peoples Act of 1963; the Indians' Education Act of 1965.

21 The Department of National Education was responsible for white schooling since 1967, the Department of education for black schooling since 1979 and the Department of Internal Affairs for coloured and Asian education since 1980.

black education was that even the inferior schooling that was available was more expensive for black parents than for whites.[22]

By insisting repeatedly on indigenous cultures[23] (a continuation of the responses of Smuts and Hofmeyr to the demand for common schooling) as the basis of limitations in the new curricula the new regime went a long way towards creating a self-fulfilling definition of ethnic delineations and barriers. The conviction underlying the implementation of this policy of impoverishment of the future work force was abetted by a high degree of ignorance, both within the state and the market of the role of a highly skilled and educated workforce in the process of development. The skills requirements for industrialisation were conceptualised in a mechanistic manner which eschewed the "Europeanisation"[24] of blacks. The implication is that the model of industrialisation which informed planning was implicitly that of a small class of technocrats overseeing a labour force whose required characteristics were docility and a modicum of taught skills which would be enhanced, as changing conditions required, by job specific in-house training. The effects on human capital formation and broad based technological capabilities was to be enduring, cumulative and devastating, and their implications for industrial development were clearly recognised by the chairman of ESCOM and the IDC in 1962 when he proposed a five percent economic growth rate as the feasible limit due to the constraints imposed by

> "... problems of social adjustments, housing conditions, town and regional planning and all the other factors that enter into development in a highly complicated multiracial society with vastly different stages of cultural and economic development ... we cannot move faster unless we train people better, unless we have more managers skilled in various directions, scientists, technologists, engineers and people with high managerial ability." (quoted in Fine and Rustomjee, 1996: 184)

---

22 The UNESCO (1969: 45) report shows the differing financial burdens of education on families, along racial lines:

> "Education is free for all White children until the end of secondary school ... the African population pay for the education of their children ... school fees for Africans increase for secondary schooling while grants for books are not payable with secondary schooling. For the individual African, the cost of maintaining a child in secondary school must affect the parental decision as to whether or not the child proceeds to secondary school."

23 See quotes from the readings of these two bills in Norval (1996: 133-134); also see Variava (1989: 273-276).

24 *ibid.*: 135

Of course the constraints listed here were integral and ineradicable constituent of the apartheid political economy. The effect of the schooling system was to deprive black students, and hence the great majority of the school population, from the quality of education available to whites. The UNESCO (1969) report estimated that the state expenditure on education, on a per capita basis, for whites was more than seventeen times that for blacks (Table 8) in 1962. The report also pointed out that the absence of compulsory education for black students beyond the age of ten, when combined with other factors, resulted in a forty percent drop-out rate at this age (UNESCO, 1969: 46). By 1981 the drop-out rate by the end of standard two (at which stage the student is considered to be semi-literate) had reached fifty two percent (Nedbank, 1983: 233). Education for whites, on the other hand, was compulsory until sixteen. A breakdown of the syllabi for black schooling up to the age of fourteen shows a heavy bias towards religious instruction, physical exercise, language instruction (English, Afrikaans and the vernacular) and manual training (UNESCO, 1969: 48-49). The UNESCO report also noted the heavy discrepancies in teacher qualifications between black and white schools (UNESCO, 1969: Ch. 8). This situation deteriorated even further over time and the De Lange commission found that in 1981 eighty five percent of black teachers were under-qualified (with a less than standard ten teacher's diploma) as against three and-a-half percent in white schools (Nedbank, 1983: 234).

The debate on education forms part of the larger race-class debate, wherein the main argument revolves around the identification of the interests which such a policy of segregated and unequal education served. A reductionist account on either side of the debate provides an impoverished analytical approach which can easily be undermined by quoting empirical evidence at some specific historical point which demolishes the hegemony of any single account. Such reductionist accounts also fail to explain the changing practices and definitions of both the racist agenda and capital. A more fruitful approach can be through the examination of the tension between institutional inertia and its changing suitability to the various goals which, both implicitly and explicitly informed the formation of apartheid institutions. The precepts of racial domination necessarily implied economic domination along racial lines. Thus the assumption of the racial inferiority of blacks, whether articulated along essentialist or culturally evolutionary discourses, contained within it the requirement for economic subjugation and education policies consistently specified both in an overt manner and through common practice.

Formal education serves two intimately related functions. The obvious one is a formal transmission of knowledge and skills. This formal aspect is, however, contingent on the successful fulfilment of another function - the socialisation of the student which, if successful, results in the internalisation of the values and norms set which constitute the identity of the structure which has appropriated the right to provide education. Thus throughout this history we can observe both convergence and divergence between the educational requirements of a racist polity and of the capitalist class with which it was intertwined. We also observe periods where education policies served to further one or the other of both broad sets of interests and periods where established policies became a net liability and required adjustment. We can also examine the nature of the adjustments and their net effects.

The obvious discontinuity in education policy that the apartheid state introduced was the general disbandment of contending providers, specifically with the dissolution of the missionary schools.[25] However, Molteno (1991) and Christie and Collins (1991)[26] point out that wide disparities in the provision of education along racial lines had been endemic in the South African polity long before the advent of apartheid, and thus challenge the proposition that apartheid marked a fundamental discontinuity in education policy.

There is however a crucial distinction in the general racist paradigms underlying education policies in the pre- and post-apartheid eras. The former, as enunciated by both Smuts and Hofmeyr, was one based on the assumption of a cultural evolutionary model which offered the possibility in some unstated distant future for blacks to satisfy the requirements for acceptance into "civilised" society. The internalisation of these norms and values are apparent in the earliest claim of the ANC for the promised recognition of the right of an "educated native" to be accorded the same privileged distance from the "raw native" as the white. Apartheid on the

---

25 Christie and Collins (1991: 162) show the expanding control over black education under apartheid:

> "Of 7000 schools, over 5000 had been missionary-run prior to Bantu education. By 1959, virtually all black schools except the 700 Catholic schools had been brought under the central control of the Native Affairs Department. ... The Christian ideals of an egalitarian and communal society, in which everyone aspired to a universalist culture which was both western and Christian, were struck a severe blow."

26 Christie and Collins (1991, Table 1) show that the ratio of per capita schooling expenditure on white schooling to black schooling rose from approximately 11:1 in 1930 to 12:1 in 1945.

other hand was founded on the presumption of essential and immutable racial differences, even when defined in cultural terms, which constituted the foundation of the separate development programme. Within this schema education for the black student could, at best, only provide an entry into the privileged ranks of the Bantustan administration.

The contrast between the implications of the two underlying assumptions can be made at several levels. Within the pre-apartheid context education was, in principle, the obvious vehicle for the entry of a black student into the ranks of privilege. In this sense pre-apartheid education policy can be seen as more pernicious in its combination of a distant promise of admission into the select category of the "civilised" and the actual paucity of resources devoted to black education. Moreover, it allowed for a degree of adaptability to address sporadic surges of resentment, as was evident in the apologist response of Hofmeyr to Matthews's critique of the premises of the "reformist" education policy, referred to in the previous chapter. This adaptability was unable to divert workers' revolt away from capital as the enemy since, while ensuring a constant supply of usually malleable workers, it also placed the black worker on the same terrain as the white one who, through effective industrial and political organisation, had ensured an extra-market position of privilege in terms of job reservation. The continued frustration of the possibility of approaching the promised goal erupted in the mine workers' strike of 1946.

Apartheid on the other hand was explicit. Black and white would never be equal within the same domain. The most that black workers could hope for was improvement within their own domain, which within the territorial definition of separate development rendered impossible any realistic aspirations towards economic improvement. The options for the black worker under apartheid were thus clear - submission or revolt. During apartheid's first two decades revolt was crushed by a regime which was convinced of its destiny, aided by favourable external conditions. But revolt reappeared on an unprecedented scale from the seventies onward, in the face of which repression, regardless of the extent of its brutality, became futile. The student inspired revolts of 1976 marked the watershed of education policy under the apartheid state. This was a watershed whose devastating structural effects on human capital development came to pose what is probably the single biggest constraint on the development prospects of South Africa even after the demise of apartheid.

An assessment

It is indicative of the acceptance of the inevitability of the constraints imposed by apartheid that successive development plans, while urging the utilisation of resources, only nominally accepted the oppressed majority of the population as a resource which could be enhanced, and consequently assumed a largely unskilled labour force as a permanent feature of the economy. Even as late as the mid-eighties the study group advising the strategic plan for industrial development, while lamenting the skills shortage, advocated a technology policy which would make "... the fullest possible use ... of unskilled and semi-skilled labour with the greatest possible saving of the scarce resources of skilled labour and capital" (DTI, 1985: 9) thus proposing an industrial development strategy which would reinforce dependence on technologies utilising unskilled labour, in a manner similar to the propagated dependence on the country's abundant mineral resources when it recommended that

> "(t)echnology in South Africa should aim firstly at making the best possible use of the country's wealth of *natural resources* in order to make full use of the comparative advantages they offer." (ibid.: 9, emphasis in quoted text)

The advocacy of an industrial development policy based on comparative advantage failed to consider that the technology intensive sectors which had become prominent in the economy, e.g. defence related industries, had emerged because the international arms embargo had forced an authoritarian regime to defy the principles of comparative advantage. Moreover, those prominent manufacturing sectors which had emerged along the dictates of comparative advantage, linked to the country's natural resources, had done so either through direct government participation, as in the case of ISCOR and SASOL (originally *Suid Afrikaanse Steenkool en Olie* - South African Coal and Oil), or, again through the stimulus offered by the defence budget as in the case of mechanical engineering and chemicals. It is noteworthy that the only specific reference to the need for support in the 1985 White Paper on industrial strategy applied to the electronics industry which had emerged as a corollary to the defence programme (ibid.: section 5.51) and which was in a state of crisis due to the structural inability of the apartheid economy to make the leap into the new techno-economic paradigm.

The move to framework autonomy and the relegation of responsibility for the attainment of ill-conceived national science and technology objectives to the market was effectively the result of a crisis of faith in the in the ability of the state to build the kind of national innovation system evident in industrialised and successfully industrialising economies. This was implicitly a loss of faith in the feasibility of apartheid. The indicators of an ailing innovation system reported in 1988 (DNE, 1988b: Annexures B and D) were the inevitable consequences of the principles on which the apartheid model was constructed. In the early sixties (UNESCO, 1969: 109-114) it was already evident that directly because of apartheid education and employment policies the sole source of scientific and technical personnel for the economy lay almost entirely within the white population, which constituted approximately nineteen percent of the total population (UNESCO, 1969: Table 2).[27] The deleterious effects of apartheid education policies on broad based capital formation have already been repeatedly noted but the effective solution to this bottleneck would have required the dismantling of apartheid and the acceptance of a general franchise.

The issue of the appropriateness of the S&T institutional framework which emerged under apartheid, and whose heritage, as argued in the previous chapters, lies in the period of segregation preceding it, can only be addressed in respect of the goal structure which constituted its referent. The emergence of technological leads within the South African economy had exhibited a generally consistent pattern throughout the period of segregation and during apartheid. This pattern was marked by a number of characteristics which became integral to the development of the national system of innovation almost since the first explicit science and technology plan in 1916.

It was, first and foremost, a system which took the general dearth of human capital as given and concentrated instead on a limited human resource development programme which applied at the higher end of the skills spectrum. Consequently technological trajectories in general followed the path of increasing physical capital intensity and progressive labour displacement. These paths were, moreover, cumulative and self-reinforcing in that they caused an incremental degradation of the human capital stock and thus offered a further incentive towards an intensification of the investment in labour substituting technological change.

Secondly, it was a system wherein the development of specific technological growth sectors was stimulated from the supply side by the

---

27 The UNESCO (1969) report noted that there were only graduates in hard science and engineering disciplines. It also notes cases where blacks coming in with eminent foreign academic qualifications were unable to find employment in a system which could not vouchsafe blacks in a position of authority over white subordinates.

determination on the part of the state to invest in their establishment and on the demand side by the guaranteed market offered by the state. During the period of segregation these initiatives were motivated by the lessons learned in the two world wars regarding the need for self-sufficiency in crucial sectors and by the imperative posed by the "poor white" problem to diversify away from the dependency on the mining and associated sectors. During apartheid the main motivation arose from the military strategic requirements of an increasingly isolated and embattled regime.

The third characteristic was the chronic inability to formulate a coherent Science and Technology planning framework. As I have argued throughout this book this deficiency was an inescapable consequence of the limitations imposed by the tenets of racial dominance. During the pre-apartheid period, especially under Smuts, the basis of the segregationist polity was under a continuous and systematic attack both from outside and from within the established governance framework. As we have seen in earlier chapters there were brief periods where economic necessity combined with Smuts' political aspirations to come close to forcing the government to opt for a path that would lead to a democratic polity. Formal science and technology planning as well as the van der Bijl period reflected the conflicts between the constraints posed by a segregated nation and the modernist aspirations of the governing elite. The advent of apartheid eliminated these contradictions in the sense that the path to modernity was effectively rejected. The epitome of this shift in policy choice was the eventual fate of the CSIR. The parliamentary debates, specifically the Ballinger critique, on the launching of Smuts' science and technology flagship captures concisely the basic deficiency of Smuts' vision, a deficiency which remained binding for the rest of this institution's history. The advent of apartheid, through the permanent elimination of debate, rapidly diminished the role and relevance of this body as the state organ entrusted with policy formulation and implementation in the area of science and technology.

Finally, as I argue in the following chapter, two crucial factors combined to block the development of the technological growth sectors. The first was the market constraint due to a combination of the limited internal purchasing power of a country with a highly skewed distribution of income and the increasingly limited access to export markets due to the growing sanctions movement. Secondly, specific techno-economic paradigm shifts, such as the microelectronics revolution, rapidly imposed a markedly increased requirement on the supply side for a broadly based highly skilled labour force, which was, as I have argued, incompatible with apartheid.

CHAPTER FIVE

THE EMERGENCE OF THE TECHNOLOGICAL GROWTH SECTORS

The distribution pattern of investment in innovation that emerged within the South African industrial sector was the product of a combination of the specificities of the industrial base of the economy which preceded apartheid and the demand patterns which arose from the effects and requirements of the apartheid economy. The first set of factors can be placed in that category of determinants considered by neo-Schumpeterian supply push approach, i.e. it can be constructed as constitutive of innovation patterns through technological opportunities which arose within an existing industrial base. This base was characterised by high levels of vertical and horizontal integration which grew dramatically under apartheid. The second set of determinants would fall in the realm of demand pull theories of technological change which were introduced by Schmookler. Within this argument the peculiar nature of the apartheid economy would have shaped the country's demand profile whose distinctive features were a highly skewed income distribution and a highly concentrated pattern of state expenditure. One should, of course, be careful not to propose a sharp distinction between the two sets of determinants, since they constitute a complex interrelatedness which is peculiar to the South African context. However this classification of determining factors, crude as it may be, can be useful in the identification of the feedback effects between industry and the apartheid state, and can consequently enable an analysis of the degree of symbiosis between state and market within the South African context.

As we have seen in earlier chapters, the main bone of contention in the debates on South African economic history has revolved around the contradictory assessments of the effects of apartheid on capital, with the liberal side claiming that it was detrimental and the Marxist revisionists arguing that there was a convergence of the interests of apartheid policies and capitalist interests. Throughout most of the literature, however, the distinction between the mining sector and secondary industries on which the liberal position was essentially based has largely been unquestioned by either side of the debate. Fine and Rustomjee (1996) were the first to contest this taxonomic division in a systematic fashion when they proposed that the core industrial base in South Africa was and still is closely linked to the mining industries through upstream and downstream linkages within a broad sector which they label as the minerals-energy complex. This sector covers electricity, non-metallic mineral products, iron and steel basic industries, non-ferrous metals basic industries, basic chemicals, industrial chemicals and petroleum (Fine and Rustomjee, 1996: Ch. 4). The linkages that Fine and Rustomjee identify indicate a minerals-energy complex that was fully integrated across the South African industrial base. The production of electricity is mostly dependant on coal, and to a lesser extent on uranium, mining activity. In its turn the mining sector accounts for approximately a fifth of the national output of electricity. Chemicals and petroleum in their turn are linked to mining by virtue of their heavy energy usage. Mining also provides the main inputs set for non-metallic mineral products, iron and steel basic industries and non-ferrous mineral products. In these cases the beneficiation processes are seen as placing the output of these sectors within the minerals-energy complex rather than in a distinct sector of manufacturing.

This reclassification of industries, in contrast to the standard primary/secondary sector classification, reinforces the representation of capitalist interests in relation to the apartheid state as structurally monolithic. It consequently implies a higher degree of stability within the industrial development process than is advocated by the liberal proposition of an embattled private sector seeking to survive within the constraints imposed by apartheid. The implications for innovation dependency patterns are obviously quite significant. Beneficiation is dependent on input volumes which are in turn dependent on extraction rates and the associated technologies. Beneficiation technologies on the other hand affect the downstream returns on the output of the mining sector. From a Schumpeterian perspective the high degree of monopoly power with the consequent high levels of vertical integration, and the increasing horizontal integration, which was stimulated by the interpenetration of capital under apartheid should have, through the internalisation of technological externalities and through the potential for attaining economies of scale in R&D, provided a significant stimulus to innovative activity within the private sector. As we shall see further on this did not prove to be the case and in this chapter I will explore some of the possible reasons for this apparent anomaly.

From a demand pull perspective the main research question concerns the identification of patterns of innovative activity which would not otherwise have emerged in their specific form except for the requirements of the apartheid polity. From this viewpoint the primary distinguishing feature of apartheid was that it placed the country on a permanent war footing within an environment - internal, regional and global - which became progressively hostile. In this case, in spite of the reservations expressed by Fine and Rustomjee which will be examined further on, the proposition of a military-industry complex has a degree of relevance as a descriptor of a unique set of determinants of innovative activity. In the previous chapter I proposed that the supply requirements of the Second World War were the source of a substantial shock to the South African economy which affected both the industrial structure and the factor markets. The war empowered in an unprecedented manner the black union movement and in spite of Smuts' recalcitrance would have provided the base for a long term shift in the balance of economic and political power towards the majority had the country continued on a path of integration within the emerging post-colonial political and economic order. The advent of apartheid radically altered the context within which this process was occurring through a commitment to a path which set the country at odds with most of the rest of the world and required an increasingly intensive armaments programme.

Thus the distinction between the military-industrial complex and the minerals-energy complex as the basis for analysing industrial and technological development can also be rendered as the difference between evolution patterns and paths which had been established before apartheid and those which emerged specifically because of apartheid and its location within the international order. In the latter case it is reasonable to assume that in the absence of apartheid the defence industry would have been less prominent and that, since defence is a main stimulant to specific intensive innovation drives, the economy's innovation system would have evolved in a significantly different manner. Again it is important to emphasise that the distinction between the two proposed approaches to the evolution of the apartheid innovation system should never be rigid. The apartheid economy, which cannot be separated from its historical antecedent, permeated every aspect of economic activity. The numerous feedback effects between the industrial structure and state policy were such as to render attempts at definitive statements on directions of causality not only implausible but highly misleading. For the same reasons that supply-push and demand-pull theories of innovation cannot be separated, theoretically, and hence empirically, the location of the explanation for the evolution of innovation patterns on either side of the state-market relationship would fall foul of the reductionism which has for so long dogged South African economic historiography. Consequently the proposed explanations of the evolution of the innovation system can never be total but should rather be presented as contingent on other, often unspecified and sometimes as yet unexplored, narratives.

R&D activity and the minerals-energy complex

The acceptance of the validity of a minerals-energy complex (MEC) category radically affects the location of R&D activity within the South African economy and a number of conclusions emerge. The first obvious one is that the MEC manufacturing industries account for the larger portion of R&D within the manufacturing sector. The second result, one which confounds a decontextualised Schumpeterian expectation, is that the brunt of R&D expenditure within these industries was borne by those performers who, as I shall argue further on, can be classified as public sector agents. Data on R&D intensity and growth rates also indicate that under apartheid it was the state that took the lead in innovation with the private sector occasionally following after some time lag. Furthermore, it was the state that initiated the quantum leap in R&D activity within the one non-MEC outlier industry, namely electronics.

An examination of the distribution of R&D expenditure within the South African economy, provided in Table 1 in Appendix A, depicts the implications of the re-classification of industries along the lines proposed by Fine and Rustomjee for the assessment of the base of R&D activity within the South African economy. If the orthodox classification of economic sectors into agriculture, mining and manufacturing were adopted, R&D expenditure data would indicate a consistent erosion of the incidence of R&D in the first two sectors and the increasing proportion of R&D in secondary industries. However, the reclassification of the core base of industries shows a relatively minor role assigned to R&D activity in those manufacturing industries which are not tied into the minerals-energy complex. If inter-industry spillovers of technology were to be taken into account, the strong linkages reported in Fine and Rustomjee (1996: Table 4.3) would render this imbalance even more significant.

Tables 2 and 3 (Appendix A) provide a classification of industries by R&D intensity, measured by the ratio of R&D to sales. This can be used as a proxy indicator of the technology bias of industries, assuming that the patterns of R&D intensity in South African industries do not differ significantly from international norms. These tables show that, in 1991, overall R&D intensity was higher in those manufacturing industries that lie within the minerals-energy complex. In the case of other industries, electronics is the main outlier and its omission from this group of industries increases substantially the difference in overall R&D intensities between the two groups of industries.

While the data in Tables 1 to 3 give an indication of the location of R&D activity, they say nothing about the source. Tables 4 and 5 (Appendix A) offer an indication of the significantly different priorities assigned to the two groupings of manufacturing industries by the different categories of R&D performers. For our purposes the different performers - government institutions, tertiary education institutions, parastatal corporations, private business enterprises and independent research laboratories - are grouped into the two categories of public and private sector performers.

The data on the financing of specific performers of R&D are available only at an aggregate level. Hence, in placing performers within the categories of public and private sectors one can miss specific instances which negate this classification. Until 1987 (the reasons for this cut-off date are discussed in Appendix C) government institutions and parastatal corporations are placed firmly within the public sector category. Private business enterprises are obviously classified as private sector performers. Overt financing for R&D in tertiary education institutions shows that in aggregate the state generally contributed more that the private sector over the period 1977 to 1987. However there is a substantial amount of cross-subsidisation across academic departments from tuition fees in these institutions and since these fees are heavily subsidised by the state, the role of public sector financing of R&D in universities and technikons substantially outweighs private sector funding. Aggregate financing figures show that in the case of independent research laboratories the main source of funding is from the private sector. The fact that in the case of aggregate figures the business enterprise sector is defined to include parastatal corporations clouds the implications slightly but since the R&D activities of both parastatal corporations and independent research laboratories are generally concentrated in different industries it is justifiable to assume minimal cross-financing between these two performer categories. Hence independent laboratories are placed within the private sector category.

Table 4 shows that government institutions, tertiary education research centres and parastatal corporations have, over the period 1977-1987, generally allocated a greater portion of their total R&D spending in the manufacturing sector to those industries which fall within the minerals-energy complex than private business enterprises. In the case of the years 1981 and 1983 where this relationship does not hold, the rising prominence of the electronics industry, as indicated in Table 5, accounts for the diffusion of R&D concentration in the case of the non-private sector agents. In the case of independent research laboratories the one case of a high concentration of R&D activity within the minerals-energy complex, in 1981, was located in structural clay products, cement and other non-metallic mineral products (other than glass products).

Tables 6 and 7 (Appendix A) each provide two sets of data for specific industrial groupings. The first is the absolute change in R&D intensity over the period 1977 to 1987 which enables a classification of industries according to the changing levels of innovative activity over time. The second data set shows the relative roles played by public and private sector performers in specific industries over this period. Table 6 shows that, over the period 1977-1987, public R&D expenditure in those manufacturing industries which lie within the minerals-energy complex accounted for the significantly larger portion (over seventy percent) of total R&D expenditure. The role played by the private sector R&D expenditure on these industries accounted for a much lower portion of total private R&D in manufacturing. The information provided in Table 6 indicates that the role played by the public sector in R&D linked to the minerals-energy complex industries far outweighed that of the private sector performers. In the case of other manufacturing industries the roles of the two performer categories are roughly equivalent over the period with public sector R&D expenditure accounting for a slightly larger portion. If the electronics industries are excluded from this group the relative positions of the two performer categories are reversed. The surge in the ratio of public sector R&D to total R&D in manufacturing industries outside the minerals-energy complex especially over the years 1981-1983 can be accounted for by a massive sudden increase in R&D spending in electronics industries by public sector performers. Table 7 shows the continued dominance of public R&D spending in electronics. Private R&D in this industrial grouping followed after a lag of a couple of years.

Table 7 shows that public sector R&D was dominant in four out of the seven industries that manifested an increase in R&D intensity and in two of the five industries which show a decrease. In the case of structural metal products the share of government and tertiary education sector R&D rose rapidly from 1984, from 26% to 71% of total R&D in this industry. In agricultural machinery, the share of tertiary education sector R&D peaked in 1983, accounting for 76% of total R&D but dropped rapidly after that reaching a low of 26% in 1987. In the case of the industry grouping labelled "other non-electrical machinery" the share of parastatal corporations' R&D was high between 1981 and 1984, rising from 74% to 84 %, but dropped rapidly after that leaving government institutions as the main source of R&D activity. In the case of the electronics industries the main source of R&D activity originated from parastatal corporations which entered with a quantum leap in R&D expenditure in 1981. In the case of transport equipment industries, government R&D was predominant in railway equipment, while R&D undertaken by parastatal corporations became dominant in "other transport equipment" since 1985, displacing government R&D. Parastatal corporations also entered the major R&D performers in the motor vehicles and components sector in 1985 and, though their share dropped since then, they still accounted for slightly more than half of total R&D expenditure in this industrial grouping by 1987.

The information on the changes in R&D intensity measures in different industries, when combined with that on the relative R&D expenditures of the two R&D performer categories, sheds further light on the different roles plated by these two sources of innovation. In five of the eight of the non-minerals-energy complex manufacturing industries that showed an increase in R&D intensity over the period the larger portion of R&D expenditure was due to public sector performers. Public R&D expenditure constituted the larger portion of total R&D in only one of the five industrial groupings which showed a decrease in R&D intensity over the period. In the case of those industries grouped under the category of "other manufacturing", which saw the largest increase in R&D intensity over the period, the main source of R&D expenditure was from independent research laboratories.

In the case of minerals-energy complex manufacturing industries this pattern is less clear. Public sector dominance in R&D is evident in only one of the five industry groupings which show an increase in R&D intensity over this period. In the case of other basic chemical products the main source of R&D expenditure comes from parastatal corporations. Public R&D expenditure also constitutes a high proportion of total R&D in other chemical products where parastatal corporations suddenly entered with a contribution 66% of total R&D in 1984, rising to 75% in 1987. In a similar example, that of non-metallic mineral products (other than glass), the main performer again is the parastatal corporations sector which also suddenly entered with a contribution 52% of total R&D in 1984, rising to 62% in 1987. Public sector performers emerge as dominant in two of the five industry groupings which show a drop in R&D intensity and in both cases they account for most of R&D expenditure. R&D expenditure patterns in basic iron and steel industries saw the contribution of parastatal corporations dropping from 66% to 38% over this period, while that of government institutions rose from 16% to 49%. In the case of non-ferrous metal basic industries government institutions accounted for over 90% of total R&D expenditure throughout the period.

All these indicators show that it was the public sector that played the leading role in R&D activity in minerals-energy complex manufacturing industries. In the mining sector, on the other hand, the major portion of R&D activity is performed by private enterprises. Moreover, in the case of the electronics sector which has emerged as the leading R&D intensive sector it was the public sector which took the lead with private enterprises following. These data shed a new light on the role played by public sector agencies in the development of core technologies and on the logical validity of the dissatisfaction which led to the reforms of public science and technology institutions in 1987. Table 8 shows the quantum leap in the prominence of private sector R&D in total R&D between 1987 and 1991. This was due to the drop in public military oriented R&D between these two dates, with the associated drop in total expenditure on R&D and in the ratio of this expenditure to GDP.

As we have seen earlier, institutions such as the CSIR were inhibited by their original charters from addressing the fundamental constraints on the development of the country's technological capabilities. They were even denied the ability to use tax incentives to stimulate private R&D activity. Their main function was therefore reduced to the performance of R&D themselves. This function was targeted, as the data provided in the tables in the appendix indicate, to leading edge technology sectors. The continuing prominence of public R&D activity in these areas is a testimony to an inadequate incentives mechanism for private sector R&D. A number of reasons can be proposed for this inadequacy, all of them interlinked within the overall framework of the apartheid economy. As far as those incentives for innovation which should be internal to industry, i.e. the supply-push factors arising from integration and monopoly power, are concerned the crucial proviso required by a Schumpeterian approach is that monopoly power should be constantly under threat. The South African industrial sector, especially with the interpenetration of capital which was promoted under apartheid, was marked by a high and protected concentration of ownership and power, thus stifling the motivation to innovate for survival. Secondly, both the internal and external markets for manufactured commodities in general were severely constrained by the effects of apartheid politics on local purchasing power and by the international sanctions policy which arose in response to apartheid.

Finally, the state eschewed the provision of fiscal incentives for R&D in favour of a direct role in its performance, thus forfeiting a basic tool in the formulation and implementation of the country's science and technology policy. This prominence of public sector R&D until the end of the eighties is directly linked to military spending and its virtual cessation with the end of apartheid caused a significant vacuum in R&D activity which took the South African system of innovation some years to address effectively. At the same time one can say that in the case of the system of science and technology, unlike the case for the wider system of innovation, the end of apartheid was indeed a major rupture which stimulated a dramatic reconfiguration of R&D activity.

R&D activity and the military-industrial complex

Once the leading role of the public sector in the national innovation effort has been established, the pertinent question concerns the motivation behind this drive and it is here that the emergence of a military-industrial complex becomes relevant. From the demand pull perspective, the country's limited internal market, combined with the decreasing access to export markets, brought government spending, through the growing military budget, to the fore as the main stimulant to innovative activity. Fine and Rustomjee question the isolation of a "military-industrial complex" as the key explanation of South Africa's industrial development patterns. They maintain that

> "... the notion of a complex as a system of accumulation, whether minerals-energy or military, must be based on the empirical identification of historically contingent linkages established between different sections of capital." (Fine and Rustomjee, 1996: 246)

thus cautioning against a reduction of analyses to a symptomatic descriptive account. In Fine and Rustomjee's thesis the "development of the defence industry has been intimately related to the interests and evolution of the (minerals-energy complex)" (ibid.: 246). While not explicitly stated, Fine and Rustomjee's argument places the weight of causality on these interests as determining the shape of the emerging defence related industries. It is perhaps futile to focus on the identification of the dominant direction of causalities in this complex relationship, especially if we consider the hypothesis that for most of this century South Africa was effectively on a low level war footing. This is especially relevant to innovation. Pre-apartheid science and technology planning was, as we have seen earlier, stimulated by the two world wars and the shortages and bottlenecks that they brought about. Apartheid entrenched the linkages between industry and military spending, with an emphasis on innovation, as a permanent feature of the political economy.

Throughout the apartheid years the country's increasing isolation, combined with rapid internal growth in specific sectors, provided niches of opportunity for investment in technology. Public planning became progressively strategic with an overall aim to render the country as self sufficient as possible in the interlinked "war essentials" sectors - armaments, energy and telecommunications - and to establish the economic base which would render the grand plan of apartheid feasible. The latter goal, because of crucial inherent contradictions in the vision primarily espoused by Verwoerd, proved more difficult to attain.

The declared and observed imperative to render the country self sufficient in armaments, futile as that objective may have been, fundamentally affected the national innovation patterns. The wide range of activities which fall under the general heading of arms industries have one thing in common, by virtue of the nature of modern warfare - they are necessarily operating at the cutting edge of technology since it is technology, more than any other factor, which determines the long term outcome of armed conflict. The growth of the defence sector affected the national system of innovation in two crucial ways. In the first place it provided the CSIR with its only long term opportunity to act as a national R&D coordinating institution. It is perhaps significant that the disillusionment with the performance of the CSIR and its redefinition came about at a time when militarism had lost its flavour as it became obvious that the cost of maintaining a long term siege economy had become prohibitively high. Secondly, it forced the country's industrial sector to go through technological paradigm leaps on a number of fronts, the foremost of which was the weapons sector, with a specific focus on electronics and communications technologies. In a perverted manner the militarisation of South Africa represented the country's closest emulation of a "big push" which marked the economic success stories of the newly industrialising countries. It was of course perverted because of the political and economic context within which it occurred. Militarisation in South Africa had the ironic effect of generating localised conditions for a modern economy while driven by the goal of maintaining a pre-modern political and economic structure. It was moreover an extremely costly programme which could only be pursued in a country where the government was not accountable to the larger portion of the population which only figured in the national economic calculus as a cheap labour resource.

From a structuralist perspective, however, the militarisation programme offers a lesson on the requirements for a quantum leap in industrial development which, however unwholesome, should have proved useful to economic planners within a democratic polity. In 1995 weapons constituted 36.5% of South Africa's exports of "high technology products"[1] (Hodge, 1997: Table 3) and was the only item in this category which exhibited a positive trade balance. If the sunken costs, both overt and implicit in terms of the opportunity costs of apartheid in its entirety, are ignored the weapons industry is a case of a successful industrial development programme. That the weapons sector is not an appropriate vehicle for overall industrial development because of its limited spillover benefits and its drain on the fiscus is not pertinent to this argument. The basic issue is that a technological and industrial growth path must be initiated and maintained in its early stages by a concerted will and direction on the part of the state as the coordinating agent. This was a lesson which held no value for the apartheid regime, given the inescapable constraints imposed by apartheid on the country's modernisation process, but which was, and is, pertinent to post-apartheid economic planning. It is a lesson which, however, seems to have been largely ignored in the ideological shift to a neoliberal approach to economic planning.

Landgren (1989) offers a basic chart of the normal stages of technological development of a military-industrial complex, covering the transition from the position of an arms importer to an arms producer and finally to an arms exporter. Essentially this is an import substitution industrial development programme over which the state has total control since it is the only local client for the product. On a broad level the South African weapons industry never quite made this transition. The few exceptions were in ammunition, where core capabilities emerged as an offshoot of the explosives industry which had developed as a supplier to the mining sector, and in military ground vehicles. In general, however, the local arms industry remained highly dependent on foreign technology and innovation was led and financed by the state.

South Africa's industrial efforts in the armaments sector started in earnest during the Second World War in the period when British war supplies dwindled. In the inter-war period the restrictions on military spending in Britain with whom the South African defence force was closely linked had curtailed the growth of the local military sector. A few

---

1 If the aerospace and computers and telecommunications sectors were added the share would leap to 73.1%. However, these other sectors exhibited substantial trade deficits, especially in the case of computers and telecommunications. (Hodge, 1997: Table 4)

training aircraft[2] and small arms ammunition were produced locally, but little else. The Second World War, with van der Bijl as the Director-General of War Supplies, saw the establishment of the South African Engineering Corps which performed extremely well on various war fronts and which stimulated the development of a number of innovations at home. The severity of the shortfalls in allied supplies, especially in the early stages of the war provided a major stimulus to the local production of weapons, munitions and the whole range of war supplies[3] and the IDC was formed in 1940 to coordinate the local war supplies sector.

The advantages which the local arms industry enjoyed were the steel and iron production capacity of ISCOR, a plentiful availability of coal and other power sources reserves, a large capacity for explosives production which had arisen from the requirements of the mining sector, a large engineering capacity, and a broad base of secondary industries (boots, textiles, food packing and canning). The war thus provided a major boost not just to the arms industry but to innovative efforts across the economy. Iron and steel production technology improved as did that of machine shops.

The establishment of the CSIR at the end of the war formalised and centralised R&D in military related technologies while the links with Britain during the fifties ensured a supply of fighter aircraft, bombers, a wide range of naval vessels, and battle tanks. Landgren (1989: 40) notes that it was in the fifties that links with US multinational computer corporations, the most prominent of which was IBM, were established, thus providing the base for the incorporation of computer equipment in the defence sector. Thus the exit of South Africa from the Commonwealth in 1961 and the imposition of the first arms embargo by the UN in 1963 were faced by a South African arms industry which was already firmly established. The more effective 1977 embargo was interpreted by South Africa as a liberty to renege on existing technology licensing agreements thus allowing local manufacturers to "further exploit and redevelop

---

2 The first aeroplane entirely built in South Africa flew in 1909. Civilian aircraft were converted to military specifications during World War Two. (Kros, 1993).

3 Landgren (1989: 38) says that

> "... the setting up of six armaments factories ... where shells, cartridge cases and bombs were locally manufactured. Several types of infantry arms and even tanks of British design were assembled locally. ... over 5000 armoured truck were produced ... as well as howitzers, mortars and ammunition. Some electronic components were also produced, mainly radar components. ... sections of the ... AECI ... were engaged in military production."

technology already purchased without any need to consult the original foreign suppliers" (Landgren, 1989: 43).

As the international boycott on arms trade with South Africa intensified the Commandant-General of the South African Defence Force asked the CSIR, through its subsidiary the National Institute for Defence Research (NIDR) which had been established in 1954, to undertake defence research. This led to the establishment of a network of institutions linked to defence R&D, including the National Physical Research Laboratory (NPRL), the National Chemical Research Laboratory(NCRL), the National Institute for Personnel Research (NIPR), the National Institute for Aeronautics and Systems Technology (NIAST), the National Research Institute for Mathematical Sciences (NRIMS), the National Institute for Telecommunications Research (NITR), the National Electrical Engineering Research Institute (NEERI), the National Mechanical Engineering Research Institute (NMERI) and several institutions involved in nuclear research.

In 1964 the arms industry was privatised under H.J. van Eck and in 1969 ARMSCOR (Armaments Development and Production Corporation) took over the Atlas Aircraft Corporation and in 1970 took over Musgrave Manufacturers and the African Explosives and Chemicals Industries (AECI) factories in Somerset West. In 1972 ARMSCOR took over the Rondens fireworks factory. It completed the navy's communications network in 1972/3. It also supplied other, non-armament, military supplies. By 1977 when the full UN arms embargo was established South Africa was fully self sufficient. By 1982 ARMSCOR entered the international markets, participating in international weapons fairs, and export earnings were funnelled to fund future R&D activity. The spillover effects of the South African defence budget on R&D activity across the economy are succinctly presented by Landgren (1989: 49-53). At the time of writing Landgren states that in the case of military engines alone South Africa had developed approximately 2000 components involving the efforts of 150 local producers. The expertise that had developed in the mining sector provided a core competence in the field of explosives technology in which, as Landgren reports, it was claimed that South African know-how was equivalent to that found in the USA and Sweden. The links with private sector corporations were always close although the R&D patterns data provided in the previous section throw doubt on Landgren's (1989: 52) proposal that "private industry actually finances a considerable part of South African military R&D".

Links with Britain were maintained for some time after South Africa's expulsion from the Commonwealth and production under license increased until 1963, when Britain started withdrawing licences and the US gave notice of arms sanctions. However, other industrialised countries quickly stepped in to fill the ensuing supply gap. Belgium provided the technology and training to manufacture assault rifles and the Israeli Uzi sub-machine gun. In 1961 South Africa started producing armoured cars for France and to innovate on established technology in this field. In the case of missile research, France started training South African scientists in 1963. France supplied South Africa with Mirage fighter aircraft[4] and Italy was the supplier of aircraft which were transformed into the Impala counter insurgency fighters. The first class of missiles, the "Cactus" missiles, were manufactured for South Africa in France.

The intensification of the arms embargo on South Africa in the seventies, combined with the impact of the international oil crisis radically altered the pressure on the apartheid regime to pursue the goal of self-sufficiency for its military requirements. Simultaneously South Africa's *cordon sanitaire* of friendly regimes started crumbling with the independence of Angola and Mozambique following the fall of the government in Portugal in 1974 and the capitulation of the Smith regime in Rhodesia in 1979. South Africa now turned into a siege economy with war on its borders and the consequent increased concern over the availability of arms and energy. The year 1975 was a watershed for South Africa's war front marked as it was by the invasion of Angola by the three flying armoured columns. Until that stage South African military equipment and training was based along NATO weapons systems and conventional warfare training. The Angolan war provided two stimuli to innovation efforts on the military front. These were a combination of the increasing effectiveness of the international arms embargo and the unconventional nature of the Angolan war, i.e. the terrain, the climate and the dispersed nature of the opposing forces. Initially the lack of supporting infrastructure for troops and arms delivery led to a flurry of road and airstrip construction across the borders in order to deliver manpower and equipment. Rapidly the combination of the two factors stimulated innovation efforts across a range of industries.[5]

---

4 Landgren (1989: 42) states that during the period 1965-1969 France supplied 45 percent of South Africa's arms imports.

5 The Cactus missile was adapted for the local conditions by local innovators and its adaptation carried significant implications for guidance systems and electronics. The launch vehicles for the missiles were developed in conjunction with the French. Until 1975 the army issue rifle was the standard NATO rifle with minor local adaptations of FN rifles (R1 and R2). The machine guns were converted .303 Bren guns (converted to 7.62 mm) and the belt fed FN light machine gun.

By the mid-eighties the drain of the war effort on the fiscus had become progressively the subject of concern and the requirements for

---

Armoured cars in current use were copies of the British Panhard. NATO mortars (60 mm and 81 mm) and Vickers machine guns (World War I issue) were also used. The medium machine gun was a .50 calibre Browning and the anti-tank weapon was a two and a half inch rocket firing bazooka (a World War II weapon which was appropriate to tank targets which obtained in that war). The main artillery piece was the WWII 25 pounder field gun of British make. Radio systems were shortwave (B2) models which were already antiquated in 1975 and which were still in use in the 1980s. The uniform webbing was based on the British model, marginally modified for South African conditions. The air force comprised Mirages at the top of the range, with two squadrons of aging Buccaneer bombers, which were a British make specifically designed for carrying nuclear bombs in the 1950s, a fleet of Canberra bombers which were long range maritime reconnaissance rescue aircraft designed for naval mine-laying, Alouette (French) and Puma (British) helicopters and large troop/cargo helicopters, the Superfrelan helicopters, all of which were antiquated in 1975. The main battle tank at the start of the war was the British Centurion 30-50 ton tank which formed the core of the armoured wing but had a high breakdown rate. The 6 ton troop and transport trucks were standard British make Bedford trucks. For general transport standard British land rovers the larger version of the American jeep were used. With all of this in place there was a concerted innovative programme on all fronts.

By 1981, in conjunction with Israel, a number of innovations in weaponry were developed. The infantry assault rifle changed from the R1 and R2 (20 clip straight magazine, with the weight of the whole weapon at seven and half pounds) to the R4 and R5 which were a smaller calibre (5.58 mm, 30 clip banana magazine, which were 6 pounds (empty weight)). The components of the weapons changed from the wood or plastic stocks of the R1 and R2 to the metal skeleton or synthetic petrochemical product stocks of the R4 and R5.

During the first offensives in the Angolan war, the capture of weapons developed in the Soviet Union (small arms, rocket launch systems, assault rifles, artillery pieces and armoured vehicles) provided the impetus for imitation and adaptation. The rocket launch system (the truck mounted multi-tube "Stalin organ") was extensively adapted with entirely new Mercedes engines loaded on a locally produced chassis, armoured steel cab and glass, and with improvements on the solid fuel and the explosive charge. The thickness and sloping of the armour plating was also an improvement on the captured weapon. The G6 artillery gun was introduced in early eighties thorough Israeli-South African research, with a calibre of 5.5cm, thus requiring changes in tooling of the barrel and shells and sighting mechanisms. It put out of range by a few kilometres all existing artillery of its size and larger. It was highly accurate and its portability and deployment and rate of fire were unique. The manpower required to operate it was less than existing field pieces. It was conveyed by an armed and armoured vehicle developed for southern African conditions.

military self-sufficiency within a context of a world that was becoming increasingly hostile to apartheid were becoming astronomical. In 1984 the chairman of ARMSCOR felt obliged to state the *raison d'être* and effects of the South African armaments endeavour in economic terms. In the first place there was the truism the munitions industry would have been much smaller in the absence of the international boycott. Secondly the returns on investment in the military sector were listed as job creation, both direct and through multipliers, standardisation and quality control which spilled over to other industrial sectors, and an increase in the country's skills and production capacity base. To these were added export earnings achieved through a sophisticated sanctions-busting trade. Within the context of apartheid this was valid enough. What was left unstated, however, was the vast range of opportunity costs entailed by apartheid within the changing global context, i.e. the phenomenon that drove the futile agenda for military self-sufficiency in the first place.

The established manufacturing sectors that were immediately affected by the war effort were those which supplied infantry weapons, small arms and ammunition, in which South Africa had already gained expertise prior to the arms embargo. These were non-electrical machinery, engineering.[6]

---

6 During the boom years of the sixties the manufacturing sector grew at a rapid rate and low (and often negative) real interest rates stimulated heavy capital investment in this sector. One of the fastest growing manufacturing sectors was in mechanical engineering. In the sixties the production of sugar milling machinery and plants for plastic and rubber industries commenced under licence from British firms. In 1962 a turnkey chemical plant was produced for Foskor at Phalaborwa. The agricultural sector became a major client in 1965 when the first sugar mills began to be produced locally. Production and innovation for the requirements of power generation, through ESCOM, had increased at a rapid rate since the thirties. Steel production had also provided significant backward linkages in the expansion of this sector.

The initial impetus for heavy mechanical engineering equipment came from the railways, shipping and the mining sector and the main manufacturer which emerged in this sector was Dorman Long Vanderbijl Corporation Limited (Dorbyl) which was formed in 1973. It was a conglomeration of a British firm, Dorman Long Limited (est. 1903) and the Vanderbijl Corporation Limited (Vecor, est. 1945).

The 1973 oil crisis boosted SASOL's role and prompted the construction of a second plant with ten times the production capacity of the original one. The demands on planning, design and engineering skills required for this investment and that planned for the third plant were facilitated by technical cooperation with the US. The construction process generated large spillovers in the form of training raw intake in pipefitting and welding. Imported human capital requirements were metal working industries, chemicals[7] and non-metallic mineral products.[8] However the embargo required the apartheid regime to acquire technologies that formed an integral part of the emerging weapons systems and the sector which was most affected by these was electronics. Landgren (1989: 135) argues that the US disinvestment from the electronics sector in South Africa was largely ineffective for three reasons. In the first place it came too late, since by the time the disinvestment process got under way South Africa had already acquired the required technological base in this sector. Secondly the acquisition of American subsidiaries by South African interests did not sever the contacts with the original mother companies. Finally in many cases the American pull-out simply allowed European and Japanese competitors who had retained their operations in South Africa to expand their market niche. The other emerging sector which came to prominence because of the siege was energy. The apartheid regime, especially after the seventies oil crisis, became obsessed with the strategic drive to become self-sufficient in terms of energy requirements. The major beneficiary of this demand was the petrochemicals sector with the coal-to-oil programme as its flagship, but the nuclear energy sector also received a considerable stimulus both because of energy provision needs and as part of a covert nuclear armament programme.

The emerging technological growth sectors

The convergence of the interests of the military-industrial and the minerals-energy complexes, as the isolating effects of apartheid on the economy increased, stimulated the indigenous technological deepening of

---

therefore minimal. SASOL2 and SASOL3 were declared by the South African Institute of mechanical engineering as the Engineering Project of the Century.

By 1980 South Africa had the biggest engineering manufacturing organisation in the Southern Hemisphere, a leader in the design and manufacture of mining equipment and a significant exporter. R&D spending by parastatal corporations grew massively from 1981 onwards as did R&D expenditure by CSIR sponsored independent research laboratories in miscellaneous manufactures received a major boost from 1983.

7 Public sector R&D increased substantially in the "other chemicals" sector from 1985.

8 Non-metallic mineral products, other than glass, saw a major increase in R&D by parastatal corporations from 1985 onwards. R&D by public corporations in basic iron and steel was consistently high throughout the seventies but started diminishing rapidly in the eighties.

specific sectors. Primary among these were electronics, petrochemicals and nuclear energy, as well as the (military) automotive sector. While the petrochemicals and nuclear energy sectors were based on an abundance of natural resources and the military vehicle sector had a long history of development, the electronics sector marked a distinctly determined foray into a new area by the state. In spite of the severe constraints imposed by the apartheid economy, it was an area whose development provided a sound base in a potentially high technology industrial sector after apartheid.

Electronics

As mentioned earlier, the main R&D intensive sector which lies outside the minerals-energy complex is electronics. The electronics sector experienced a dramatic leap in R&D expenditure in 1981 which derived entirely from the public sector (government and parastatal corporations). R&D by private business enterprises in this sector followed after a two-year lag. Goode (1995b: 48-49), among others, traces the sources of this activity to ARMSCOR, the CSIR and the South African Posts and Telecommunications, with the military sector accounting for the largest portion.

The initial impetus to establish a local telecommunications industry arose in the fifties and was motivated by military concerns about South Africa's dependence on foreign suppliers, especially in light of the growing international opposition to apartheid. Prior to this, telecommunications equipment was almost entirely imported. The main recommendation of the Electronics Committee, under the aegis of the Defence Resources Board, was that the South African Post Office should guarantee purchases of equipment manufactured locally. In response, the existing suppliers/importers agreed to commence local production. The year 1958 saw the initiation of long term Manufacture and Supply Agreements (two ten- year agreements and a fifteen-year one commencing in 1979) which guaranteed the market for local suppliers while regulating it. Kaplan (1990: 33) attributes the rapid rise in the local content of manufactured telecommunications products over the first ten-year period to two factors, apart from the guaranteed public sector market. The first was the high degree of protection implicit in the differential between the prices that the state paid and those paid on the international markets (specifically those prevailing in Britain). Secondly, the technology governing telecommunications products was mature, hence requiring moderate acquisition costs and "keep-up" costs.

The seventies saw dramatic changes in telecommunications technology because of the move from analogue to digital systems, which was due to the advent of the microelectronics age. Kaplan (1990) points out that South Africa was exceptional as the only country where the state led the market in the transition to the adoption of the new digital technology.[9] This state led initiative was to create a unique relationship between the foreign supplier (Siemens) of a technology still in a development stage and a recipient which was itself acquiring expertise and in the process staying on the leading edge of the new technology. However, while South Africa was quite capable of coping with the old mature analogue technology,[10] the sudden acceleration of innovative activity required by the leap into the new technological paradigm posed a challenge for which the country was structurally unprepared. The major constraint the industry now faced within the new technology was that of a restricted local market and the consequent economies of scale problem in an area which suddenly became characterised by requirements for heavy capital investments, a high R&D cost incidence, short product life cycles, due to rapid technological obsolescence, and a rapid widening of the range of telecommunication products and services. The local enduring skilled labour shortages ensured that the rapid rate of technological advance in this field generated a consistently widening technology gap.

The range of products of the electronics sector which rapidly became crucial for the armaments programme had to provide for command, control, communication and intelligence programmes, avionics, radar and telecommunications systems, lasers and navigational optronics, and training and simulation systems. The inputs for these requirements covered the whole semi-conductor and integrated circuitry industries, the microwave industry, as well as the associated software development. The requirements from the electronics sector escalated rapidly as competitive advantage in weapon systems became increasingly defined by the ability to employ state of the art electronic systems. By 1984 the South African

9 Kaplan (1990: 38) points out that

> "...(w)hereas in the USA and Europe the telecommunications industry had developed digital products prior to their acceptance by the telecommunication authorities, in South Africa it was the telecommunication authority ..., which took the decision in favour of digital and the local telecommunications industry which followed suit."

10 Kaplan (1990) quote the low levels of R&D activity that were required, the ease of licensing from foreign suppliers and the cheap cost of black labour and the lack of effective labour unions in a labour intensive industry as the main reasons.

Post Office and ARMSCOR accounted for 70% of the South African electronic equipment industry (Chataway, 1990a: 245-246).

In 1984 a special committee, consisting of the CSIR, the IDC, ARMSCOR, ESCOM and NUCOR, was established to formulate and implement an integrated strategy to develop the local electronics industry. The basic strategic tools which were proposed were the employment of the state's buying power to provide a guaranteed market and state support of local R&D activity in this sector. This replicated the industrial development programme which had been implemented in the inter-war period and which had provided the base for the establishment of ISCOR and ESCOM. At the same time the specific constraints imposed by apartheid on the economy were clearly recognised. Thus the motivation to increase self-sufficiency in this sector was qualified by cautionary admonitions about the dangers of isolation and the consequent distancing of the local industry from the latest international developments in this area. Another *caveat* on the local development programme concerned the recognised severe skills constraint, especially with regard to engineers. The potential cost of these two factors was that the local industry would be caught up in replicating the development process of technologies which had already been established elsewhere and for which South Africa simply did not have the required human capital capacity. The development of the telecommunications industry contained many of the characteristics of the hothouse R&D environment created by the apartheid war economy. The 1986 BTI report clearly highlighted the decreasing competitiveness of the local electronics industry, in terms of its low level of local content, low levels of private R&D and the increasing reliance on imported technology. Chataway (1990a: 236) says that while "...in the mid-1980s the electronics industry was growing at nearly 11% a year in real terms ... the real growth rate of domestic production was under 3% a year". The attempt by the state to increase capacity within the electronics sector through the creation of the South African Micro Electronics Systems (SAMES), a joint venture between the IDC and a number of private corporations proved to be counter productive since the establishment of its monopoly position as a supplier of integrated circuitry, mostly as a manufacturer, increased the cost of this crucial input to the sector, unaccompanied by any significant increase in exports. This attempt at an infant industry programme was doomed to failure given the underlying systemic constraints, mainly with respect to skilled labour. This particular and crucial constraint on the development of an indigenous set of capabilities is noted by Chataway (1990a: 243-244) when she reports on the results of a survey carried out as late as 1986 which asked corporations within the sector to list and rank twenty possible policies that could be implemented to diminish the effects of sanctions. While the economies of scale constraint in R&D was given a high priority through the proposal for the establishment of a joint R&D institution, the provision of training programmes for black employees was assigned a low priority. Chataway reports that the designer of the survey himself was taken aback by this finding, especially given a history of poor training programmes for black and female employees in this sector. The extent to which South African policy was still firmly embedded within the apartheid sub-text is evident in the BTI's proposition that self-sufficiency in military electronic equipment could spill over onto other sub-sectors and "... serve as a catalyst for the rest of the local electronics manufacturing effort ..., *just as was the case in Israel*" (BTI, 1986: 16, emphasis added). This statement was made with no recognition of the implications of the radically different structural contexts, especially in terms of the human resource capacities, in the respective economies. Further on in the report the massive gap between the skills base of the South African and Israeli electronics industries is noted, but assigned a relatively low priority as a determinant of technological capabilities and the development of core competences.[11]

The case of the television industry, which has been recorded in detail by Bauman (1995), is indicative of the formidable structural limitations on attempts by the state to establish core industries outside the base minerals-energy complex. With the introduction of television broadcasting in the late seventies the television industry was identified by government as a

---

11 The BTI (1986: 37) report states that

> "... the largest part (89% in 1984) of the labour corps in the South African electronics manufacturing industry had received no tertiary technical training. In 1984, only 2.7% of the labour corps in this industry represented scientists and engineers (as against 23% in Israel) and 8.1% of technicians and technologists (as against 22% in Israel)."

with the consequence that

> "The inability of the South African electronics industry to successfully enter the export market must largely be ascribed to the low ratio of engineers and technically trained personnel ... [which] hinders the development of unique products by applied and product-oriented R&D. Nonetheless there is a sensible utilisation of professional engineers and scientists ... on R&D. ... 44% of the engineers, scientists, technicians and technologists in the electronics industry in 1984 were employed on R&D."

This statement ignores the skills level of the general work force as a factor in developing competence and by quoting the utilisation rates of the low skilled worker component sidelines the issue of human capital from the analysis of constraints.

strategic industry on the grounds of the expected internal market for televisions, and the perceived potential of this industry to offer technical skills training which would spill over to other domestic electronics industries. This new industry was regulated by a number of measures which could well be reminiscent of a South Korean experience. The number of licensed manufactures was limited and each of them was bound to engage in a joint venture with an international manufacturer in order to assure state of the art technology transfer. The licensed firms had to guarantee in-house training for their workforce. Firms were moreover bound to local content clauses in order to maximise backward linkages with local component manufacturers. The range of products to be produced was also limited in order to assure viable production runs within the constraints of the local market. Tariffs on imported sets were set up at high levels but with the proviso that this was a short term measure to allow the learning period necessary to achieve a sustainable level of competitiveness against imports. This effort proved to be fruitless and costly to the economy,[12] primarily because even the limited number of firms was too large to achieve economies of scale within the local market and because upstream local supply fell far short of its expected contribution, hence requiring a high import content. For these reasons local production consisted mostly of assembly and the generation of skills within this industry was consequently minimal. Bauman's assessment of the resulting situation of the local television industry is extremely pessimistic:

> "Two decades later (since its inception), the industry remains essentially unchanged. Its net contribution to the economy is heavily negative; its products are uncompetitive with imports; it is still a net importer of components. It has also failed to serve as the basis for a wider electronics industry for the simple reason that assembly of imported components is a simple procedure which generates few skills and requires little local input. Firms which have gone beyond simple assembly face significantly higher costs than importers and the fly-by-night firms which have taken advantage of the BTI's 1989 programme to assemble semi-knocked-down ... kits at low cost, selling them as locally manufactured." (Bauman, 1996: 195).

Bauman identifies the focus on the television industry as distinct from the wider electronics and components sector as constituting the major flaw

---

12 Bauman quotes a 1984 BTI report which assesses that "... local manufacturing of televisions cost the economy 1.2 times more foreign exchange than was gained in added value ..." (Bauman, 1996: 186).

of the industrial and trade policy which had been designed and implemented for its promotion. In the process the necessary adjustments in upstream industries were neglected and economies of scope with respect to complementary product lines ignored.

Petrochemicals

On the energy front, the synthetic fuels programme received a major boost during the period of the preparation for the siege economy under apartheid. Anglovaal, which had operated a company since before the Second World War to produce petrol from torbanite was granted a licence in 1947 to develop an oil-from-coal project. The terms of the licence laid down the condition of exclusive South African ownership and top management of the company. The result was SASOL which became a public company in September 1950 and which was privatised in 1979. SASOL grew rapidly in terms of both its size and of its product range. Kros quotes an export figure of four billion Rands for 1990 and SASOL rapidly became a world leader in many lines of beneficiation - fertilisers, industrial gas, synthetic rubber and catalyst preparation and utilisation.

The original basis of the South Africa chemicals industry was driven by the requirements of the mining industry for explosives and of the agricultural sector for fertilizers. Crompton (1995: 69) sees two developments, both occurring in 1932, which entrenched the reliance of the South African chemical industry on coal as a feedstock, away from the progressive shift of the world industry towards oil and gas feed stocks which began during the Second World War. Crompton (1995: 76) points out that the inflexibility of the cost structure of the coal based producer relative to that of the oil based one constitutes a main feature of the technology choice peculiar to the South African petrochemicals industry.

By the late sixties three companies dominated the chemicals sector - AECI, Sentrachem and SASOL. The expansion of SASOL's operations was substantially stimulated by the oil crisis of the early seventies, complemented by a reinforcement of the UN call for an international embargo on oil supplies to South Africa. This led to the building of SASOL2, a much larger operation than the original plant. The collapse of the Shah's Iran in the late seventies prompted the building of SASOL3. Crompton (1995) points out that the enormous investment in what was, by the global yardstick, an alternative energy source (including the Mossgas operation which started in 1987 to synthesise petrol from natural offshore gas) was unparalleled anywhere else in the world and was driven by the reaction of an embattled regime to a historically brief oil shortage on the world markets. He charts the progression from SASOL1 to 2 and 3 and finally to Mossgas as the increasingly aberrant domination of the national economic fiscus by military concerns. The creation of SASOL was driven by the strategic reasons of the siege mentality of the apartheid regime at the cost of commercial feasibility. It is only relatively recently, within a democratic and open political economy that SASOL is proving to be a competitive enterprise. This follows those many cases where military vulnerabilities, real or perceived, have driven an R&D and industrial development programme which would never have been initiated by the private sector.

In the case of SASOL a substantial portion of the engineering design had been done abroad. In the case of Mossgas a greater design autonomy was achieved. One of the means to ensure a more permanent technology transfer was through joint ventures between local and foreign companies. Mossgas was set up in 1987 to exploit offshore natural gas reserves for the production of synthetic fuel. It also offered the opportunity to provide the economies of scale required to promote local engineering and technical capacity and to provide powerful backward linkages, especially to the manufacture of machinery and steel. The local content was thus very high. As in the case of SASOL the training implications were substantial. The Mossgas initiative was almost a caricature of extreme wastage of public funds. Cromptom (1995: 71) gives an opportunity cost measure for Mossgas by quoting comparisons made at the time which showed that the equivalent investment would have been enough to replace the country's entire existing refinery capacity or that half of that investment could have electrified all the houses in South Africa. The investments in SASOLs 2 and 3 fixed the sector's commitment to coal based feed stocks while Mossgas focussed the country's natural gas reserves on the production of petrol instead of petrochemicals, thus forcing a reduction in the range of petrochemicals produced countrywide. South Africa's entry into the production of petrochemicals was comparable with similar concurrent developments in South Korea. While the South Korean plants were smaller the range of chemicals that they produced was much wider than their South African counterparts

Crompton (1995) identifies the source of the woes of the South African chemical, specifically the petrochemical, sector as an economies of scale constraint which has prevented local manufacturers from attaining the low-cost structures and runs of the top world producers (USA, Europe and Japan). This was due to an effectively small internal market, import substitution policies and a reliance on coal (instead of oil or gas) as feedstock, both of which policies were driven by military strategic imperatives, and low labour skills on the shop floor which, when combined with historically low R&D levels has concentrated the product mix in the upstream region of the petrochemical to plastics product chain. With the collapse of apartheid, the product mix narrowed, with an increasing concentration on speciality chemicals aimed for export markets and the consequent increases in R&D levels. There has also been a significant increase in worker training and a higher degree of consultation at shop floor level. The political commitment to satisfy the basic needs requirements of the general populace offered significant new internal market potential with the consequent implications for overcoming economies of scale constraints in a range of low-cost speciality chemicals. In the nineties South Africa started to show an internationally competitive R&D competence in biotechnology.

Nuclear energy

The development of nuclear power was again mostly boosted by the siege planning framework. The Uranium Enrichment Corporation of South Africa (UCOR) was established in 1970 to develop enrichment technologies. In 1982 the A was formed as the umbrella body within which all nuclear research and power generation would be coordinated. In 1985 NUCOR and UCOR were liquidated and the Atomic Energy Corporation became the sole institution in charge of the nuclear power sector in South Africa.

The viability of South Africa's nuclear programme, outside the policy requirements of apartheid, has been questioned on the basis of the claim that nuclear power can be imported cheaper than the local product. The list of local innovations and technological advances seems to be impressive (see SAIMechE records) but the spillover and linkage effects are limited.

Transport equipment

The war also had extensive implications for the transport sector. The pre-1975 aerial and geological surveys of southern Africa had already established the conditions (e.g. soil type, porosity, vegetation cover) which troop carriers and other vehicles would have to operate in. The design and development of troop carriers and light tanks were specifically designed to be appropriate to these conditions. The Rhodesian war experience with anti-mine vehicles fed into the design of South African vehicles. The production of motor vehicle parts started in 1960. With the intensification of the Angolan war and the introduction of a wide range of troop carriers and armoured vehicles, R&D spending by parastatal corporations in motor vehicles and transport equipment, other than railway equipment, saw a quantum leap from 1985 onwards. The spillovers of this sector of the military-industrial complex to non-military industries is however limited.

The specificity parameters of the apartheid system of innovation

By the end of the eighties, and at the end of apartheid one can indeed talk about a national system of innovation that was specifically an apartheid construct. The fact that it was a capitalist economy allowed the seamless transition to the post-apartheid system of innovation. However, the very smoothness of that transition carries implications for the possible endurance of its foundations. The industrial structure that was inherited by the democratic government had been shaped by the peculiarities of apartheid over the previous few decades.

The primary legacy was the endemic skills shortage which shaped the structure of the economy to accommodate for it through investment in capital intensive, low skilled industries and technologies. This legacy still proves to be an insurmountable obstacle to the transformation of the South African system of innovation and its depth and extent is perhaps unique in post-colonial history. This was due to the social engineering model of apartheid which lasted for generations and which affected the myriad dimensions of the human capital development process of the majority of the population. As I argue in the following chapter, the failure to understand the totality of the degradation of human capital has strongly compromised the effectiveness of various fragmented policy initiatives to enhance the overall skills base of the post-apartheid system of innovation.

The heritage of the minerals-energy complex as the basis for the South African economy is still significant. The international embargo on the sale of armaments to South Africa that determined the rapid development of the electronics sector was to a large extent due to the siege economy and the drive for some form of self-sufficiency in strategic areas. The development of the petrochemical sector was also a result of this drive. While the original impetus for the development of these industrial sectors disappeared with the end of apartheid they now remain as viable sectors. However, the structural constraints of the apartheid heritage severely limit their potential spillovers and linkages across the economy.

This is where the apparent ease of the economic transition to democracy may have been dangerously misleading. While the extreme injustice of the apartheid economy and its effects on the living conditions of the majority of the population, was obviously recognised and addressed in the legislation of the new democratic economy, little was done to alter the foundations of the apartheid system of innovation. There was too much of a concern not to be seen to be impeding the capitalist engine and not enough of an appreciation of the fact that many of the successful varieties of capitalism in industrialised and industrialising economies are managed and restricted on several levels by the state. In the case of South Africa it was unreasonable to expect that the private sector would, to any significant measure, alter the structure within which it had evolved and matured. The specificity of the apartheid system of innovation was implicitly ignored with the adoption of the assumption that the elimination of a racist political system and the liberalisation of markets would be sufficient to attain the development objectives of the new democracy.

CHAPTER SIX

THE POST-APARTHEID SYSTEM OF INNOVATION

South Africa was transformed into a democracy virtually overnight. However, while the codified components of a demographic nation state are in place, there is still insufficient evidence of a working democracy in a number of crucial aspects. In this respect South Africa constitutes one of the more unusual cases of what, for want of a better term, we may call the "post-colonial" governance crisis. The codified components of the new democratic state are in place. They include a constitution and a bill of rights which offer a comprehensive protection of individual rights (including property rights), backed by a parliamentary democracy, an independent judiciary and a free and critical press. Moreover, the post-apartheid system of innovation started of with a sound infrastructural base, both physical and institutional, which with the advent of democracy immediately placed the nation as the foremost economy in Africa and the recognised economic superpower on the continent. Overtly, therefore, South Africa had that most desirable combination of a democratic polity with all the constitutional guarantees for the maintenance of democracy, with a sound base for growth and development. Its transport systems, in terms of roads, rail, ports and air, are those of an industrialised economy. Its banking and financial systems, and its stock exchange provide an easy platform for industry and commerce. It has pockets of technological excellence backed by specific pools of highly skilled scientists and engineers. Its R&D and innovation indicators, after the initial drop in the early nineties due to the cutting down of military R&D, now place South Africa comfortably within the OECD average range of economies. South Africa, due to a large extent to the size and sophistication of its economy, also rapidly emerged as the main launching pad for economic integration across sub-Saharan Africa. South African corporations rapidly extended their operations across Africa, altering patterns of foreign direct investment and competing for this space with industrialised and emerging economies.

However, it is the tacit components of a democratic state, most of which are the result of history, which set the context within which the codified components are placed and which determine their power to engender an effectively functional democratic state. Throughout the history of South Africa the relationships within civil society and between civil society and the state were forged under segregation and apartheid. A universal franchise in the post-apartheid era is of course a necessary condition for the transition to a functional democracy. It is not however a sufficient one and an insufficient regard to the tacit components of the apartheid heritage is now posing one of the biggest obstacles to the emergence of an economically democratic state. In the absence of the required transformation to this end the evolution of the national system of innovation is severely compromised.

The main theme of this book has been the analysis of continuities and ruptures in the evolution of the South African system of innovation. Undoubtedly, the most dramatic rupture in this country's political history was the demise of apartheid and its replacement by a democratic government. However, from a systems perspective we also need to assess the degree to which this significant break with the political past translates into a systemic shift in the evolution of the South African system of innovation. In conjunction with this investigation we also need to evaluate the suitability of the post-apartheid system of innovation to the development needs of the new democracy. In this case we need to refer back to the biological metaphor of the system of innovation approach to economic development. Early in the book, this metaphor was used to allow a specific type of evaluation of the success of innovation systems in terms of their ability to reproduce, to mutate and to grow. We also have to qualify this type of evaluation by clearly specifying what may be called the "suitability parameters". By this I mean the suitability of systems for specific objectives. Thus, for example, the viability of the system of innovation which emerged under apartheid may only be properly assessed in relation to stated goal sets. The two obvious goal sets are those determined by the political objectives of apartheid as distinct from the development goals of a democratic political economy. Two such fundamentally different contexts will inevitably yield significantly different evaluations of the same system. Thus, the basis for the analysis of the post-apartheid system of innovation has to be clearly articulated prior to analysis and assessment. Otherwise, the interpretation of measures of success can be severely obscured. In this respect, therefore, the performance of macroeconomic indicators does not necessarily reflect the health of the system of innovation. Indicators such as the growth rate in GDP per capita, fiscal health, enhanced export performance, low inflation rates, low unemployment rates, and a deepening of the technological base of the economy were as much the goals of the apartheid economy as they are of the post-apartheid one. One can also argue that the gap in the quality of life between blacks and whites in terms of income and other constituents was an inevitable consequence of the logic of the apartheid system of innovation. As I have argued earlier, had the disenfranchised section of the South African population been a small minority, legislated racism would not necessarily have diverted the evolution of the system of innovation on to what may be termed a regressive, anti-modern path. That hypothetical system may well have followed that of successfully industrialising economies. In that case, the demise of a racially defined political economy may have held much less of a significance for the evolution of the system of innovation. On the contrary, the specific conditions of the South African case under apartheid generated a direct causality between the political regime and the national system of innovation. Thus, in the case of South Africa fundamental political change towards a truly democratic economy is inextricably bound with a fundamental change in the national system of innovation. The one defining feature of democracy is that it eradicates constitutionally the racial barriers to mobility in the several interlinked meanings of the term. Its success, within the South African context can only be assessed in terms of the degree to which the constitutional change affects the actual life conditions of the majority of the population.

We also need to expand on the discussion of the institutions that form the networks that constitute an innovation system. In Chapter 1, I referred to the distinction between formal institutions and informal ones. The former represents those planned structures within public and the private sector, both national and international, whose terms of reference and whose manner of engagement with a specific system of innovation is mostly explicit and codified. Informal institutions refer to sets of established practices, routines and the non-codified rules of engagement between the various sets of agents in a specified context. The next step in the analysis of the South African system is to explore the possible modes of interaction among the various institutional sets. To do that, we have to look at the relationship between policy and the planned transformation at the formal institutional level, as well as the evolution of the informal institutional underpinning. Here the term underpinning is used to denote explicitly the assumption that the base foundation of a specific system of innovation is constituted of its informal institutional network. We may, in fact, think in terms of meshing networks with varying possibilities of cohesion and dislocation. If that assumption holds then policy may best be assessed by the manner in which and the extent to which the transformation of the formal institutional structures affects the informal institutional base. Work cultures, the relationship between employers and employees, the short term planning horizon of the average family, to name a few cases, are all stamped by the peculiar history of apartheid. Unless these are fundamentally altered, productivity levels, the absorptive capacity for innovation and human capital development will still remain in place as severe limitations on the efficacy of S&T, education and labour policies in terms of their ability to shunt the South African development path on to the knowledge economy route.

Furthermore, this analysis has to be set within the changes in the political context through the still brief history of South Africa's democratic period. The one salient feature of this history since the breakdown of the Government of National Unity in 1996 is that South Africa is essentially a legitimate one party state. It is a legitimate state in terms of free and fair elections, a vocal and unrestrained opposition front, an independent judiciary and the strong presence of highly critical news media. It is also, at the same time, in effect a one party state because of the extreme improbability of any contending party successfully challenging the parliamentary majority of the ANC. This is to a large extent the result of the nature and history of the ANC and to the post-apartheid political environment. From the early 1980s onward the ANC emerged as the most effectively organised anti-apartheid movement. While the Black Consciousness Movement and the Pan African Congress probably held the intellectual core of the revolution, the ANC was much more effective in its organisation of local resistance to apartheid and in its international mobilisation of the anti-apartheid movement. Progressively, the core of the intelligentsia from other resistance movements drifted to the ANC as the more effective platform for the overthrow of apartheid. The other outstanding feature of the ANC was that it was all encompassing of ideology. Its one defining, and unifying, identity was the revolt against apartheid and the mission to bring in a democratic government. From an ideological perspective, in terms of the options for the reformation of the economy, it was an umbrella organisation which contained some very disparate and potentially polarised ideological positions on the nature of the post-apartheid political economy.

The demise of apartheid and the democratisation of South Africa mark the most significant ideological rupture in the country's entire history. However, in terms of governance, the effective one party model is redolent of the pre-democratic era. From its election to power in 1948 the National

Party was, within the context of the racially defined polity, the permanently entrenched government during apartheid with little possibility of its dislodgment. The only variable in the political system was the official opposition which oscillated between the liberal faction and the extreme right wing coalitions. In the case of the post-apartheid era, the ANC is, for the foreseeable future the ruling party with the possibility of shifts in the official opposition. In both cases it was the intra-party conflicts and alliances that shifted policy. The main implication for the informal part of this particular type of governance is a permanence of structures and of patronage systems, with the most effective controlling mechanisms located within the ruling party rather than imposed from outside. The radical difference between the two eras lies in the formal governance structures which derive from an authoritarian predatory regime that had placed the country in a permanent low level state of war on the one hand and a democratic normal government on the other. Thus, in the post-apartheid era the constitutional independence of the judiciary, the official exclusion of political censorship of the media and a full freedom of movement of resources and of association are assured by relatively inviolable sets of extra-parliamentary control mechanisms.

The failure of opposition parties on the left to offer a credible alternative to the ANC in terms of governance has left them out in the political hinterland, in spite of their historically appealing ideological stance. The official opposition that finally coalesced in the Democratic Alliance went through an initial turbulent history of failed mergers and coalitions. It is, moreover, still seen as a largely ethnically defined political organisation mostly representing a White and Cape Coloured constituency. Moreover, it is a party that is decidedly neoliberal and thus shares the political economic goal set of the ANC. Its claim as a valid opposition essentially rests on issues of corruption and the effectiveness of government, and not on principles. The tripartite alliance between the ANC, the South African Communist Party (SACP) and the Congress of South African Trade Unions (COSATU forms the ruling coalition of the party. In reality however, the ANC, which has until recently embraced a neoliberal macroeconomic policy, has been the dominant partner with the other two movements playing the role of vociferous but, until December 2007, largely powerless partners. The election of the new ANC structures at the end of 2007 marked a dramatic overthrow of the neoliberal faction which had coalesced around the state president by a coalition representing COSATU, the SACP and other left wing lobby groups which had for long been marginalised from the core of the decision making processes within government. The avalanche defeat of the entire array to the members of the ANC who formed the cabinet, including the state president, and core stalwarts who were identified as strongly adherent to the current government was the result of the long gestating and a deepening ideological rift within the ruling party. As such it does mark the beginning of the possibilities of a break in the dominant political economic ideology that still determines the overall context of development planning in South Africa. On another level, it will almost certainly result in a new set of patronage networks within the ruling party. Given the experience of almost a decade and a half of democratic governance set firmly within the context of continental and global systems of innovation, the criteria for the formation of new patronage networks may have more relevance for the capacity requirements of a government that is increasingly concerned about the role of the state in the economy and about the overall failures of the state's delivery systems.

Periodisation of the post-apartheid era

In terms of economic policy of the post-apartheid period can be broken down into three stages, with a fourth stage in the offing after the historic election of the new ANC structure in December 2007. That there should have been so many stages in such a short span of time is indicative of the highly contested ideological terrain of the articulation of the vision for the new democratic South Africa, with numerous coalescences of vested interests and power positions vying for the authority to be the architect of the emerging system of innovation.

The first stage, until the publication of the *Growth, Employment and Redistribution: a Macroeconomic Strategy* (GEAR) White Paper in 1996 was the period of intense debate between a Keynesian intervention approach towards the restructuring of the South African economy and the neoliberal one which ultimately won the day. In the early 1990s the ideological basis for the economic plan for the development of the newly democratic South Africa was a highly contested terrain. The original approach was an essentially Keynesian programme that required a strongly interventionist role by government to address high unemployment, an economy that was still based on the institutional relations established under apartheid, sluggish growth and a high public debt. The initially adopted economic policy agenda of the new government, drawn prior to the 1994 election was the *Reconstruction and Development Programme* (RDP) and this was formalised in the RDP White Paper (September 1994). From a developmental perspective the RDP proposed a broad-based programme of investment in the country's depleted stock of human capital. It contained a strong redistributive element in its proposed delivery of housing, water, hygiene, power, policing, medical services, education and land reform for the poor. From a system of innovation perspective this would also have been the pivotal long term strategy to correct the core structural fault that apartheid bequeathed to the new democratic government. The plan was careful to factor in a degree of fiscal discipline that was to be brought about through an increased efficiency in tax revenue retrieval, an addressing of inefficiencies in state enterprises and a realignment of public spending towards social needs. However, following the collapse of the Soviet Union and the extreme reaction against most forms of direct involvement of the state in the economy which had formed global conventional economic wisdom since the eighties, this was an unfriendly period for economic policies that allotted any significant restructuring role to the state.

The countervailing ideology which ultimately defined the country's development programme was neoliberal economics, which in its moderate version limited the role of the public sector to addressing issues of externalities and public goods. A draft *National Growth and Development Strategy* document was presented in February 1996, departing substantially from the Keynesian paradigm on which the RDP had been based. In June 1996 the shift in the official national economic policy was finally articulated in the GEAR document, whose main policy recommendations were to reduce government spending, control wage increases and reduce tariffs. The overt immediate rationale behind GEAR was the precarious state of the economy in the early 1990s. It was an economy marked by a large budget deficit, perilously low foreign exchange reserves, double digit inflation and a high rate of unemployment. These factors were set against a background of a strong degree of political uncertainty about the nature of the political shift, large outflows of currency and a four-year decline in the economy. The seductively pragmatic view was that the macroeconomics had to be put right before the structural distortions of apartheid could be addressed.[1]

1 However, Adelzadeh (1996) objects to the validity of a number of the accepted "pragmatic" arguments for the adoption of GEAR. Specifically, he questions the overwhelming concern with the fiscal deficit relative to GDP, maintaining that it was well within internationally accepted limits and could even rise according to World Bank planning scenarios for the South African economy. He also questioned theoretically the "crowding out" effect argument for cut backs in public spending, as well as pointing out that South Africa's public debt to GDP ratio was lower than most OECD economies.

This overwhelming concern to address the immediate economic crises was reinforced by an acceptance of the longer term prospect of the curative effects of "market rationality" for the South African economy. The underlying assumption of the neoliberal approach in South Africa at the time was that apartheid constituted a prime example of market distortion and consequently that a policy aimed at liberating market forces would be the logical way to start addressing the structural effects of apartheid on the economy. Put differently, the race side of the race class debate became, at least implicitly, the accepted explanation of apartheid economic history. The "trickle down" tenet at the core of the neoliberal programme proposed that in largely untrammelled, and therefore flourishing, capitalist economy, the benefits of growth would cascade down to the general population in the form of increased employment, remuneration and upward mobility. The final articulation of this approach was the GEAR plan of 1996. The fundamental attraction of this plan for the new government charged with the monumental task of re-engineering the economy and the entirety of the public service was the sheer simplicity of its proposed strategy. The relatively simple programme of market liberation would, by virtue of the assumption of necessarily efficient competitive markets, solve the development issues of the country. The objectives of GEAR by the year 2000 were a 6% per annum growth rate and the annual net creation of 400,000 jobs. The main recommendations of GEAR were summarised as follows:

> "(G)overnment consumption expenditure should be cut back, private and public sector wage increases kept in check, tariff reform accelerated to compensate for the depreciation and domestic savings performance improved. These measures will counteract the inflationary impact of the exchange rate adjustment, permit fiscal deficit targets to be reached, establish a climate for continued investor confidence and facilitate the financing of both private sector investment and accelerated development expenditure." (GEAR. 1996: 5)

The factor that was left out of the analysis is that it is rarely the business of business to alter structure. It is rather the business of the state to alter the structure, the rules of the game, within which business operates. The adoption of GEAR marked the start of the rift between the labour movement and government. This rift was based on the explicit argument that GEAR did not offer a distinct break with the macroeconomic policy of apartheid, allowing, of course for the entry of South Africa into the global market.[2]

The third period of the brief history of the post-apartheid era is marked by the review of GEAR that started in 2001 where it was accepted that while successes were achieved in economic growth, fiscal discipline and inflation rates, none of this seems to have had much effect on the high levels of unemployment or on the quality of life (apart from the important fact of political freedom) of the majority of the population. The official review of the first four years of GEAR concluded that, while macroeconomic stability had been achieved, growth, investment and savings were still too low, foreign direct investment was consistently negative, education was falling behind the country's skills requirement, and that unemployment and poverty had not been significantly addressed. While the GDP growth rate has improved appreciably since then, there has been no significant reduction in unemployment. It is now widely recognised that the persistent levels of unemployment are largely due to the inherited shortage of human capital, a shortage that has not been significantly addressed, in combination with an economic structure which has little absorptive capacity for low skilled and unskilled labour.[3] These therefore became the two main challenges that the new policy orientation has to address - how to increase the employment of the low skilled and the unskilled portion of the labour force while simultaneously increasing the skills level of the labour force. The recognition of the failure of GEAR in this area led to a series of initiatives, culminating in the *Accelerated and Shared Growth Initiative for South Africa-AsgiSA* (RSA, 2004) programme,[4] which arose from the recognition of the need for direct

---

2 Thus Adelzadeh (1996: 67-68) states that GEAR

> "... represents a recourse to the policy goals and instruments of the past apartheid regime, and to the failed adjustment strategies being imposed on other countries under IMF and World Bank tutelage"

and that it would "... fail in meaningfully addressing let alone transforming the inherited inequities of the apartheid system".

3 The employment of low skilled labour in South Africa has no significant effect on the long term prospects for human capital development. As Altman (2006: 6) puts it:

> "There is evidence to show that the wages of low skill and semi-skill formal sector workers is stagnant or falling and that these jobs are becoming increasingly precarious in character. This is consistent with the path of industrial development, which has increasingly leaned to the outsourcing, the real expansion of services, and of the informal sector."

4 The overarching objectives for AsgiSA were specified as follows:

• Reduce the unemployment rate from 30% to 15% by 2014.

integrated state intervention on a number of fronts in order to address the development challenges of the country. The shortage of skills assumed a priority among the constraints to growth and led to the establishment of the *Joint Initiative on Priority Skills Acquisition -JIPSA* (RSA, 2006),[5] which was formulated specifically to strengthen and co-ordinate the activities to address the shortage of skills.

Since then, a more interventionist approach has been advocated, but this has been done in an almost apologetic manner and certainly a fragmented one. The proposal of a dual economy picture of South Africa (Mbeki 2003), arising out of a deep frustration at the failure of the South African economy to address significantly redistributive issues, is still anchored within a neoliberal paradigm. The portrayal of a division of the South African economy into two compartments, one modern, efficient and affluent and the other seriously underdeveloped and caught up in a low level poverty equilibrium trap may be a reasonable portrayal of the deep inequalities in the conditions of life in South Africa. However, as an understanding of the structure of the economy and hence as the basis for policy prescriptions, it would be seriously misleading. The South African system of innovation has always been a specifically integrated one within a context of legislated racial inequality which, with the demise of apartheid has progressively mutated into a class-based inequality. Even within the ideological requirements for the separation of (racially defined) classes under apartheid, the uniquely integrated nature of the South

---

• Reduce poverty from one-third to one-sixth of the population by 2014.
• Increase the annual GDP growth rate from the then average of 3% to 4,5% per year for the period 2005 to 2009 and to 6% for the period 2010 to 2014. This target should create a sustainable annual growth rate of 6%.

The list of binding constraints to the achievement of the growth rate required to reduce poverty significantly were identified as:

- Volatility and level of the currency.
- The cost, efficiency and capacity of the national logistics system
- Shortage of suitably skilled labour
- Barriers to entry, limits to competition and limited new investment opportunities.
- Regulatory environment and the burden on small and medium businesses
- Deficiencies in state organisation, capacity and leadership.

5 AsgiSA identified the following medium- and long-term interventions to address the skills shortage, which became the broad mandate of JIPSA:
• Build a strong foundation in public schooling.
• Focus on areas of greater priority in tertiary education and training.
• Initiate and improve work-based training programmes and scarce skills initiatives.

African economy excluded an effective model of "separate development". The modern sector of the South African economy is not an enclave economy. It is rather defined and determined by the complex sets of permeating interdependencies with the overall system of innovation and the foundations of that system are still largely those that were laid down in its pre-democracy history.

The case of that most negligible parts of the economy, domestic work, may be used to illustrate the interdependencies that permeate the fabric of the South African system of innovation. Cheap and abundantly available domestic service is one of the permanent features of the South African family from lower middle income upwards. It is generally a poorly paid employment which can take up as much as eighty hours per week and separate a woman from her family for up to eleven months of the year. In the early 2000s legislation was introduced to bring domestic labour into the formal market economy by requiring domestic workers who were employed over a minimum amount of hours per week to be registered for the state unemployment insurance fund. A minimum wage structure was simultaneously established. The objective of this legislation was to address particularly exploitative labour practices and improve the working conditions of one of the poorest segments of the labour market. There are however other considerations that would have evaluated the economic role of South African domestic labour. On the one hand there is the valuation of the service offered by domestic labour to the employer. Should that service be withdrawn, the employer would have to take on the household maintenance and child rearing functions of the domestic worker. Given the time that these roles would take up, the real value to the employer could be estimated in terms of foregone earnings and the value of lost leisure time. From an overall systems approach the cost of domestic labour to the economy would also have to be estimated in terms of its effects on human capital formation. The absence of the domestic worker from her family for protracted periods of time reduces the time that is devoted to child rearing in the families of domestic workers and hence negatively affects one of the more important components of the stability of the family structure. These effects have a negative impact on the human capital formation process within the family, an impact that does not carry a market value but which is nevertheless a substantial cost to the economy. These two factors, the direct opportunity cost to the employer and that for the economy, should enter the formulation of labour legislation within this sector. They also provide an indication, for a relatively unimportant economic sector, of the complexity of the interdependencies of the two sides of the proposed "dual economy" of South Africa.

These sets of interdependencies also carry specific policy recommendations which are distinct from those formulated within a neoliberal framework. The more important one is that the objectives of policy and policy strategies should not be mis-specified. From a systems approach, the separation between the measurement of the goals of development (income per capita, employment, equity, etc.) and the instruments of development (investment, public spending, monetary policy, etc.) can be dangerously misleading. Rather, we should develop a measure of development that contains both the means and the end, the goal, of the development process. If human capital formation is accepted as the main determinant of the competitive advantage of nations, then it would be invalid to treat the upliftment of the poor in an economy such as South Africa solely as the goal of policy. It should also, simultaneously, be the main development strategy. In other words, in the South African context the only way to address the longer term problem of the low level poverty equilibrium trap is to eradicate the conditions of poverty in the short term. This apparently contradictory proposition actually addresses the main systemic fault in the South African system of innovation. The human capital constraint, which has not been relieved in any significant measure, and which arguably cannot be addressed from a neoliberal framework, is the single most important impediment to the transition from an apartheid system of innovation to one which delivers the requirements for a broad-based long term sustainable development path.

The issue of appropriate technology and of the innovation system within which it is fostered has been the main recurring theme in this study. Its treatment has consistently been marked by contradictions arising from the difficulty of identifying the prevalent motive force, the prime client, of the overtly racist regimes, both prior to and during apartheid in South Africa. In the post-apartheid era the broad political objectives, insofar as the need to redress the inherited economic inequalities, are explicitly stated and, for the first time, are supported by the large majority of the population. There is also a broad-based consensus that the economic heritage of apartheid is the main obstacle to the attainment of these objectives. The crucial area where the consensus breaks down is the choice of strategies required to repair the damage done by apartheid to the country's development base. The increasing rift and the escalating conflict, between organised labour and business after GEAR is the symptom of the crisis facing the South African economy and constitutes the cause of its progressive deepening. The state, now viewed by the union movement as largely on the side of business, was faced by extremely stringent resource constraints on every front simply by virtue of the sudden requirement that structures and budgets effectively designed for the benefit of approximately five million whites had to be adapted to the needs of a constituency approximately nine times that size. This may provide a partial explanation for the political *volte face* from the pre-election draft RDP of 1993 to GEAR in 1996. The departure from the broad based consultative process which informed the original RDP with the imposition of GEAR was inevitable and constitutes a serious aggravating factor in the current confrontation between organised labour and the state. An examination of the post-war histories of Japan and most of the South East Asian economies offers ample evidence that the consensus which is so obviously lacking among the main stakeholders in the South Africa's future development is the crucial prerequisite of the ability to embark on development paths which defy the predictions of economic orthodoxy. In terms of this consensus, the current conflict within the ANC, its nature and the uncertainty of its outcome, has portentous implications for the evolution of the country's system of innovation.

The post-apartheid system of science and technology[6]

To a large extent, the changing role assigned to S&T planning in the post-apartheid era reflects the shifts in the country's economic planning context. The planning period up to 1994 saw S&T planning located in the Department of Arts, Culture, Science and Technology (DACST), combined with Arts and Culture. The minister in charge was a member of the Inkhata Freedom Party and the deputy minister was an ANC member whose standing within the party was at the time perceived to be on an irreversible path of political decline. These two factors - the location within a combined department and the political choice of its top managerial appointments - provide some indication of the priority that S&T planning held within the overall planning context at the time. The *White Paper on Science and Technology: Preparing for the 21st Century* policy statement came out in 1996 along with GEAR and the strong neoliberal planning environment severely constrained the application space of the country's first national S&T plan since the First World War. It is ironic that the second S&T plan at the end of the 20th century should have allotted lower priority to innovation policy within the national policy framework than the first plan at the beginning of the century that had

6 Kahn (2008) provides a succinct and comprehensive history of the evolution of Science and Technology (S&T) policy since the early 1990s.

placed it at the core of industrial policy. However, the main difference between the two historical points was that positioning of S&T within the overall economic planning framework declined progressively after the first S&T plan while that of the second plan has become increasingly integrated with, and strengthened within, macroeconomic policy. Although the White Paper refers consistently to the national system of innovation, a novel concept at the time, the overall economic policy context limited S&T policy strictly to the formal science and technology sectors within the economy. The White Paper correctly defined the NSI as "a set of functioning institutions, organisations and policies which interact constructively in the pursuit of a common set of social and economic goals and objectives" (DACST, 1996:20). However, the list of the type of institutions that were to be included in this definition was what really determined the ambit of S&T and innovation planning. A number of well-conceived S&T policies and initiatives were planned and implemented but the demarcation lines severely inhibited DACST from having any significant effect on the national system of innovation, as distinct from that of science and technology.

At the time of the drafting of South Africa's first White Paper on S&T policy by the country's first democratically elected government, the policy formulation framework in this field was in a state of disarray.[7] This was symptomatic of a wider malaise. R&D expenditure was low by international standards and had been steadily decreasing over the previous seven years with the dismantling of the military strategic programmes of apartheid. Trade patterns indicated that the country's exports of manufactured goods were intensive in physical capital and unskilled labour, whereas it imported commodities which exhibited high intensities of technology and human capital.[8] By most definitions, economic policy under apartheid had relegated the country's system of innovation to the periphery within the global framework.

The task of the White Paper of 1996 was therefore to redefine national S&T policy in line with the requirements of the political economic system emerging from the rupture in the country's history marked by the elections

---

7 The assessment of the White paper on the innovation system that was inherited from apartheid is quite explicit:

> "... we have in place an ailing national system of innovation. It is fragmented and is neither co-ordinated within itself nor within national goals; innovation capacity is not being built but is being eroded; national investment in R&D is not increasing relative to GDP, but falling." (DACST, 1996: 46)

8 See Scerri (1990, 2003a).

of 1994. This process of redefinition depended for its articulation on the definition of the preceding structure and of the economic paradigm which underlay it. Thus the genealogy of the 1996 White Paper must be sought in the history of S&T planning in South Africa and, since any historiography is, as already argued, a contentious discipline, different genealogies can be constructed. Different renditions would in turn result in differing assessments of the degree to which the White Paper represents a rupture in the paradigmatic language encompassing the history of S&T planning in South Africa.

The starting point of the 1996 White Paper was the recognition of the paucity of the S&T planning framework which had been inherited from apartheid. This assessment was partially based on the review of South Africa's national system of innovation undertaken by the International Development Research Centre (IDRC) in 1993. Apart from the obvious observation that S&T policy in South Africa had been determined by the requirements of apartheid, particularly in the emphasis on defence, the IDRC report identified the lack of coordination within the country's national system of innovation as one of the main features which needed to be addressed.[9] Thus the focus of the reform became the issue of coordination but this still left the level at which coordination was to be defined vague. In the three-year period between the publication of the IDRC report and the submission of the White Paper a significant change occurred in the context of national planning within which S&T policy articulation is set. The shift was from a relatively interventionist position in the RDP to a more neoliberal one, in the GEAR document, which largely confined the role of the state to that of a facilitator for market forces. This fundamental shift redefined the role that should be played by

---

9 The report succinctly identifies the overall coordination vacuum in the immediate post-apartheid economy:

> "... individual institutions trying to adapt are doing so in a policy vacuum at the highest levels of the present South African government. It may be that in the past, during the days of the National Party government's 'Total Strategy', there was strong coordination and shared purpose among the institutions of the white dominated state. If that was the case then, we found no evidence of it being the case now. Rather, we saw a series of institutions, each trying to define for itself a role in a 'new' South Africa ..." (IDRC, 1993: 5) "There are no articulated economic or social goals towards which various institutions could apply their efforts. ... as a consequence of the policy vacuum, resource allocations are essentially frozen, subject only to minor variations approved by officials within a system which is non-consultative and non-transparent, even to other high-level government officials." (IDRC, 1993: 22-23, emphasis added)

the state in the country's reconstruction and development process. In the process, strategic intervention as pertaining to the identification and the interventionist promotion of potential growth sectors was largely abandoned. Thus the planning level within which the improvement in coordination was envisaged became largely restricted to an intra-bureaucratic realignment of existing institutions, primarily aimed at reducing duplication of research efforts within the goal framework of the newly fledged democracy.

That the White Paper was cognisant of the need to integrate S&T policy within the overall national planning framework is clear when it stated that

> "Governments of the industrialised countries recognised, at the beginning of the 1980s, that one of the challenges of promoting technological innovation was in devising means to ensure that government actions across all fields - in trade, education, labour laws, environmental protection, to name but a few - be taken with due consideration of how these actions would affect the climate for innovation." (DACST, 1996: 22)

However, beyond this general statement it contained no specific provisions for affecting industrial and trade policy. Indeed, it cannot have had any since the national planning framework, as spelled out in GEAR, excluded any provision for trade and industrial policy.[10] There was therefore little scope in using such policy tools to promote the development of growth sectors. Thus, for example, instead of strategically intervening to reverse the inherited trade patterns, the policy on trade that emerged was one of accelerating trade liberalisation[11]. The White Paper

10 Adelzadeh (1996: 81, parentheses added) has this to say about trade and industrial policies under GEAR:

> "Section five of the Document (GEAR), on 'Trade, Industrial and Small Enterprise Policies', is thin on what the proposed trade policies, industrial policy and small enterprises are to be. On trade, the proposals appear to do away with any policies, as fast as possible. Some small enterprise policies are listed and there is a complete absence of any proposal for an industrial policy or strategy."

Earlier (Adelzadeh, 1996: 71) he points out that an export based growth plan which did not provide for strategic intervention was meaningless in an economy whose non-gold export-GDP ratio was higher than that for most industrialised economies.

11 "The evidence to support the proposition that import liberalization is automatically good for growth is weak—almost as weak as the opposite proposition that protectionism is good for growth." (UNDP, 2005: 119).

was therefore set within a tension between the definition of objectives and its general incapacity, beyond its curtailed coordination function, to attain those objectives. This incapacity was the result of the general move towards a neoliberal prescriptive approach to the process of transformation. Adelzadeh (1996: 81) argued that the GEAR growth rate objective for non-gold exports was unrealistic in the light of international experience. What should have been of concern was rather the composition of exports of manufactured goods rather than aggregate figures. In the introductory section on the effects of opening up to the international markets, the White Paper argued for a policy which maintained "... an appropriate balance between opening up the economy to global competitiveness and nurturing local initiatives" (DACST, 1996: 5), but the absence of a strategic trade and industrial policy rendered the ability to pursue the "nurturing local initiatives" side of the balance effectively particularly weak.

The capability of the state to stimulate and direct private R&D expenditure through indirect fiscal incentive programmes was eschewed, even though the White Paper acknowledges the extensive use of this tool in industrialised economies. Fiscal incentives were limited to direct subsidies on a matching grant basis. One of the reasons quoted for the exclusion of tax incentives was that the Katz Commission had previously ruled out the use of this tool because of its negative impact on the tax base. The other reason that was advanced was the difficulty of administering such incentives, especially since the CSIR, the body best suited for certifying R&D expenditure which qualifies for such incentives, had itself since 1988 been a competitor for R&D contracts in the private sector. The use of this institution as a certifying body would therefore lead to a conflict of interest, but in the absence of a comparable certifying body this left a serious gap in the ability of the state to influence the levels and patterns of R&D expenditures. This shortcoming was a legacy of the decision taken in 1987 to redefine the CSIR as a market player, a decision which, as we have seen in the previous section, can be traced to the progressive fossilisation of that institution since its re-definition by the apartheid government in 1948.

Consequently, deprived of the possibility of using most of the tools required for strategic intervention, the recommendations in the White Paper focussed on enhancing intra-governmental information flows and coordination as well as the formalisation of a dialogue with the private sector, with the aim of achieving a relocation of the public S&T in line with the country's development goals. Proper coordination of S&T policy across the broad spectrum of the public service would be entrusted to the

Ministers' Committee on Science and Technology which comprised all focussing ministers whose portfolios contain a significant S&T component. The National Advisory Council on Innovation (NACI), a council of experts from diverse fields and sectors, representing various stakeholder bodies, was established as an advisory body for DACST. This council was designed to address some of the objections to the Scientific Advisory Council articulated in the IDRC report (1993: 25-27). The most important innovation was that, as opposed to the Scientific Advisory Council, the terms of reference and the areas covered by NACI were to be public knowledge.

The White Paper objected to the inherited public funding system for S&T on the basis that it was partial, applying only to DACST and the Science Councils and short-term in that it was based on an annual budgetary system. The White Paper proposed instead a Science Budget which would incorporate the spending on S&T by all government departments and which would be put within a multi-year fiscal framework. The main tool for the financing and control of specific R&D projects would be the newly proposed Innovation Fund. The budget allocation for this fund would be drawn from a process of reallocation of science funding across government. It was proposed that DACST would cooperate with the Department of Trade and Industry (DTI) which administered the Support Programme for Industrial Innovation. The project choice criteria were aimed at three main goal sets which marked a significant break with past S&T funding policy. Project prioritisation criteria included the following:

> -projects which addressed the needs of the previously disadvantaged (initially half of the funding was to be directed at such projects);
> -large, long-term projects, in order to reverse the trend towards short planning horizons;
> -projects which manifested strong links between innovation, diffusion and use, thus reducing endemic fragmentation and delivery bottlenecks.

These priorities have remained largely intact through the several transformations of the S&T planning structures since 1996. What has changed is the capacity of the state organ entrusted with S&T planning to address these priorities. The White Paper also contained a specific proposal for DACST to address the development of an indigenous technology initiative, in collaboration with the DTI, by focussing on the technology requirements of small, medium and micro-scale enterprises through the setting up of pilot projects.

A further source of R&D funding would come through a redefinition of the state procurement policy in order to provide a demand-side stimulus to technology intensive industries. This procurement policy had been launched with the first S&T policy statement in 1916 but had subsequently deteriorated to an undiscriminating promotion of all local industries regardless of their technological capabilities content. In consequence it had often tended to encourage patterns of industrial development which manifested a low technology and a low human capital content. These patterns had become entrenched in the apartheid system of innovation.

The White Paper proposed the introduction of a comprehensive management system which would encompass all government science, engineering and technology institutions. These fall into two categories - science councils and department-based institutes. Science Councils had been established in 1987 under Framework Autonomy. The rationale behind this system was to address the constraints imposed by bureaucratic management due to the integration of S&T agencies within the main body of the public service. As discussed in a previous chapter, prior to the introduction of framework autonomy there was a deep division between the management structure of these bodies, composed as it was mostly of civil servants, and the scientific and technical core staff. This policy shift required that science councils move progressively towards private sector funding through contract work in order to attain growth budgets over and above the baseline funding scheme. The White Paper accepted the basic rationale behind Framework Autonomy primarily on the grounds of the higher degree of managerial flexibility within the councils and of the reduced strain on government funding, due to contract R&D programmes. The two main disadvantages of the existing system were the gaps between the R&D policies of individual councils and national development priorities and the tendency to crowd out private sector R&D performers through costing practices which did not reflect overheads. The 1993 IDRC report noted that the reliance on private sector clients introduced distortions in S&T policy since only the larger corporations and some government departments could afford to commission R&D projects, thus excluding the requirements of small enterprises and the problems of historically disadvantaged groups.

The White Paper addressed these objections by proposing that science councils as well as department-based institutes should operate within a national goal framework with an increased level of coordination in order to reduce the fragmentation of research programmes. The government's commitment to Framework Autonomy was evident in White Paper's proposal that more department-based institutes should make the transition to the science council category or should become part of existing science councils. The driving force behind this argument was the need to escape the budgetary constraint under which department-based institutes were operating, thus permitting them to recruit qualified research personnel at competitive remuneration rates. The check on the possible increasing deviation of the R&D activity of these institutions from national objectives lay in their accountability to an institutional review process wherein the role of specifying the criteria would be the responsibility of DACST and the line department governing the particular institute. It was, however, unclear how national priorities were going to be enforced, given the planned increased dependence on private sector funding. As an aid to designing the guidelines for the investment of public S&T funds, DACST initiated Research and Technology Foresight Exercises aimed at identifying "...potential technological trends and trajectories of significance to the social and economic development of South Africa" (DACST, 1993: 21). However, though the paper stated that the results of this exercise would be used to guide both public and private R&D investment, the absence of fiscal R&D incentives and of incentives emerging from related policy areas, severely restricted the ability of the state to affect private investment patterns.

The White Paper explicitly recognised the crucial role of human capital in the development process and it broke with the history of S&T planning in that human capital was defined as covering all aspects of human resource development, rather than focussing on the generation of scientists and engineers. It referred to the six human resource development objectives laid out in the National Growth and Development Strategy (1996) plan and specified the role of DACST as an advisory one in order to bring an S&T perspective into education programmes. DACST was already collaborating with the Department of Education in a programme which focussed on the establishment of curricula in science, technology, engineering and mathematics at pre-tertiary education levels and the development of the teaching capacity to deliver these programmes. The national research grant system had been refined to address the historical imbalances in research capacity across the tertiary education sector. The focus was on capacity building within historically disadvantaged institutions. The White Paper also proposed the establishment of a National Qualifications Framework which would act as the accreditation mechanism across the country, thus eliminating the tiered pre-tertiary education system, while raising qualification standards across the board.

The role allotted to DACST was an advisory one to develop curricula for pre-tertiary education levels, as well as for adult training programmes. The National Research Foundation was to act as the coordinating body for research funding in the tertiary education sector and was to operate through four agency divisions - natural sciences and engineering, social sciences and humanities, health sciences, agricultural and environmental sciences. The foundation would also administer the National Facilities for Research.

The heritage of apartheid *vis-à-vis* the country's national system of innovation can therefore be characterised by two main features which, though distinct, are inter-related. The foremost one was obviously that of a system of innovation geared towards the needs of the country's privileged white minority and the maintenance of the white supremacist agenda. The other characteristic, to a large extent derivative of the first one, was the absence of a coherent national plan on the development of the country's system of innovation in line with the development requisites of a democratic political economy. While the 1996 White Paper was formulated within the context of an entirely different goal set, its proposals on institutional reform failed to address the fragmentation of the S&T planning framework and the definition of the perimeters of S&T planning were therefore not altered substantially. What occurred was rather a refinement of the inherited structure within a democratic context where the whole of the population was to be considered as the beneficiary of state planning. Therefore the extent to which the 1996 White Paper constituted a break in the country's Science and Technology planning history became the resultant of the tension between the impact of a fundamentally redefined national goal set and the adherence to the inherited programme of economic liberalisation and privatisation. Within the confines of its terms of reference the White Paper provided a sound plan for the overhaul of the institutional basis for the development of a sound S&T base. It was the failure in the implementation of some crucial ancillary policies that lay within the jurisdiction of other ministries and departments that prevented the S&T policy from extending to an innovation policy that would radically alter the national system of innovation.

The reactive move to an unmitigated embracing of the pre-eminence of market forces had resulted from the disillusion with the failure of a planned economy to deliver an evidently sustainable apartheid economy. It amounted to an abnegation of the state's role to redefine structure. This loss of faith on the part of the apartheid regime marked the last stage of an embattled polity and the dawn of a new era. With the emergence of democracy, the new government was put under severe pressure by the overtly expressed fear by local and international capital[12] of state intervention which in any way constrained the market forces. It was this misplaced fear of the volatility of capital which, combined with an understandable dearth of decision making capacity, caused public policy to swing towards the libertarian camp in a manner which the late apartheid regime had come to hold as its salvation. A class-based historiography would see this policy shift, or a reinforcement of the previous policy path, as the ultimate victory of capital which, now legitimated under a democratic label, had managed to engineer a freedom of operation which it had for so long sought in vain.

The review of GEAR in 2001 was followed by a radical administrative reorganisation of S&T planning. In 2002, DACST was split into two departments with the Department of Science and Technology (DST) as the new, prominent agency for S&T planning. The new policy statement on S&T policy (DST, 2002) allocated a significantly expanded coordinating role over various aspects of R&D for the new department. The new minister in charge of DST was also from an opposition party, but this time it was from the Azanian People's Organisation (AZAPO), the main descendant of the Black Consciousness Movement from which a significant portion of the top rank of the ANC had come and which was consequently held in high regard by the ruling party. The sheer size of the

12 It is ironic that, in spite of an extremely market friendly policy environment, foreign direct investment data shows net outflows, except for specific acquisitions, over the past ten years, with FDI for 2006 at an unprecedented negative of R47.3 billion, as the following quotation shows:

> "Foreign Direct Investment (FDI) has not been a major part of our foreign capital inflows not including for some exceptional years like 1997 (Telkom privatisation), 2001 (De Beers restructuring) and 2005 (purchases of several major South African companies, including Absa). This calculation shows the net and the negative trend in 2005 - 2006 that is due to a number of South African companies investing abroad. Most of our foreign investment is received as purchases of shares in South African companies on various stock exchanges and not reflected as FDI. South Africa is the third highest recipient of equity (share) portfolio investment among developing countries behind China and India in 2005 and China and Brazil in 2006, but FDI needs to be strengthened too." (SA Development Indicators 2007, 7).

South Africa has consistently achieved low rankings in the World competitiveness surveys. The main reasons behind this are the low availability human resources, in terms of skills, poor education, work culture, crime and skilled emigration. The addressing of most of these factors lies almost entirely within the domain of public policy.

staff complement of the department has grown considerably since then. Several R&D functions which were located in other ministries and departments have been located within the DST. The most notable was the transfer of the CSIR from the Department of Trade and Industry to the DST in 2005. However, the planning context of the DST is still largely limited to science and technology planning. Thus, for example, human resource development is largely the domain of the Department of Education (DoE) although the influence of the DST over the funding of higher education has grown considerably over the past few years. The two departments now collaborate to a degree that marks a significant sea change in human resource development policy. However, the influence of DST over primary and secondary education policy formulation and implementation is still limited. Overall, the role of the DST is still defined by the generally neutral intervention stance of the supply side economic policy environment that still dominates development planning in South Africa. In this role it acts as a facilitator for the mobilisation of R&D resources but was, until recently, mostly prevented from designing and implementing strategic intervention initiatives and "picking winners". Again, this penumbra policy formulation space following the formation of DST reflected the still hesitant and fragmented state of economic planning following the implicit loss of faith in GEAR.

The National Research and Development Strategy (NRDS) document (DST, 2002) identified some key systemic fault lines within the national system of innovation that needed to be addressed. It is worth quoting the text in full:

> $ The termination of key technology missions (such as military dominance in the subcontinent and energy self-sufficiency) by the previous government between 1990 and 1994. This resulted in a drop in national R&D spending from 1,1% in 1990 to 0,7% of Gross Domestic Product (GDP) in 1994.[13] **This reduction happened at a time when the National System of Innovation needed to expand to cope with the needs of 40 million people as opposed to a mere 5 - 6 million.**
>
> $ Strategic considerations, from human, economic and security perspectives. Adequate responses to new diseases and to old forms of new diseases, whether these diseases affect humans or animals, need to be informed by local research programmes. From a security perspective, even being a smart buyer of rapidly

13 However, the ratio of gross expenditure on R&D relative to the GDP has been rising steadily since 1997/1998 and is comparable to that of Poland, Portugal and Hungary (Kahn and Blankley, 2006).

> developing technology rather than a developer requires a critical mass of local scientists doing research in relevant areas. The S&T capacity of the country is running as fast as it can, but is still losing ground.
>
> $ Human Resources. Our human resources for science and technology are not being adequately renewed. An overwhelmingly white, male and aging scientific population is not being replaced by younger groupings more representative of our demographics.
>
> $ A complex set of factors driven largely by globalisation has resulted in reduced levels of both investment and performance by the South African private sector in R&D. This could result in a loss of local control of the developing knowledge base that underpins the success of our most competitive companies.
>
> $ Inadequate intellectual property legislation and infrastructure. New developments in biotechnology have increased our vulnerability with respect to the exploitation of our biodiversity, and inventions and innovations from publicly financed research is not effectively protected and managed.
>
> $ Fragmented governance structures. Although research institutions have been reviewed and key performance indicators put in place, the roles of different departments in governance and in setting output targets for government research institutions is [sic] not clear or synergistic. From a budget perspective there is no holistic view of science and technology spending by government. (DST, 2002: 15-16)

This assessment indicates a significant shift in public thinking about the shape and direction of the system of science and technology that had been inherited from apartheid. The creation of the DST in 2002 was due to a re-thinking of the role of innovation in South Africa's development process. It marked an unprecedented shift in national S&T policy which has had a significant effect on S&T indicators since the beginning of the (21st) century. The R&D surveys have been resumed since the early 2000s and, along with a number of independent surveys, have restored a data base that is essential to planning after a gap of some years (Kahn, 2008). Since 2003 the DST has dramatically increased its funding for the biotechnology sectors, marking a shift to strategic "picking winners" intervention. Enhanced tax incentives for R&D expenditure were introduced in 2006. Overall, S&T policy has now acquired a sustained focus and direction that are supported by an increased budget and human resource complement. Its coordination role was redefined and enhanced since 2002 (Kahn, 2008).

The most recent statement on the shape and direction of S&T policy was articulated in the DST's ten year plan (DST, 2007). This plan is an explicit commitment to move S&T planning more specifically towards innovation and to shift the base of the economy from natural resources to the knowledge economy. It identifies an endemic "innovation chasm" in the national system of innovation, i.e. a failure of R&D, especially state-sponsored R&D, to be translated into outcomes which have a significant economic return. It identifies the main constraints on the path to the knowledge-based system of innovation as human capital development, low R&D levels and intensities, a poor knowledge infrastructure and sub-optimal levels of ancillary functions, such as finance, that impede the flow from R&D to innovation. The plan has also set up priority areas for R&D support on the basis of the contribution of these areas to the transformation and development of the national system of innovation.[14] The identification of these areas represents a shift away from neutral intervention towards the type of strategic role of what Kahn (2008: 153) calls "the mission-oriented push of the three decades of the apartheid wars in Angola, Mozambique and the then Rhodesia". Within the context of the post-apartheid innovation system this strategic intervention should, if sustained, provide the required quantum leap in the transformation of the system of science and technology that was impossible to achieve under apartheid. This shift to "picking winners" also takes cognisance of the core elements of successful state-supported R&D projects. These are listed as the need to achieve critical R&D mass (lumpiness of R&D capital), a systems approach with due regard for the required complementarities with skills development, physical capital investment and services, and the long term nature of such R&D programmes which takes into account the depreciation of knowledge.

The system of science and technology has altered dramatically since 1996. The White Paper had indeed placed S&T policy within the national system of innovation context but the neoliberal approach to economic planning at the time severely restricted the implementation of an innovation policy as distinct from a science and technology policy. The crisis of faith in the neoliberal agenda around the turn of the century brought about a focus on several core aspects of the national system of innovation. However, innovation policy, as it is currently being formulated, still mostly focuses on technological innovation with institutions that do not directly affect science and technology being treated

14 These priority areas are biotechnology and bio-industry, space science and technology, energy security, global climate change science, and human and social dynamics (the role of science in stimulating growth and development).

at best as "enablers" rather than sources of innovation in their own right. Thus, the ability to affect the innovation system as a whole still largely lies outside the ambit of the DST and lacklustre achievements on several other fronts are still proving to be major obstacles in the required reform of the system.

There is little doubt that the post-apartheid government has as yet failed to engineer the overall structural transformation of the economy that was required to foster the type of national innovation system that is required for sustainable development. There may indeed be spurts of moderately high growth, as have been seen since 2002 but the fundamentals of the economy have been wrongly identified. In consequence, the single-minded drive for immediate macroeconomic stability, in terms of inflation, fiscal caution and a manageable public debt, and a relatively stable export-promoting exchange rate has displaced the concern with altering the core elements of the inherently unstable innovation system inherited from apartheid. The failure to read history correctly and to distinguish between fashionable, ephemeral economic paradigms and those which were both theoretically sound and empirically validated has seriously flawed the development agenda of the democratic economy.

It is not that the historian should have opted necessarily for the dominance of one or the other sides of the race-class debate. The contingency of the two accounts was accepted by most economic historians by the late eighties. Rather, there should have been a strong awareness at the start of the democratic era of the need to address both racism and the nature of the particular variation of capitalism that had evolved to flourish under segregation and later on under apartheid, concurrently. By focussing almost entirely on dismantling a racist polity and neglecting the long-standing effects of that polity on the fundamental structure of the South African economy, the democratic development agenda has failed to alter substantially the life prospects of the larger part of the population. In the process it has seriously compromised the emergence of a national system of innovation that is appropriate for the human capital development requirements of a democratic South Africa.

The reading of South African economic history was also flawed in regard to the role of the state *vis-à-vis* economic development paths. The shifting of the economy on to a rapid industrialisation path with an emphasis on secondary industries in the inter-war period was directly due to the state stepping in where the market had failed. The emergence of the military-industrial complex under apartheid and its stimulus to a range of high-technology industrial sectors was also a public sector demand-led transformation of the apartheid system of innovation. The fact that these initiatives occurred in a political economy that was legislatively racist was, of course, the main obstacle to the long term transformative effect of state intervention on the national system of innovation. It was this factor, as I have argued earlier, that generated the anomaly of an innovation system characterised by cutting-edge infrastructure and numerous concentrations of technological capabilities which was, at the same time, progressively anti-modern and divergent from the global trend of economic successes built on the basis of broad based human capital platforms. Even before apartheid and the retreat from modernity, the race issue had caused the development of formal S&T institutions, such as the CSIR to lag behind those of comparable commonwealth countries such as Canada, Australia and India. This was the main structural flaw that should have been addressed in all its complexity in order to alter the development path of the post-apartheid economy. It was this priority that should have determined the over-riding policy imperative within which other macroeconomic policies would have been set. The remedy for the flawed system of innovation that had been shaped by the extensive intervention of the apartheid state should not have been a general renouncement of state intervention in the market, but rather a re-shaping of the form of intervention in order to effect the required structural change of the economy.

Human capital, growth and development

In today's global economy the old distinction between growth and development has lost most of its relevance. Growth used to be applied to mature industrialised economies, while development theory was relegated to the challenges faced by the "non-industrialised" or "industrialising" nations. In the era of unprecedented technological change, global mobility of resources and globally integrated financial markets all economies are now in a process of often radical structural transformation and hence development. This renders the task faced by countries that used to be classified as "third world" even more onerous since the development goal is nowadays a rapidly shifting one, receding as we move towards it, with critical threshold levels ever more difficult to cross.

Through the modern reassessment of the determinants of growth and development we are now fully aware that most development policy initiatives are strongly dependent on the availability of a rich and rapidly growing base of skills and knowledge embedded in the population as a whole. This is now seen as the prime prerequisite for sustainable development. In the case of South Africa, given its specific history, we can therefore identify human capital as the major bottleneck in the path towards sustainable growth. As indicated in the NRDS document, at the higher end of the education there are indications that the age group of active researchers has been steadily drifting upwards since 1990. The number of full-time equivalent researchers stayed roughly constant between 1992 and 2004, with those employed in the private sector increasing while those in higher education institutions and in government employment dropping in that period.[15] The conditions in the feeder sector for universities, i.e. schools, make the prospects for academia even more bleak. Over the period 2000 and 2002, South Africa ranked the lowest out of forty countries that were surveyed on the knowledge of mathematics and science among Grade 8 students. South African Grade 4 students ranked the lowest in numeracy in a survey of African countries (Perry and Arends, 2003 and reported in Kraak, 2004). The matriculation pass rate has been dropping since 2003, as has the pass rate in Higher Grade mathematics. This has broader implications for the technological capabilities stock of the population and the absorptive capacity of the general labour force for innovation. It is a trend that has troubling long term inter-generational effects on the potential of the national system of innovation to evolve out of the apartheid mould.

Moreover, certain broad indicators of the context for the development of human capital in South Africa indicate a worrying degree of deterioration or at best a stagnation of human capital development over the past few years. Overall life expectancy dropped from 54.6 years in 2001 to 50 years in 2006, largely due to the HIV/AIDS pandemic (SA Development Indicators 2007, 26). While the percentage of the population living below R 3000 (at 2000 prices) dropped by almost 7% between 1993 and 2006, mainly due to increasing social transfers, South Africa still ranked low, at eight place from the bottom, out of 26 countries in terms of

---

15 Kahn (2008) shows that the largest percentage of researchers in the higher education sector is in the 45-54 age bracket, with the equivalents standing at the 25-34 age bracket in the case of business and 35-44 in the case of Science Councils. In terms of the actual research output of the higher education sector, in terms of scientific publications, the data (quoted in Kraak, 2004) show that there is indeed an aging population of researchers, with the percentage of publications of academics who are fifty and upwards increasing from 20% in 1990 to 47% in 2000. The explanation for this may be found in the changing conditions of academic work where functions other than research are taking priority in an academic sector where shrinking subsidies linked to throughput rates for students are rapidly shrinking the academic space of the average academic.

income inequality for the year 2003 (UNDP 2005). In fact, income inequality as indicated by the Gini coefficient has deteriorated progressively since then (SA Development Indicators 2007, 21)[16]. The Human Development Index has dropped between 1990 and 2003 (UNDP, 2005). The official effective unemployment rate reported for March 2007 stood at slightly above 37% of the economically active population. By any measure this level of unemployment is much too high and official statistics show little signs of its alleviation.

Development policy should seek to identify critical bottlenecks at various stages of development and seek measures to ease them. In the case of post-apartheid South Africa we can then conclude that, up to a certain stage of development, policy should be "bottom-up" in the sense that the strengthening of the resource base of the population would provide the motive force for the right growth process. A "trickle-down" approach to policy may become feasible at later stages in the development process. The term *measure* is here used in both of its two main meanings - as an indicator of levels of achievement and as the means towards achievement. This is in itself an innovation in the analysis of the growth and development process for policy purposes. In particular, the focus on the family unit, however that may be defined, as a diagnostic tool derives specifically from the system of innovation approach to the growth and development problem. This approach places human capital formation, in its various dimensions, at the centre of the development process and it is within this context that the concept of the family is placed at the core of the economy.

There are three related propositions on human capital formation that are relevant to this discussion. The first two propose human capital development as a core element in the engine of growth. In the first case human capital is seen as the main input in the evolution of the national system of innovation. Given the increasing importance of skills and knowledge in the global economy, human capital is perhaps the main driver of economic growth and development. Secondly, given that human capital formation requires an increase in the effective demand of individuals and families, this process can be a stimulus of the growth of local demand with its consequent incentives for the process of industrialisation. The constrained local demand under apartheid,

---

16 It is interesting to note that while the measure of income inequality has decreased over the period, the one for within racial classifications has increased (SA Development Indicators 2007, 21). This may be interpreted as a belated argument for the progressive emergence of class, rather than race as the defining parameter of inequality in the post-apartheid South Africa.

combined with an often incomprehensible tariff structure placed severe constraints on the effects of the import-substitution industrial policy of apartheid. It has consequently severely handicapped the shift to export oriented industrial policy since the 1990s. In the case of the pre-democracy South Africa, given this local demand constraint, List's infant industry argument would have probably only been applicable to a few sectors at the heart of the military-industrial complex, but certainly not to the broader economy. The same systemic flaw was evident internally in the case of the bantustans and homelands where the dismantling of the subsidy schemes in the 1990s rapidly de-industrialised the artificial local economies that had been established by apartheid in the vain pursuit of a credible model of separate development. Even in the era of globalisation and the rapid erosion of tariff barriers, there is still ample scope for the deployment of an increasing local demand base as a major strategic tool for industrial development. The combination of the enduring skills constraint and the limited internal demand severely limits the success potential for South Africa's system of innovation. A sustained and integrated human capital development programme would address both constraints simultaneously. Finally human capital, encompassing as it does most of the factors that make up the quality of life and the well being of the population, may be used as a composite indicator of the success of the development process. In this respect the same measure may be used to assess the implementation of policy and the results of policy.

It is now commonly accepted that the competitive advantage of nations is no longer determined so much by natural resources as by knowledge. Today we talk about the "knowledge economy" to emphasise the clear fact that value is added to natural resources only through the investment in human capital. However, knowledge never stands still and the "learning economy" has replaced the "knowledge economy" (see Archibugi and Lundvall, 2002) in the economists' lexicon to emphasise the historically unprecedented rate at which knowledge is becoming obsolete. All economies now have to innovate faster to retain their place in the global market. The days of the lifelong job and even of the lifelong career are long gone and workers are faced with the necessity of lifelong learning, re-skilling and upgrading in order to survive in the modern labour market and for the economy to thrive in the global market. It is this factor that has fundamentally altered development planning. As long as the knowledge base of industry was relatively stable and constant, the focus on human capital formation was less pronounced. The skills base that was required for a thriving economy was relatively constant and only changed gradually over the long term. The focus was rather on physical capital investment.

As the various radical techno-economic revolutions took off at rapidly decreasing intervals in the second half of the twentieth century, the existing skill bases also started becoming obsolete at an accelerated rate. It was soon understood that economies needed a more rapid rate of investment in human capital not only at the upper end to develop new technology but also across the labour force in order to absorb it.

Consequently for some time now the focus of development economics has shifted to the generation of knowledge and skills on the back of human capital development as the core determinant of the development and growth process. The skills and knowledge base of an economy shape its technological capabilities, i.e. its propensity to develop, adapt and adopt innovations. Technological capabilities are not generated in a vacuum. They grow, and are grown, within an institutional network that gives rise to the concept of innovation systems. Given that the informal institutional component is crucial to the development of technological capabilities, and that innovation systems become specific and native, located in time and space, technological capabilities have to be home grown to be successful. Thus we can safely say that the burden, and hence the economic costs, of the development of technological capabilities through human capital development has never been higher. The question then arises as to whom, which agent, should bear these costs. This is related to, but distinct from, the question of the location of human capital development. The word "capital" is applied to what is otherwise known as "human resources" in order to identify this factor, arguably the most crucial and the source of all productive resources, as an asset that can be increased and enriched through investment, but also one that can depreciate and become obsolete. However, unlike other productive resources the enrichment of human capital is also the goal of development since it can stand as a proxy for rising standards of living and the quality of life.

The development of human capital

The precise definition of human capital is an elusive one. It can be defined as knowledge embedded in human beings and the ability to apply that knowledge to the production of goods and services. Knowledge in turn is classified as codified knowledge and tacit knowledge. The former type can be made specific, in writing, blueprints, plans, etc., and can therefore easily be transferred. Tacit knowledge on the other hand is ephemeral and cannot be made explicit. It is developed primarily through specific cultural practices of problem solving. Its development is complex and long-term and it is specifically this aspect of human capital development that requires it to be seen as a costly long-term investment process. It is costly because it requires a large diversity of inputs whose supply must be guaranteed and secure over time. It is a long-term process because the modern knowledge-based economy requires a broad base of human capital of a magnitude and a diversity that is historically unprecedented. The history of successful development indicates that state participation in human capital development is critical to the social internalisation of the returns of human capital formation. There are a number of characteristics of human capital development, listed below, which strongly influence the path of that development and help determine the relevant policy implications.

- ***The value of human capital*** - Human capital is both a private and a public good. It provides returns for the individual or a group of individuals who own it. It can be bought or hired and provide a return for its employer. However it is also essentially a public good in that its availability is crucial to the economic well-being and development prospects of the nation. In this aspect it offers returns that cannot be appropriated entirely by any single individual who owns it, buys it or rents it. As such it has two distinct and integrated stakeholders - the private and the public. In alternative economic terms it has large potential externalities, i.e. those returns that cannot be captured by the individual but can only be appropriated by society at large. We should note here that human capital formation is not necessarily conducive to public welfare. In the first place in the absence of the right opportunities for employment this type of capital can leave the country of origin. The brain and skills drain from developing to industrialised economies is endemic in a number of countries.[17] Secondly, human capital may, again in the absence of appropriate conditions, be applied to antisocial activity in the form of organised crime and widespread corruption. Finally, if the generation of human capital falls below specific thresholds it will be impossible to achieve its sustainable reproduction and development, and the returns on it will mainly be private with little or no spillovers to the economy at large.

- ***The constituents of human capital*** - One of the fundamental characteristics of human capital is its complexity. This is tied in with

17 South Africa has been experiencing a steady net skills drain since 1994 (Kraak, 2004).

the difficulty that we experience when we try to arrive at a precise definition. We can see human capital and its formation as the resultant of a convergence of various elements. Among these we can list education, health, social responsibility, secure basic needs provision, etc. In economic terms we can see human capital formation as a production process with several inputs that can be combined in different ways to produce a complex output. From within this language we can say that the productivity, or the effectiveness, of any single input is highly dependent on the nature and the availability of others. Thus, for example, the effectiveness of public spending on education, the return on Rands spent, is contingent on basic needs provision in terms of the availability of food and the access to water, housing, connectivity, medical facilities, etc. The lower the availability of these other inputs, the less able will be the return on resources allocated to education. The cultural specificity of human capital formation enters in the combinations of the inputs in their specific context. The cultural specificity of human capital formation is analogous to the technological specificity of the production function. It is this aspect that renders the tacit knowledge base particular to a specific context or, in other words, "native" and difficult to transfer.

- ***The "investment function"*** - Successful human capital development is the result of a long-term investment, ideally lasting between eighteen and twenty-two years before the "output" enters the economy as a fully fledged productive factor. As the result of an investment process, it is also subject to depreciation as the production of new knowledge renders old knowledge obsolete. As discussed above, the defining feature of the modern age is that the rate of obsolescence of knowledge is rapidly accelerating. Hence so is the rate of depreciation of human capital stocks. This factor increases the need to invest thus raising the cost and burden of human capital formation. There are two main implications of this argument that we need to consider. The first is the issue of the returns on investment. From this perspective investment choices are based on a comparison of the returns on outlays among various investment options. The premise that human capital formation now occupies pride of place in the evolution of innovation systems implies that the returns on investment on this type of capital rank among the highest. In the case of South Africa this proposition is further supported by the urgent need to reverse the long-term deleterious effects of apartheid on human capital stocks. The second implication is that the long-term nature of this investment requires a set of stability conditions that would guarantee long planning horizons. Not only would the political climate have to be stable, a condition that has only been fulfilled for a relatively short space of time in South Africa, but the stability conditions of the average family would also have to be guaranteed. From this perspective the family unit which is seen as the custodian of future generations must be guaranteed the ability to "produce" citizens equipped with the skills and knowledge required for a modern economy. This guarantee must guard the family unit from the vagaries of economic fluctuations. From this perspective a welfare system that guarantees adequate housing, health care, food and education is not only a right but also a basic requirement for the country's development.

- ***The role of the family*** - The location of human capital formation is often contingent on cultural, political and economic factors. In most cases it is the family that is the main formative context for human capital. There have of course been some notable political experiments, for example during China's "Great Leap Forward", where the state undertook a significant direct role in the raising of children. These measures have been disastrous on a number of levels, not the least of which is the human rights one, in terms of their widespread destruction of human capital bases. It is now generally accepted that the family is the proper context for the raising of children, thus becoming the most appropriate focus for human capital development. In the case of South Africa the impact of apartheid, and segregation before it, on the family unit was prolonged and devastating, with forced removals, institutionalised and widespread migrant labour, job reservation and separate education effectively degrading the country's broad-based stock of human capital. This is not a simple proposition, however. In the first place, the definition of the family is quite flexible. In most parts of the world the nuclear family is far from the norm, both for cultural and for economic reasons. In South Africa specifically the family is generally extended, often trans-generationally and increasingly impoverished of parents due to the HIV/AIDS pandemic. It is marked by an inherited and now institutionally entrenched system of migrant labour with absent men, fathers and husbands as well as the absent women, wives and mothers. In the rural areas extended families are often headed by grandparents. In urban areas the prevalence of single parent families is increasing and, against the backdrop of abject poverty, this is seriously prejudicial to human capital development. In the second place, the average family unit is currently much too vulnerable to shifting conditions in its environment to allow for long-term planning. For the average family, burdened by a low skill base, jobs are hard to find and are insecure when they are found. In the absence of adequate support systems, the loss of employment has disastrous effects on human capital formation, often interrupting or delaying education streams. Thirdly, a family structure that is typically constantly under attack by the conditions of endemic poverty is always threatened with disintegration. This factor, the impermanence of the family structure, has a highly adverse effect on the socialisation of children and on the proper internalisation of society's values. This socialisation process is the ground in which formal education takes root. It is the foundation of the human capital formation that is required for sustainable development. It is also the most vulnerable component of human capital.

- ***The role of the state*** - The factors that have been discussed above should indicate that role of the state is crucial to the human capital development process. In a way, the acceptance that the family is the best location for human capital development implies a form of privatisation, but it is the degree of privatisation that is the issue. In most countries the rights of parents over the rearing of children are severely circumscribed. Laws against child labour, mandatory education laws and laws against the sexual abuse of children are all limitations on the power of parents over children. From an economic perspective we can see the state as determining the context within which the family performs its role as the producer of human capital. The less the involvement of the state, the more costly it is for the family to perform this function and hence the less likely it is to perform it. Given the long-term nature of this particular form of investment, an "absent state" will result in human capital formation becoming entirely a private good, belonging to the privileged few. Human capital formation is a costly process, too costly for all but the wealthiest families to bear and certainly much too costly, in terms of the inability to appropriate the returns on it, to be contemplated by the business sector. However, all sections of society reap the rewards of this type of investment and it is this combination of cost that cannot be borne by any single agent and the returns that are enjoyed by all that makes the case for extensive and permanent state involvement and intervention. The responsibility for a country's human capital formation thus lies fundamentally with the state. Business enterprises normally operate within more or less given structures to maximise returns. They rarely have the ability or the motivation to alter the foundations of the structure that they operate in. On the other hand it is the business of the state to affect, through legislation, fiscal policy and other means, the structure within which the business sector operates. In the case of post-apartheid South Africa, business operates within the context of a factor market that is still very much an apartheid construct. The main characteristic of this market is a widespread scarcity of skills among the labour force and the poor institutional infrastructure necessary for human capital formation. In this regard it is the family, as the bedrock institution, that is the damaged link in the human capital formation chain.

- ***Human capital formation as a measure for increasing effective domestic demand*** - Internationally the history of the economic success stories indicates that the viable path towards successful industrialisation often depends critically on the development of internal markets. Export earnings often constitute a small portion of GDP and sound export performance is usually built on the back of the development of a sustainable and growing internal market. From this perspective, an integrated policy aimed at broad based human capital investment would cause substantial changes in the magnitude and patterns of the local demand for goods and services. Moreover, such a policy would introduce an element of permanence and stability in the internal market, thus promoting the potential for long-term investment planning horizons in a number of manufacturing and service industries. The investment, income and employment multiplier effects would be considerable, sustained and self-reinforcing. Given the commitment by the state to an ongoing investment in the family unit, the internal markets thus generated would enjoy a long term stability that, in turn provides a long term demand for skilled labour. It would also greatly enhance the demand for home grown innovation and R&D.

- ***Human capital formation as a measure of development*** - The goal of economic growth and development is a constantly sustained improvement in the material conditions of the whole of the population of a country. The achievement of this goal can be measured in a number of ways. The simplest is GDP per capita. It is however commonly agreed that this measure has to be qualified by several others, such as income and wealth distribution, measures of individual freedom and civil rights, and other indicators of the quality of life. The commonly accepted Human Development Index is a weighted composite of three components which are (a) longevity measured by life expectancy at birth, (b) educational attainment measured by the adult literacy rate and the combined gross enrolment rates at primary, secondary and tertiary levels, and (c) comfortable lives measured by a GDP Index. The ability to invest in human capital in a consistent and stable fashion may easily act as a proxy for most measures of economic well-being. In effect, the guaranteed provision of the requirements for human capital formation, as discussed above would constitute a significant increase in the real income of the average South African family. This increase would, given the preceding arguments, have to be based on an ongoing transfer of funds for the foreseeable future. Through the logic of the argument, it will take a generation before the bulk of the population would be able to bear a significant portion of the human capital investment burden. In any case the experiences of industrialised and successfully industrialising countries show that an efficient welfare system is crucial to guarantee steady human capital investment streams.

- **Policy implications** - The main elements of the arguments sketched here may be outlined in the following four points:
  - $ Human capital development is the prime mover in the process of growth and development.
  - $ The family is the location of human capital development and economic policy prior to the advent of democracy has fundamentally damaged the structural integrity of the average family.
  - $ The focus of national policy should be on the redressing of past institutionalised generalised disintegration of the family's ability to fulfil its human capital formation function.
  - $ From this argument there follows the requirement that national policy should be judged on the basis of its effects on the long-term institutional and economic integrity of the family unit.

The main policy implication of these arguments is the fusion of policy ends and means. The increasing well-being of the family unit is both a robust measure of the objective of development policy and the main mechanism towards the achievement of the objective. The acceptance of this proposition will require a fundamental re-prioritisation of the various development policy measures. It will also enable the development of an integrated policy framework in that various sectoral policies will be assessed in terms of their estimated contribution towards the establishment of a programme of human capital investment that is sound, broad-based and sustainable.

A convergence of policy

From a national system of innovation perspective, innovation, if defined to extend far beyond technological innovation, becomes the very fabric of the economy and of economic development. Economic progress and the assessment of economic policy can then be rendered in terms of the health of the national system of innovation and its appositeness to the development requirements of specific economies. Altman and Mayer (2003) point out that industrial development in South Africa has been handicapped by the dual curse of an economy which is rich in mineral resources and one which has evolved under apartheid. The development paths of minerals rich economies typically tend to bypass the progression from labour absorbing, low skilled manufacturing to a labour absorbing, skills and technology intensive manufacturing and services base. In the case of South Africa, this path was inevitable and irreversible under apartheid because of the specific bind of the apartheid polity on the economy. As Fine and Rustomjee (1996) argue, South Africa never shifted decisively from its minerals-energy complex base, with the exception of the electronics sector, which was due to military strategic considerations.

The health and vigour of the national system of innovation are nowadays considered the prime determinant of the well being, of the developmental capacity and of the competitiveness of economies. In turn, the main common component of a healthy system is a broad base of human capital which provides the economy with a broad and deep pool of technological capabilities. In other words, a highly skilled and highly educated population is nowadays the *sine qua non* of development. It is from this perspective that I believe that we can best judge the economic cost of apartheid and the manner in which the economic prospects of South Africa have been compromised by this history. Apartheid was unique due to the combination of three important aspects. It was formalised in legislation towards the end of the imperial order and of traditional colonialism and lasted far into the twentieth century. It was a thoroughly and intricately legislated racist regime which affected all aspects of human behaviour, human interaction and of the life prospects of its populations. Finally, under apartheid, the oppressed constituted the large majority by far of the population and of the workforce. The convergence of these three aspects progressively rendered the South African economy regressive and anti-modern within the second half of the twentieth century. Its logic required that the majority of the population was legislatively excluded from the provision of an education that would provide them with an equal footing *vis-à-vis* white labour. Over generations, the devastating effect of what was effectively a process of disinvestment of human capital culminated in an economy that now faces monumental developmental obstacles. It is precisely the reversal of the long process of disinvestment in human capital that should now be the one of the foremost overall priorities of economic planning.

From a systemic perspective, human capital development on the scale that is required to address the long-term structural faults of the South African economy would be simultaneously a supply-side and a demand-side approach to industrial and broader economic policy. The implications of the demand-side aspect of the policy would also address the apparent conundrum that the long-term solution of poverty requires its short term alleviation. A concerted development programme aimed at the progressive re-establishment of the family unit as the stable guaranteed incubator of human capital, with extensive state support, would mark a massive broad-based increase in local demand for a wide array of goods and services. If properly managed, the envisaged surge in local demand would far outweigh the mission oriented spending of the military-industrial complex under apartheid, in terms of the mobilisation of local production, of spillovers and of R&D. Historically, one of the major impediments to the development of an indigenous appropriate technology base has been an economies of scale constraint imposed by a relatively small internal market, which was, as we have seen, largely a heritage of apartheid. This was mainly due to the endemically low purchasing power of the majority of the population and the increasing difficulties experienced by corporations operating under the apartheid regime in accessing export markets. Consequently, in the post-apartheid era there are two corresponding factors which can contribute towards the easing of the economies of scale constraint.

The first is the drive to provide for the basic needs of the majority of the South African population. Given the huge inherited gap in the provision of basic housing, water, electricity, telecommunication facilities, education and medical services to households, the potential internal market is large and should be fundamentally guaranteed because of the political commitment to address poverty in all its aspects. The scope of developing, for example, a building technology that is appropriate to the local physical environment and to the purchasing power of low-income households is consequently also significant. In the call of tenders for such provision this type of technological requirement can be included as a qualifying criterion. In this regard we should note that the development of most of the high tech industries in South Africa (iron and steel industries, energy, telecommunications and electronics, and armaments) was stimulated by a guaranteed local market driven by the exigencies of apartheid. The constraints on their development were, in turn, largely due to the broader internal and external market constraints which were the result of apartheid policies.

The second, linked, factor is the consideration of a regional sub-Saharan market in the investment planning framework used by both the private and the public sectors. Now that South Africa has become a legitimate economic partner in the region, the possibilities for trade and investment have increased dramatically. Regional infrastructural projects on transport, communications and energy carry a significant implication for the development of technology appropriate to the region. In this case the knowledge accumulated in the local provision for basic needs can, insofar as the local requirements for the supply of such needs is mirrored in other countries in the region, expand the potential market for local innovations considerably, with the consequent implications to economies of scale in R&D.

The crucial importance of human capital development for overall economic development is now fully accepted. However, the policy approach to this factor is still highly fragmented with several of its components being subject to often contradictory policy directions. One possible way out of the current policy confusion is to place human capital, in its entirety, at the top of the development planning agenda and firmly within the context of an innovation system planning framework. It is only within this framework that the various formative elements of human capital and the diverse determinants of these constituents can be brought together in a coherent overarching policy programme. The system of innovation concept would then become the organising framework of development planning. That would mark the required decisive rupture with the apartheid system of innovation.

As may be seen through this brief outline of the development path of the post-apartheid system of innovation, there is a rising wave of disquiet and disenchantment with the original neoliberal development programme.

A number of initiatives have been launched on several policy fronts that clearly indicate a new commitment by the state to intervene directly where the market has failed to alter significantly the apartheid economic heritage. These initiatives are still fragmented, however, and stand a poor chance of achieving the desired effect on the quality of life and the life chances of the larger population as long as they are fragmented.

Here I return to the question posed at the beginning of this chapter concerning the tension between ruptures and continuities between the apartheid and the post-apartheid systems of innovation. This question is the central concern of this study since the related assessment determines the policy direction, and hence the prospects for the South African economy. The answer to this question depends critically on the definition of the system of innovation, specifically with respect to the concept of innovation that is adopted.

If innovation is regarded as technological innovation, then the system would refer to those institutions that affect, directly and indirectly, the level and patterns of the generation, adaptation and absorption of technology. Those institutional changes which are not directly related to science and technology, but which define its setting, will then be viewed largely as contextual determinants but not as innovations in their own right. In this case we may talk more of a system of science and technology and the assessment of the shift from the apartheid to the post-apartheid systems would decisively conclude that there was indeed a fundamental rupture. The nature and role of S&T planning shifted fundamentally with the publication of the 1996 White Paper. It was the first time since the end of the First World War that an integrated S&T policy was placed on the national planning agenda. The evolution of S&T policy and the growing prominence of the DST since then is a vindication of the merit of the original vision as the compartmentalisation of S&T within the overall economic planning framework has been rapidly eroded. In the same vein, the rising ratio of R&D expenditure to GDP since 1998 (RSA, 2007) would also be seen as an indicator of the development of the South African system of innovation within the narrow definition. In this case the relevant human capital indicator that would be considered would relate directly to education, and more specifically to the top end of the spectrum of education, especially with regard to scientists and engineers. The performance of the "contextual determinants" of the development of science and technology would then be seen as enhancing or retarding the evolution of the national system of innovation. From a science and technology perspective the post-apartheid system of innovation has performed well. After the initial sharp drop in the ratio of R&D

expenditure to the GDP, largely due to the fall in military related R&D, this indicator has risen consistently since 1997/98 to reach 0.95% by 2006/07. South Africa compares well with Spain and with other emerging economies such as Argentina, India,, Hungary and Brazil (RSA, 2008). Most of the indicators provided in South Africa's first innovation survey, listed in Appendix C below, place the South African system of Science and Technology squarely within the representative EU economy. From the perspective of the narrow definition of systems of innovation South Africa is doing well. It has managed to effect the required structural transformation in the science and technology sector in shifting the base away from its linkages to the military-industrial-complex to a growing private sector entrenchment. The one area where South Africa lags behind the EU average is that of public funding support for R&D, but again this may be seen as testimony of the success of the structural transformation that commenced in 1996.

This particular depiction of the national system of innovation is, however, disturbing on two related counts. In the first place, this depiction seems to be detached from the set of indicators that reflect the quality of life of South Africans, which can also be used as indicators of the development capacity of the economy, following the human capital argument. The implication of this detachment is twofold. On the one hand it indicates a worrying causal decoupling of the system of science and technology from the expected effects of a successful development path. On the other hand it is emblematic of a development path where the fundamentals of the development capacity of the nation, in terms of long term, broad based human capital development is not significantly affected by the performance of the private sector. In this case the prospective development path of the South African economy would be that of an enclave, export-oriented, and possibly successful, private sector base against a third world economy backdrop. The implications for such indicators as income distribution and poverty levels, while mitigated by social grant transfers, would be worrying. This brings in the second related aspect of this type of development. This is the disturbing structural similarity between the apartheid and the post-apartheid systems of innovation. While structural transformation within the science and technology sector has indeed occurred, due to a combination of a sound S&T planning framework and the effects of the legitimisation of the private sector, following apartheid, the relationship between this sector and the general economy has remained to a large extent unchanged. This therefore further strengthens the argument for the essential continuity in the evolution of the system of innovation from apartheid to democracy.

This attests to the failure of a fragmented approach of innovation policy in the post-apartheid period to alter the foundations of the inherited system of innovation. Precisely because of the legitimisation of the South African economy, this particular development path will tend to be reinforced by its delimited successes.

If, on the other hand, those aspects which are classified as "contextual determinants" within the narrow definition of the system of innovation are brought into the definition of innovation, now expanded to cover all institutional change, applicable to both formal and informal institutions, the concept of the national system of innovation would extend to cover all aspects of the political economy. In this case the concept would provide the basis for an alternative general approach to the analysis of economic change. From this perspective it is difficult to see clear signs of a decisive rupture in the transition from the apartheid to the post-apartheid system of innovation. The core argument for this alternative assessment lies in the identification of the main lasting effect of the apartheid innovation system as the human capital constraint. Here we can see few signs that this factor has been significantly addressed since the end of apartheid. The original cause of this failure of policy was the choice of a neoliberal economic plan, specifically as the vehicle for transformation. The continuation of this failure is currently due to an enduring fragmentation of policy, with the several diverse aspects of this complex phenomenon being addressed by a variety of largely uncoordinated agencies of the state. This lack of coordination is itself due to a continuing adherence to economic orthodoxy which fundamentally separates the understanding of the economy from that of social and political dynamics. It is this separation that mistakenly defines the macroeconomic fundamentals in terms of the standard elements of fiscal and monetary stability. This restricted definition and the consequent failure to excavate to the deeper layers of the bedrock of the political economic system, will continue to restrict the ability to alter the evolutionary course of the South African system of innovation.

ENDNOTE

Occasionally, when writing a contemporary history, there is a chance that history may overtake the author and there is a distinct possibility that this may have happened in the case of this book. One of the main concerns of this work has been the identification of continuities and ruptures in the history of the South African economy, as rendered through the language of innovation theory. Until recently the transition from apartheid to the post-apartheid economy was the last significant break in the political history of South Africa around which the arguments regarding the possibilities of continuity or rupture of the national system of innovation could be built. There is now a new break in the country's political history that, while much less significant than that of 1994 in purely political terms, provides the possibility for the re-direction of the evolution of the national system of innovation.

The origins of a possible rupture in the evolution of the South African system of innovation lie in the rift between the state and labour movements that started with the unilateral declaration of GEAR as the sole economic planning paradigm for the post-apartheid South African economy. This unequivocal stance firmly aligned the ANC with big business against COSATU and the SACP. This rift grew over time but was contained by the historical allegiance of COSATU to the ANC. Eventually that allegiance could not resist the groundswell of revolt of the aggrieved "left" against an administration that was seen to have betrayed the spirit of the alliance. The coup that effectively ended what can be legitimately termed the "Mbeki era" as far as economic planning is concerned happened within the internal structures of the ANC.

The 52nd conference of the ANC marked a dramatic shift in the power base of the ANC. The consequent, though unexpected, removal of Thabo Mbeki as the country's president, months before the scheduled 2009 general election and the early reconstitution of the cabinet have added a sense of urgency and uncertainty regarding the transition to what is effectively a new ruling party. These events obviously constitute a rupture in the post-apartheid political history. It is, however, far too early to judge whether the political change will also cause a rupture in the evolution of the national system of innovation. The emerging government is now, through planning and through unforeseen developments, significantly different from the one that had been in place at least since 1996. The new government which will coalesce with the national election in 2009 has a radically different power base from the previous one, with the ascendancy of organised labour, in conjunction with the SACP, as the emerging major political backer. Whether this political change does indeed constitute a disjuncture in the evolution of the post-apartheid system of innovation is still uncertain and if such a disjuncture does indeed happen it will take considerable time to be effected. All that we can discuss at this point in history are the conditions that can transform the forthcoming political change into a significant break from the trajectory of the national system of innovation that has been established since 1996.

One of the unintended consequences of the internal coup against the "Mbeki hegemony" within the ANC is the probable fundamental alteration of the location of the ruling party within the South African political economy. Until the end of 2007, the ANC was the ruling party of what was effectively a democratic one party state. This was due to the historic positioning of the ANC as the most prominent and best organised liberation movement that ultimately saw in the democratic era, and the absence of any viable contesting political party with the same liberation credentials. The formation of a significant break away portion of the ANC after the recall of Mbeki from his post as president will destroy the "democratic one party state" model and usher in an era of effective electoral contestation among political parties and coalitions of parties. This exposure of parties to the vicissitudes of the electoral process should introduce a more effective control mechanism over the efficient implementation of policy by the various agencies of government. The other related, but perhaps even more significant consequence is the introduction of ideological choice in the South African political system. As I have already mentioned, one of the characteristics of the ANC which engendered its hegemony was the fact that it was all inclusive of ideology. Ideological contestation occurred within the confines of this "umbrella" party, but was not within the choice set of the electorate. The division of the ANC is now largely along ideological lines, however broadly they may be articulated. The alliance that brought about the coup in 2007 is clearly placing itself to the left of the GEAR paradigm that had continued to inform economic policy even after the announced misgivings about the failure of this plan to attain stated objectives. The new ANC is now shaping up to fill the vacuum on the left, which opposition parties had failed to do effectively. The "breakaway" part of the ANC is clearly adhering to the neoliberal development programme. This externalisation of the ideological battles that had hitherto occurred internally within the party not only creates a more democratic polity; it also forces an ongoing process of examination of policy and of the underlying theoretical foundation of policy.

As I discussed in the last chapter of this book, the damaging effects of the post-apartheid management of the South African economy can be summed up in the effects on human capital, in the various ramifications of the concept. This was due to a combination of two main factors. The first was that the social and economic engineering of apartheid fundamentally altered the human capital development trajectories of the greater part of the population. Secondly, the accelerating global rate of change in the knowledge economy has led to unprecedented demands on the skills pools of countries, a demand which is now seen as the primary necessary requirement for sustainable development. The combination of these two factors required that human capital investment, in all its complexity, should have been the prime focus of post-apartheid economic planning. This in turn required a strong and comprehensive interventionist policy on the part of the state. For a variety of possible reasons which have already been discussed, the foundation economic planning paradigm articulated in GEAR relinquished the task of the restructuring of the economy to the market and in this pursuit sought to remove as many of the constraints on the activities the private sector as possible. The effect of the fallacy of a number of the core premises of GEAR on broad based human capital development has consequently been devastating and this is the basis for the argument for the continuity in the evolution of the innovation system from apartheid to democracy. Unfortunately, over time the founding doctrine informing economic planning has established structures, practices and network systems, both local and global, which tend to lock in the economy into the neoliberal paradigm. Within the context of the GEAR programme there are sufficient shortfalls, specifically in the case of public sector delivery systems that can be used as the generic scapegoat for the failure of the programme to deliver on its promised objectives. These delivery failures divert the analysis of the general failure of economic policy away from the paradigm to the implementation. As a consequence of the entrenchment of the GEAR paradigm the definitive alteration of the current evolutionary path of the national system of innovation depends on three broadly related conditions.

The first, which is the primary pre-condition for the possibility of a rupture, is the ideological shift away from the neoliberal planning paradigm. The basis for this shift has been growing with the progressive disenchantment with GEAR and its “trickle down” premise that started with the review of the effects of that plan around the turn of the century.

The most vocal and explicit refutation of the GEAR philosophy came from organised labour and from the SACP and it was this rebuttal that formed ideological basis for the coup within the ANC. This condition has therefore been fulfilled. However, policy which has been established since the birth of the democratic South Africa and one which is continuously reinforced by approval from capital and the international institutions of capital, both local and global, is not easy to dislodge. There will therefore be a strong countervailing force that will tend to dampen down reform to rhetoric and reduce it to the smoother implementation of established "social development" programmes.[1]

The second condition is the design of policies specifically aimed at the long term development of the human capital base of the South African economy. The "new" ANC has indeed put a "pro-poor" programme at the top of its planning agenda. However, specific projects to deliver on basic needs and general working conditions may not be enough on their own to generate a long term sustainable process of the broad based human capital development of a magnitude and type to shunt the evolutionary trajectory of the innovation system decisively away from its present course. The new language of reform is still grounded primarily in context of social justice, but this may not be enough for the sustainability of such reforms in the face of globalisation and intensified competition from emerging markets such as China and India. In this new harsher globalised economy, such reforms may well eventually founder on the rocks of the apparently pragmatic requirements of the internationally competitive economy. In order to prevent this potential reversal, the motivational basis for the proposed reforms must be shifted to the core of economic planning and redefined as the instruments of development, rather than solely as the objectives of development. I have argued the rationale for this proposition in the previous chapter, but its implications for policy bear further elaboration.

As I argued in the previous chapter, human capital is a complex multi-faceted concept which requires a an integrated multi-pronged programme

---

1 The *Statement of the Alliance (GEAR, SACP and COSATU) Economic Summit* (issued 19th October 2008) provides an explicit statement of the formal economic planning agenda after the 2009 elections. The statement contains a clear intention to shift to a strategic approach to trade, industrial and procurement policies, specifically with the aim of employment creation and the shifting of the competitive advantage of the South African economy away from low wage (and low skilled) labour component. The various aspects of human capital development are, however, still placed solely in the category of social rights and as the objectives of macroeconomic policy.

for its development. The central role of human capital development in the healthy evolution of national systems of innovation is now generally accepted among development economists and needs no further elaboration here. It is rather the possible constraints that may prevent the implementation of human capital development programmes of the required scale that need to be discussed here. Generally these constraints fall into two categories. The first is the fiscal constraint on the amount of tax revenue that can be transferred to families to provide the basic components of the human capital development programme on a long term guaranteed basis. In this case the counter argument should be based on the expansionary multiplier effects of programmes which are aimed at providing basic needs such as housing, energy, water, education, etc., to the majority of the population. These effects, if properly managed, should lead to the expansion of several related sectors and to innovation within those sectors. The second category concerns labour market reforms, in terms of minimum wages and working conditions. These reforms are often opposed on the basis of the relationship between the labour component of per unit cost and international competitiveness. In the case of concerns about competitiveness, the counter argument is that in the short run the proper provision of basic needs is essentially a transfer from the fiscus which eases the demands for higher wages due to the increase in the average household's real income.

This easing of the pressure on wages would be further enhanced by pricing policies which directly affect the cost of living for the average household. These would include price ceilings for quotas of agricultural produce allocated to local consumption, accompanied by the requisite subsidy structures, for locally produced energy sources, and for transport. The enforcement of competition policy which directly addresses the pervasive practice of collusion and price fixing would also act to ease the pressures on the cost of living of poor households, and again consequently the pressure on wages. In the long run the significant alteration of the foundations for international competitiveness depends on the availability of broad based human capital. This is the only factor that would decidedly shift the export profile of the economy away from the resource rich and low skilled exporter to the knowledge based exporter with all the benefits of the latter. This shift should be further reinforced by a selective targeting incentives policy which would be aimed at promoting through various measures those sectors which exhibit high contents of technological capabilities.

The third condition for the decisive alteration of the evolutionary path of the system of innovation is the addressing of the urgent need to reform the state delivery systems so as to eliminate rampant corruption, patronage and inefficiency. Corruption has always been endemic in South Africa. Apartheid structures, in their bizarre complexities, were certainly well suited to the development of elaborate sets of patronage, with the consequent implications for corruption and inefficiency. Indeed, this may have been partially recognised as a necessary price for the maintenance of apartheid. The relatively sudden change to a democratic state allowed for the possibility of a continuation, through transformation, of some of the previous patronage systems as well as providing the institutional space for the rapid development of new forms. The provincial map that was drawn up after apartheid provides a prime example of a combination of the two effects and, as a consequence has led to massive disparities in the conditions of life among the various provinces (Scerri, 2008). The sudden shift to a radically new ANC, in combination with years of accelerating public dissatisfaction with widely reported corruption and the prevalent experience of the shortfalls in the promised delivery of basic needs may open up the window to the possibility of the required cleansing reform of governance structures.

The urgent requirement to leapfrog the development process in South Africa cannot be attained by piecemeal reforms. Rather, it requires a comprehensive effort within an integrated planning framework. All of the three sides of the required reform that I have briefly outlined here have to be addressed concurrently since the failure on any one front would severely compromise the structural effects of successes on the others.

PART 3:

APPENDICES

APPENDIX A:

PATTERNS OF R&D

Source: Resources for R&D
MEC: Minerals-energy complex
R&D expenditure refers to R&D in the natural sciences
1966-1975 figures refer to applied research and development; from 1977 onwards figures refer to total R&D, including basic research.

Table 1: Share of Applied R&D by Sector (%) in Total Applied R&D

YEAR	SECTOR						
	Agriculture, Forestry and Fisheries	**Energy and Energy Sources**	**Mining**	**Total Manufacturing**	**MEC Manufacturing**	**Non-MEC Manufacturing**	**Total MEC**
1966	38	7.5	15.5	23.6	13.5	10.1	36.5
1968	31.2	4.4	23.1	23.7	10.7	13	38.2
1969	29.2	2.7	19.6	31.1	15.8	15.3	38.1
1970	26.2	2.6	17.1	33	18.8	14.2	38.5
1971	26	na	17	34	na	14	39
1973	22	na	13	28	na	14	33
1975	17	na	15	27	na	12	37
1977	15	na	15	28	na	14	36
1979	18	na	10	31	na	17	30
1981	13	na	13	38	na	19	41
1983	12	na	10	37	na	27	36
1985	na	na	na	na	na	na	na
1987	12	na	10	29	na	16	28
1991	12	na	11	29	na	18	26

na: not available

Table 2: R&D/Sales (%) by Industry: 1991

INDUSTRY	R&D/SALES
Food, beverages and tobacco	0.17
Manufacture of textiles	0.21
Wearing apparel except footwear	0.01
Leather products, including footwear	0.01
Wood and wood products, including furniture	0.26
Paper and paper products	0.07
Printing and publishing	0.02
Rubber products	0.14
Pottery, china and earthenware	0.00
Glass and glass products	0.23
Metal products, except machinery and equipment	0.36
Machinery, except electrical	0.62
Electrical machinery	2.27
Transport equipment	0.40
Jewellery and related articles	0.13
Other manufacturing industries	1.90
TOTAL NON-MEC	0.45

TOTAL NON-MEC (excluding electronics)	0.33
Fertilizers and pesticides	0.59
Synthetic resins and plastic materials	0.11
Paints, varnishes and lacquers	0.57
Medicinal and pharmaceutical preparations	0.39
Cosmetic and toilet preparations	0.17
Other chemical products	0.58
Other basic chemical products	1.60
Other plastic products	0.14
Structural clay products	0.05
Cement	0.10
Other non-metallic mineral products	0.54
Iron and steel basic industries	0.21
Non-ferrous metal basic industries	1.07
TOTAL MEC	0.49

Table 3: R&D/Sales (%) by Specific non-MEC Industries: 1991

INDUSTRY	R&D/SALES
Food, beverages and tobacco	
Food manufacturing	0.19
Beverage industries	0.13
Tobacco products	0.34
Metal and metal products	
Cutlery, hand tools and general hardware	0.03
Furniture and fixtures of metal	0.00
Structural metal products	0.26
Other metal products	0.48
Machinery, except electrical	
Engines and turbines	0.29
Agricultural machinery	0.38
Metal and woodworking machinery	2.10
Special industrial machinery	0.16
Office and accounting machinery	0.01

Other machinery, except electrical	1.06
Electrical machinery	
Electrical industrial machinery	0.97
Radio, television and communication equipment	5.66
Electrical appliances and house ware products	0.53
Other electrical apparatus	1.12
Transport equipment	
Railway equipment	0.91
Motor vehicles and parts	0.20
Other transport equipment	2.21

Table 4:Share of MEC R&D in total Manufacturing R&D, by Performer

YEAR	PERFORMER					
	Government	Tertiary education	Private business	Parastatal corporations	Independent laboratories	TOTAL
1977	50.3	42.5	39.0	99.2	2.7	50.7
1979	50.2	44.0	38.7	97.1	0.2	44.6
1981	44.6	55.0	59.0	43.1	68.5	48.8
1983	45.6	40.2	49.0	22.6	1.7	29.8
1985	51.7	44.9	33.9	47.0	1.6	39.4
1987	55.2	45.1	26.7	60.1	2.5	42.6

Table 5: Electronics R&D/Total Manufacturing R&D, by Performer

YEAR	PERFORMER					
	Government	Tertiary education	Private business	Parastatal corporations	Independent laboratories	TOTAL
1977	9.2	13.7	6.8	0.0	0.0	6.2
1979	9.2	22.8	16.0	0.0	0.0	9.8
1981	17.3	19.5	8.1	28.0	0.0	19.8
1983	8.0	21.1	12.8	36.9	0.0	23.0
1985	9.0	14.9	32.9	25.9	0.0	21.5
1987	10.8	19.0	35.1	19.7	0.0	21.0

Table 6: Change in R&D/Sales and Performer Share (1977-1987)

INDUSTRY	% CHANGE IN R&D/SALES	%PERFORMER SHARE	
		PUBLIC	PRIVATE
Food, beverages and tobacco	-0.018	38.00	62.00
Textiles	0.017	88.76	11.24
Wearing apparel, except footwear	-0.004	35.40	64.60
Leather products	-0.049	3.83	96.17
Wood and wood products	0.021	81.24	18.76
Paper and paper products	0.006	30.38	69.62
Printing and publishing	-0.044	0.40	99.60
Rubber products	0.000	21.56	78.44
Glass and glass products, etc.	0.014	53.43	46.57
Metal and metal products	0.080	51.56	48.44
Machinery, except electrical	-0.196	67.58	32.42
Electrical machinery	1.490	62.10	37.90
Transport equipment	0.140	50.09	49.91
Other manufacturing industries, except jewellery	5.038	20.89	79.11
TOTAL NON-MEC	0.124	53.42	46.58

TOTAL NON-MEC (excluding electronics)	0.048	48.86	51.13
Fertilizers and pesticides	0.066	7.22	92.78
Plastic materials	-0.159	11.22	88.78
Other basic chemical products	1.142	77.66	22.34
Medicinal and pharmaceutical preparations	-0.829	37.52	62.48
Cosmetic and toilet preparations	-0.136	6.10	93.90
Other chemical products	0.308	48.74	51.26
Other plastic products	0.052	15.70	84.30
Other non-metallic mineral products	0.543	47.09	52.91
Iron and steel basic industries	-0.272	90.05	9.95
Non-ferrous metal basic industries	-0.013	95.01	4.99
TOTAL MEC	0.100	70.10	29.90

Table 7: Change in R&D/Sales and Performer Share (1977-1987):Non-MEC

INDUSTRY	CHANGE IN R&D/SALES	PERFORMER	
		PUBLIC	PRIVATE
Food, beverages and tobacco			
Food manufacturing	-0.018	39.23	60.77
Beverages	-0.036	50.34	49.66
Tobacco products	0.041	0.29	99.71
Metal and metal products			
Structural metal products	0.072	94.58	5.42
Other metal products	0.064	39.28	60.72
Machinery, except electrical			
Agricultural machinery	-0.718	32.11	67.89
Other machinery	-0.109	71.71	28.29
Electrical machinery			
Electrical machinery, except electronic equipment	0.302	39.60	60.40
Electronic equipment	3.779	64.24	35.76
Transport equipment			

Railway equipment	0.917	81.53	18.47
Motor vehicles and parts	-0.101	31.66	68.34
Other transport equipment	2.222	78.38	21.62

Table 8: Share (%) in Total Applied R&D by Performer

Year	Government	Tertiary	Parastatal	Private	Independent
1966	65.3	2.9	4.7	24.5	0.9
1968	65.4	3.3	7.4	12.9	11
1971	62.5	3.3	7.5	24.9	0.6
1973	58.1	15.5	5.1	22.1	1.7
1975	57.3	11.3	4.8	24.2	0.7
1977	56.5	6.4	6.9	19.7	10.4
1979	51.5	8.5	9.4	20	10.4
1981	44.9	8	22.4	14.5	10

1983	30.6	7.8	37.2	15	10.2
1987	37.2	12.3	23.4	16.7	10
1991	29.3	10.8	5.1	47.4	7.1
1993	30.5	6.4	18.1	39.6	4.9

APPENDIX B

INDUSTRIAL GROUPINGS BY SIC CATEGORY

Food manufacturing (SIC 311)
Beverages (SIC 313)
Tobacco products (SIC 314)
Textiles (SIC 321)
Wearing apparel, except footwear (SIC 322)
Leather products include footwear (SIC 323; 324)
Wood and wood products include furniture (SIC 331; 332)
Paper and paper products include pulp, paperboard and containers (SIC 3411; 3412; 3419)
Printing and publishing (SIC 3420)
Fertilisers and pesticides (SIC 3512)
Plastic materials include synthetic resins, plastic materials and man-made fibres, except glass products (SIC 3513)
Other basic chemical products include petroleum and coal products (SIC: 3511,353,354)
Medicinal and pharmaceutical preparations (SIC: 3522)
Cosmetic and toilet preparations (SIC: 3523)
Other chemical products include paints, varnishes and lacquers (SIC: 3521; 3529). R&D data for the sub-sectors are only available for 1991 and hence appear separately in Table 5.2, but not in Table 6.2
Rubber products include tyres and tubes (SIC: 3551; 3559)
Other plastic products (SIC: 356)
Glass and glass products, etc. include pottery, earthen ware and china (SIC: 361; 362). R&D data for the sub-sectors are only available for 1991 and hence appear separately in Table 5.2, but not in Table 6.2
Other non-metallic mineral products (SIC: 391) include structural clay products, cement and other non-metallic mineral products (SIC: 3691; 3692; 3699). R&D data for the sub-sectors are only available for 1991 and hence appear separately in Table 5.2, but not in Table 6.2
Basic iron and steel industries (SIC: 371)

Non-ferrous metal basic industries (SIC: 372)
Structural metal products (SIC: 3813)
Other metal products include cutlery, hand tools and general hardware and furniture and fixtures of metal (SIC: 3811; 3812; 3819). R&D data for the sub-sectors are only available for 1991 and hence appear separately in Table 5.2, but not in Table 6.2
Agricultural machinery (SIC 3822)
Other machinery includes engines and turbines, metal and woodworking machinery, special industrial machinery and office and accounting machinery (SIC: 3821; 3823; 3824; 3825; 3829). R&D data for the sub-sectors are only available for 1991 and hence appear separately in Table 5.2, but not in Table 6.2
Electrical machinery includes electrical industrial machinery, electrical appliances and house ware products (SIC: 3831; 3833; 3839). R&D data for the sub-sectors are only available for 1991 and hence appear separately in Table 5.2, but not in Table 6.2
Electronic equipment includes radio, television and communication equipment (SIC: 3832)
Motor vehicles and components (SIC: 384)
Railway equipment (SIC: 3852)
Other transport equipment includes ship building and repairing and the manufacture of aircraft (SIC: 3851; 3855; /3859)
Other manufacturing industries, except jewellery, include professional, scientific, measuring and controlling equipment and photographic and optical goods (SIC 386, 3902-9)

APPENDIX C

NOTES ON R&D DATA

R&D data were first published in 1964. For this and the following year the published data referred to R&D expenditure by government (government departments, provincial administrations and state research institutions such as the CSIR) and tertiary education institutions. From 1996 onwards data applied research and development expenditure were published for all performers. Over the period 1968 to 1971 the publication "Resources for R&D" was issued annually. Since then it has come out every alternate year. Since 1977 basic research was included in R&D expenditure figures. Until 1989 the survey on R&D in the natural sciences and the final compilation of the report was the responsibility of the CSIR. This function was taken over by the FRD for the year 1991 but after that the survey and compilation was done by private consultants.

The period that is considered extensively in this book covers the years 1977 to 1987 since there were significant discontinuities between this period and the one preceding it and the following years. As already mentioned, prior to 1977 basic research was excluded. After 1987 the change in science and technology policy and the extensive institutional change that followed significantly altered the classification of performers that has been used in this study. The wave of privatisation of parastatal corporations started around this time and as discussed in this chapter the CSIR became more of a market performer than a government institutions. Hence the demarcation lines between public and private sector performers were blurred. Moreover, the demise of apartheid altered the context within with data reported in the 1991 and 1993 surveys were placed.

The *National Survey of Research and Experimental Development (R&D)*, based on the Frascati Manual methodology re-established the official R&D data base for South Africa from 2001/2002 onward on an annual basis. In 2005 the *South African National Innovation Survey*, covering the period 2002-2004 became the first official innovation survey in South Africa. Its methodology was based on that of the Eurostat Community Innovation Survey (CIS4). The results of this survey placed the innovation activity of the South African private sector within the same category as Sweden, the UK, Portugal, Denmark, Ireland and Austria, and above the EU average. The main indicators supporting these results were the percentage of enterprises engaged in innovation activity, the percentage of innovative enterprises which introduced new or improved products to the market, the percentage of turnover generated by the sale of products which were an innovation in their specific market, and R%D expenditure as a percentage of turnover. In terms of public funding for innovation, South Africa fell below the EU average. In terms of the origins of innovations, South Africa exhibits the same profile as the EU average, with most of the innovations developed in South Africa.

BIBLIOGRAPHY

Adam, H. (ed.) 1971a. *South Africa: Sociological Perspectives.* (London: Oxford University Press).

—. 1971b. "The South African Power Elite: A Survey of Ideological Commitment", in Adam (1971a).

—. 1972. *Modernizing Racial Domination: The Dynamics of South African Politics.* (USA: University of California Press).

Adelzadeh, A. 1996. "From the RDP to GEAR: The Gradual Embracing of Neoliberalism in Economic Policy", *Transformation*, 31: 66-95.

Altman, M. 2006. "Low wage work in South Africa." *Paper presented to IZA/World Bank Conference on Employment & Development Berlin, Germany, 25 - 27 May 2006.* (SA: HSRC Press).

Altman, M. and Mayer, M. 2003. "Overview of Industrial Policy.", in Kraak and Perold (eds.).

Anderson, B. 1983. *Imagined Communities.* (USA: Verso).

Ansell-Pearson, K., Parry, B. and Squires, J. (eds.) 1997. *Cultural Readings of Imperialism: Edward Said and the Gravity of History.* (London: Lawrence & Wishart).

Archibugi, D. and Lundvall, B-Å. (eds.) 2002. *The Globalizing Learning Economy.* (UK: Oxford University Press).

Arrow, K. 1962. "Economic Welfare and the Allocation of Resources for Inventions", in *The Rate and Direction of Inventive Activity*, ed. R. Nelson. Princeton University Press.

Asheim, B. and Gertler, M.S. 2006. "The Geography of Innovation: Regional Innovation Systems.", in Fagerberg et al (eds.).

Ballinger, M. 1969. *From Union to Apartheid: A Trek into Isolation.* (New York: Praeger Publishers).

Balzat, M. And Hanusch, H. 2003. "Recent Trends in the Research on National Innovation Systems". *Volkswirtschlaftliche Diskussionsreihe*, 254: 2-18. (Germany: University of Augsburg).

Basson, N. 1996. *Passage to Progress: The CSIR's Journey of Change 1945-1995.* (Johannesburg: Johnatan Ball Publishers).

Bauman, T. 1995. *An Industrial Strategy for the Household Electrical Durables Sector.* (Cape Town: UCT Press).

Bauman, Z. 1998. *Globalization: The Human Consequences.* (UK: Polity Press).

Becker, G.S. 1993. "Nobel Lecture: The Economic Way of Looking at Behaviour." *Journal of Political Economy,* 101: 385-409.

Beilhartz, P., Robinson, G. and Rundell, J. 1992. *Between Totalitarianism and Postmodernity.* (USA.: MIT Press).

Bell, T. 1986. "The Role of Regional Policy in South Africa.", *Journal of Southern African Studies*, 12: 276-292.

Bernstein, J.I. 1988. "Costs of Production, Intra- and Inter-Industry R&D Spillovers: Canadian Evidence", *Canadian Journal of Economics*, 21: 324-347.

—. 1989. "The Structure of Canadian Inter-Industry R&D Spillovers, and the Rates of Return to R&D", *The Journal of Industrial Economics*, 37: 315-328.

Bernstein, J.I. and Nadiri, M.I. 1988. "Interindustry R&D Spillovers, Rates of Return, and Production in High-tech Industries", *American Economic Review (Papers and Proceedings)*, 78: 429-439.

Bernstein, J.I. 1989. "Research and Development and Intra-industry Spillovers: An Empirical Application of Dynamic Duality", *Review of Economic Studies*, 56: 249-269.

Blankley, W., Scerri, M., Molotja, N. and Saloojee, I. (eds). 2006 *Measuring Innovation in OECD and non-OECD Countries.,* (South Africa: HSRC).

Board of Trade and Industry (BTI). 1986. *Investigation into the South African Electronics Industry.* (Pretoria: Report No. 2455).

Boshoff, N. and Mouton, J. 2003. "Science Policy Indicators." in Kraak and Perold (eds.).

Brown, A.C. (ed.) 1977. *A History of Scientific Endeavour in South Africa.* (South Africa: The Rustica Press).

Buckland, P. 1991. "Technism and de Lange: Reflections on the Process of the HSRC Investigation.", in Kallaway, P. (Ed.), op. cit.

Buhlungu, S., Daniel, J., Southhall, R. and Lutchman, J. (eds.) 2006. *State of the Nation: South Africa 2005-2006.* (South Africa: HSRC Press).

Campbell, G. (ed.). 2003. *The Indian Ocean Rim: Southern Africa and Regional Co-operation.,* (Routledge-Curzon: London & New York):123-42.

Chataway, J. 1990a. "The South African Electronics Industry." in Hanlon (ed.), op cit.

—. 1990b. "The South African Motor Industry.", in Hanlon (ed.), op cit.

Chesnais, F. 1988. "Multinational Enterprises and the International Diffusion of Technology.", in Dosi et al. (eds.), op. cit.

Christie, P. and Collins, C. 1991. "Bantu Education: Apartheid Ideology and Labour Reproduction.", in Kallaway, P. (ed.), op. cit.

Coase, R.H. 1937. "The Nature of the Firm.", *Economica*, 4:386-405.

Cohen, W.M. and Levin, R.C. 1989. "Empirical Studies of Innovation and Market Structure.", in Schmalensee and Willig (eds.), op. cit.

Cohen, W.M. and Levinthal, D.A. 1989. "Innovation and Learning: The Two Faces of R&D.", *Economic Journal*, 99: 569-596.

Cooke, P., Uranga, M.G. and Etxebarria, G. 1997. "Regional Innovation Systems: Institutional and Organisational Dimensions.", *Research Policy*, 26: 475-491.

Conrad, T. 1990. "High-Tech Sanctions: More Bark Than 'Byte'?", in Edgar (ed.), op. cit.

Cordes, J.J. 1989. "Tax Incentives and R&D Spending: A Review of the Evidence.", *Research Policy,* 18: 119-133.

Coricelli, F. and Dosi, G. 1988. "Coordination and Order in Economic Change and the Interpretative Power of Economic Theory." in Dosi et al., op. cit.

Crompton, R. 1995. *An Industrial Strategy for the Commodity Plastics Sector.* (South Africa: UCT Press).

Dallago, B. 2002. "The Organizational Effect of the Economic System". *Journal of Economic Issues*, 36 (4): 953-979.

Danziger, K. 1971. "Modernization and the Legitimation of Social Power.", in Adam (ed.)

Davenport, T.R.H. 1981. *South Africa: A Modern History, 2nd edition.* (South Africa: Macmillan).

—. 1987. *South Africa: A Modern History, 3rd edition.* (South Africa: MacMillan).

Davies, J. 1991. "Capital, State and Educational Reform in South Africa.", in Kallaway, P. (Ed.), op. cit.

Davies, R. 1979a. *Capital, State and White Labour in South Africa: 1900-1960.* (UK: Redwood Burn Ltd.).

—. 1979b. "Capital Restructuring and the Modification of the Racial Division of Labour in South Africa.", *Journal of Southern African Studies*, 5: 181-198.

Department of Arts, Culture, Science and Technology (DACST). 1996. *White Paper on Science and Technology: Preparing for the 21st Century.* (Pretoria).

Department of Industries (DI). 1971. *White Paper on the Report by the Inter-departmental Committee on the Decentralisation of Industries.* (Pretoria).

Department of Finance. 1996. *Growth, Employment and Redistribution: a Macroeconomic Strategy* (GEAR) White Paper. (RSA: Department of Finance).

Department of National Education (DNE). 1988a. *A System of Framework Autonomy for Scientific Councils.* NATED 11-007 (88/04).

—. 1988b. *The Science Policy and System of the Republic of South Africa.* NATED 11-005 (88/06).

Department of Trade and Industry (DTI). 1985. *White Paper on Industrial Development Strategy in the Republic of South Africa.* (Pretoria).

Department of Science and Technology (DST). 2002. *South Africa's National Research and Development Strategy.* (South Africa: DST).

—. 2007. *Innovation towards a Knowledge-Based Economy: Ten-Year Plan for South Africa: 2008 – 2018.* (South Africa: DST).

De Kiewiet, C.W. 1968. *A History of South Africa: Social and Economic.* (London: Oxford University Press).

Diawara, M. 1998. "Toward a Regional Imaginary in Africa.", in Jameson and Miyoshi, op. cit.

Dosi, G. 1982. "Technological Paradigms and Technological Trajectories", *Research Policy*, 11: 147-162.

—. 1991. "Perspectives on Evolutionary Theory." *Science and Public Policy*, 18: 353-361.

—. 1997. "Opportunities, Incentives and Collective Patterns of Change.", *The Economic Journal*, 107 (444): 1530-1547.

Dosi, G., Freeman, C. Nelson, R., Silverberg, G. and Soete, L. (eds.). 1988. *Technological Change and Economic Theory*, (London: Pinter).

Dosi, G. and Orsenigo, L. 1988. "Coordination and Transformation: An Overview of Structures, Behaviours and Change in Evolutionary Theory." in Dosi et al., op. cit.

Dosi, G. and Soete, L. 1988. "Technical Change and International Trade." in Dosi et al., op. cit.

Dosi, G., Pavitt, K. and Soete, L. 1990. *The Economics of Technical Change and International Trade* (New York: Harvester Wheatsheaf).

Edgar, R.E. (ed.). 1990. *Sanctioning Apartheid.* (US: Africa World Press Inc.).

Edquist, C. 2001. "The Systems of innovation Approach and Innovation Policy: An Account of the State of the Art.", paper presented at the DRUID conference, Aalborg. http://www.druid.dk/uploads/tx_picturedb/ds2001-178.pdf

—. 2006. "Systems of Innovation: Perspectives and Challenges", in Fagerberg et al.

Evangelista, R., Iammarino, S., Mastrostefano, V. and Silvani, A. 2002. "Looking for Regional Systems of Innovation: Evidence from the Italian Innovation Survey." *Regional Studies*, 36 (2): 173-186.

Fagerberg, J. 1988. "Why Growth Rates Differ." in Dosi et al., op. cit.

Fagerberg, J., Mowery, D.C. and Nelson, R.R. (eds.) *2006. The Oxford Handbook of Innovation* (Oxford University Press).

Feller, I. 1990. "Universities as Engines of R&D Based Research: They Think They Can.", *Research Policy*, 12: 1-22.

Feyerabend, P.K. 1970. "Consolations for the Specialist" in Lakatos and Musgrave, op. cit.

—. 1975. *Against Method*. (UK: NLB).

Fieldhouse, D.K. 1986. *Black Africa: 1945-1980*. (UK: Unwin).

Fine, R. and Davis, D. 1990. *Beyond Apartheid: Labour and Liberation in South Africa*. (South Africa: Ravan Press).

Fine, B. and Rustomjee, Z. 1996. *The Political Economy of South Africa: From Mineral-Energy Complex to Industrialisation*. (Johannesburg: University of the Witwatersrand Press).

Fine, B. and Stoneman, C. 1996. "State and Development.", *Journal of Southern African Studies*, 22: 5-26.

Foucault, M. 1970. "Orders of Discourse.", Lecture delivered at College de France, 2 December 1970. R. Swyer (trans), *Soc. Sci. Inform*, 10 (2).

—. 1977. *The Order of Things: An Archaeology of the Human Sciences*. (London: Tavistock Publications).

—. 1984. *The History of Sexuality: Volume I*. (UK: Peregrine Books).

—. 1994. *The Archaeology of Knowledge*. (UK: Routledge).

Freeman, C. 1982. *The Economics of Industrial Innovation*, 2nd ed. (London: MIT Press).

—. 1991. "Networks of Innovators: A Synthesis of Research Issues", *Research Policy*, 20: 499-514.

—. 2002. "Continental, national and sub-national innovation systems - complementarity and Economic Growth", *Research Policy*, 31: 191-211.

Freeman, C. and Lundvall, B.-Å. (eds.) 1988. *Small Countries Facing the Technological Revolution*. (London: Pinter).

Freeman, C. and Perez, C. 1988. "Structural Crises of Adjustment, Business Cycles and Investment Behaviour." in Dosi et al., op. cit.

Freeman, C. and Soete, L. 1997. *The Economics of Industrial Innovation, 3rd ed.* (USA: MIT Press).

Gellner, E. 1983. *Nations and Nationalism*. (UK: Basil Blackwell).

—. 1987. *Culture, Identity, and Politics*. (UK: Cambridge University Press).

—. 1994. *Encounters with Nationalism*. (UK: Basil Blackwell).

—. 1996. *Conditions of Liberty: Civil Society and its Rivals.* (UK: Penguin Books).

Goode, R. 1995a. *An Industrial Strategy for the Electrical Distribution Equipment Sector.* (Cape Town: UCT Press).

—. 1995b. *An Industrial Strategy for the Professional Electronics Sector.* (Cape Town: UCT Press).

Goto, A. and Suzuki, K. 1989. "R&D Capital, Rate of Return on R&D Investment and Spillover of R&D in Japanese Manufacturing Industries", *Review of Economics and Statistics*, 71: 555-564.

Griliches, Z. 1979. "Issues in assessing the contribution of research and development to productivity growth", Bell Journal of Economics, 10: 92-116.

—. 1980a. "R&D and the productivity slow-down", *American Economic Association (Papers and Proceedings)*, 70: 343-348.

—. 1980b. "Returns to Research and Development in the Private Sector", in *New Developments in Productivity Measurement and Analysis*, ed. J.W. Kendrick and B.N. Vaccara (Chicago: University of Chicago Press).

Griliches, Z. and Lichtenberg, F. 1984. "R&D and Productivity Growth at the Industry Level: Is There Still a Relationship", in *R&D, Patents and Productivity*, ed. Z. Griliches (University of Chicago Press for National Bureau of Economic Research, Chicago).

Gutting, G. 1989. *Michel Foucault's Archeology of Scientific Reason.* (UK: Cambridge University Press).

Hancock, W.K. 1968. *Smuts: The Fields of Force, 1919-1950.* (UK: Cambridge University Press).

Hanlon, J. (ed.). 1990. *South Africa - The Sanctions Report: Documents and Statistics.* (London: The Commonwealth Secretariat)

Hare, P. and Wyatt, G. 1988. "Modelling the Determinants of Research Output in British Universities", *Research Policy,* 17: 315-328.

Hirsch, A. 1991. "Industrial Decentralization and the Spatial Economy of Apartheid", in Konczacki et al. (eds.), op. cit.

Hirschman, A.O. 1958. *The Strategy of Economic Development.* (USA: Yale university Press).

Hodge, J. 1997. "South African Trade in High Technology Products.", *Trade and Industrial Policy, Working Paper,* No. (Johannesburg).

Hodgson, G.M. 1998. "The Approach of Institutional Economics." *Journal of Economic Literature*, 36 (1): 166-192.

—. 2000. "What is the Essence of Institutional Economics?" *Journal of Economic Issues*, 34 (2): 317-329.

—. 2003. "The Mystery of Routine: The Darwinian Destiny of an Evolutionary Theory of Economic Change.", *Revue Économique*, 54 (2): 355-384.

—. 2007. "Evolutionary and Institutional Economics as the New Mainstream?" *Evol. Inst. Econ. Rev.* 4(1): 7–25.

Holemans, B. and Sleuwaegen, L. 1988. "Innovation Expenditures and the Role of Government in Belgium", *Research Policy*, 17: 375-379.

Horwitz, R. 1967. *The Political Economy of South Africa.* (London: Weidenfeld and Nicolson).

Houghton, D.H. 1969. *The South African Economy.* (Cape Town: Oxford University Press).

Houghton, D.H. and Dagut, J. 1972. *Source Material on the South African Economy, Volume II: 1899-1919.* (Cape Town: Oxford University Press).

Houghton, D.H. 1973. *Source Material on the South African Economy, Volume III: 1920-1970.* (Cape Town: Oxford University Press).

Howe, J.D. and McFetridge, D.G. 1976. "The Determinants of R&D Expenditures", *Canadian Journal of Economics*, 9: 57-61.

Hulsman-Vejsova, M. and Koekkoek, K.A. 1980. "Factor Proportions, Technology and Dutch Industry's International Trade Patterns", *Weltwirtschlaftliches Archiv.*, 116: 162-177.

IDRC (International Development Research Centre). 1993. *Towards a Science and Technology Policy for a Democratic South Africa: A Report to the ANC, COSATU and SANCO* (South Africa).

—. 1999. *Framework for Regional Cooperation in Science and Technology.* (Cape Town: Edunet Consulting).

Jacobs, A. 1948. *South African Heritage: A Biography of H.J. van der Bijl.* (Pietermaritzburg: Shuter and Shooter).

Jaffe, A.B. 1986. "Technological Opportunity and Spillovers of R&D: Evidence from Firms' Patents, Profits, and Market Value", *American Economic Review*, 76: 984-1001.

Joffe, A., Kaplan, D., Kaplinsky, R. and Lewis, D. 1995. *Improving Manufacturing Performance in South Africa: The Report of the Industrial Strategy Project.* (South Africa: UCT Press).

Jameson, F. and Miyoshi, M. 1998. *The Cultures of Globalisation.* (USA: Duke University Press).

Johnes, G. 1988. "Determinants of Research Output in Economics Departments in British Universities.", *Research Policy*, 17: 171-178.

Johnson, B. 1988. "An Institutional Approach to the Small Country Problem." in Freeman and Lundvall, op. cit.

Johnson, B. and Lundvall, B-Å. 2001. *Why all this Fuss about Codified and Tacit Knowledge?* DRUID conference paper, Copenhagen.

http://www.druid.dk/uploads/tx_picturedb/dw2001-396.pdf

Johnstone, F.A. 1976. *Class, Race and Gold: A Study of Class Relations and Racial Discrimination in South Africa.* (U.S.A.: University Press of America).

Jones, S. and Müller, A. 1992. *The South African Economy, 1910-1990.* (New York: St. Martin's Press).

Kahn, M. 2008. "Science and Technology Policy.", in Kraak, A. And Press, K. (eds.).

Kahn, M. and Blankley, W. 2006. "The State of Research and Experimental Development: Moving to a Higher Gear.", in Buhlungu et al (eds.).

Kahn, M.,, Blankley, W., Maharajh, R., Pogue, T.E., Reddy, V., Cele, G, and du Toit, M. 2004. *Flight of the Flamingoes: A Study on the Mobility of R&D Workers.* (South Africa: HSRC Press).

Kallaway, P. (ed.) 1991. *Apartheid and Education: The Education of Black South Africans.* (Johannesburg: Ravan Press).

Kamien, M.I. and Schwartz, N.L. 1978. "Self-financing of an R&D Project.", *American Economic Review*, 68: 245-260.

Kaplan, D. 1976. "The Politics of Industrial Protection in South Africa.", *Journal of Southern African Studies*, 3: 70-91.

—. 1990. *The Crossed Line: The South African Telecommunications Industry in Transition.* (Johannesburg: Witwatersrand University Press).

—. 1996. "Science and Technology in a Democratic South Africa: new Challenges and new Policy Directions.", *Science, Technology and Society*, 1: 101-127.

Keck, O. 1993. "The National System for Technical Innovation in Germany.", in Nelson (ed.), op. cit.

Kingwill, D.G. 1990. *The CSIR - The First 40 Years.* (Pretoria: CSIR).

Kleu, S.J. 1983. *Report of the Study Group on Industrial Development Strategy.* (Pretoria).

Konczacki, Z.A., Parpart, J.L. and Shaw, T.M. (eds.) 1991. *Studies in the Economic History of Southern Africa, Vol II: South Africa, Lesotho and Swaziland.* (UK: Frank Cass & Co. Ltd.)

Kozul-Wright, R. 1995. "Transnational Corporations and the Nation State.", in Michie and Smith, op. cit.

Kraak, A. 2004. *An Overview of South African Human Resources Development.* (South Africa: HSRC Press).

Kraak, A. and Perold, H. (eds.)) 2003. *Human Resource Development Review 2003: Education, Employment and Skills in South Africa.* (South Africa: HSRC Press).

Kraak, A. and Press, K. (eds.) 2008. *Human Resource Development Review 2008: Education, Employment and Skills in South Africa.* (South Africa: HSRC Press).

Kros, J. 1993. *A Century of Mechanical Engineering* (The South African Institute of Mechanical Engineers).

Kuhn, T.S. 1970a. *The Structure of Scientific Revolutions.* (Chicago: The University of Chicago Press).

—. 1970b. "Logic of Discovery or Psychology of Research." in Lakatos and Musgrave, op. cit.

Lakatos, I. and Musgrave, A. (eds.). 1970. *Criticism and the Growth of Knowledge.* (UK: Cambridge University Press).

Landgren, S.1989. *Embargo Disimplemented: South Africa's Military Industry.* (UK: Oxford University Press).

Lall, S. 1981. *Developing Countries in the International Economy.* (London: The Macmillan Press).

—. 1981. "Technology and Developing Countries: A Review and an Agenda for Research", in Lall, op. cit.

—. 1987. *Learning to Industrialize: The Acquisition of Technological Capability by India.* (London: Macmillan).

—. 1992a. "Technological Capabilities and Industrialization.", *World Development*, 20: 165-186.

—. 1992b. "Technological Capabilities and the Role of Government in Developing Countries.", *Greek Economic Review*, 14: 1-36.

—. 1993. "What Will Make South Africa Internationally Competitive?", paper delivered at the ASPEN/IDASA *Conference on South Africa's International Economic Relations in the 1990's.*

—. 1994. "Industrial Policy: The Role of Government in Promoting Industrial and Technological Development." UNCTAD Review.

—. 2001. *Competitiveness, Technology and Skills.* (UK: Edward Elgar).

—. (ed.) 1996. *Opening Up, and Shutting Down?: Import Liberalisation and Industrial Technology in Sub-Saharan Africa.* (INTECH).

Lall, S. and Latsch, W. 1996. "Import Liberalisation and Industrial Performance: Theory & Evidence.", in Lall (ed.), op. cit.

Lall, S. and Pietrobelli, C. 2002. *Failing to Compete: Technology Development and Technology Systems in Africa.* (UK: Edward Elgar).

Lancaster, K. 1966. "A New Approach to Consumer Theory", *Journal of Political Economy*, 84: 132-157.

Legassick, M. 1974. "Legislation, Ideology and Economy in Post-1948 South Africa.", *Journal of Southern African Studies*, 1: 5-35.

Levin, R.C., Klevorick, A.K., Nelson, R.R. and Winter, S.G. 1987. "Appropriating the Returns From Industrial R&D", *Brookings Papers on Economic Activity*, 783-820.

Levy, D.M. and Terleckyj, N.E. 1983. "Effects of Government R&D on Private R&D Investment and Productivity: A Macroeconomic Analysis", *Bell Journal of Economics*, 14: 551-561.

Lichtenberg, F.R. 1984. "The relationship between Federal Contract R&D and Company R&D", *American Economic Association (Papers and Proceedings)*, 74: 73-78.

—. 1987. "The Effect of Government Funding on Private Industrial Research and Development: A Reassessment", Journal of Industrial Economics, 36: 97-104.

—. 1988. "The Private R&D Investment Response to Federal Design and Technical Competition", *American Economic Review*, 78: 550-559.

Lipton, M. 1986. *Capitalism and Apartheid: South Africa, 1910-1986.* (UK: Gower Publishing Company Ltd.).

List, F. 2005. *National System of Political Economy, Vols 1-III: The History.* (USA: Cosimo).

Lodge, T. 1983. *Black Politics in South Africa since 1945.* (Johannesburg: Ravan Press).

Lundvall, B.-Å. (ed.). 1992. *National Systems of Innovation. Towards a Theory of Innovation and Interactive Learning.* (London: Pinter).

—. 2002. *Innovation, Growth and Social Cohesion: The Danish Model.* (USA: Edward Elgar).

Lundvall, B.-Å., Johnson, B., Anderson, E.S. and Dalum, B. 2002. "National Systems of Production, Innovation and Competence Building.", *Research Policy*, 31:213-231.

Luke, T.W. 1990. *Social Theory and Modernity: Critique, Dissent, and Revolution.* (USA.: Sage Publications).

Lyotard, J.F. 1989. *The Postmodern Condition: A Report on Knowledge.* (Manchester: Manchester University Press).

Macdonald, S. 1986. "Theoretically Sound: Practically Useless? Government Grants for Industrial R&D in Australia.", *Research Policy,* 15: 269-283.

Magubane, B.M. 1979. *The Political Economy of Race and Class in South Africa.* (US: Monthly Review Press).

Mansfield E. 1984. "R&D and Innovation: Some Empirical Findings." in *R&D, Patents and Productivity*, ed. Z. Griliches (University of Chicago Press for National Bureau of Economic Research, Chicago).

—. 1986. "The R&D Tax Credit and Other Technology Policy Issues.", *American Economic Association (Papers and Proceedings),* 76: 190-194.

Mansfield E. and Switzer, L. 1985. "The Effects of R & D Tax Credits and Allowances in Canada", *Research Policy*, 14: 97-107.

Marglin, F.A. and Marglin, S.A. (eds.) 1990. *Dominating Knowledge: Development, Culture and Resistance*. (Oxford: Clarendon Press).

Marglin, S.A. 1990a. "Towards a Decolonisation of the Mind.", in Marglin and Marglin (eds.), op. cit.

—. 1990b. "Losing Touch: The Cultural Conditions of Worker Accommodation and Resistance.", in Marglin and Marglin (eds.), op. cit.

Marks, S. and Rathbone, R. (eds.) 1982. *Industrialisation and Structural Change in South Africa: African Class Formation, Culture and Consciousness 1870-1930.* (U.S.A.: Longman).

Maskell, P. and Malmberg, A. 1999. "Localised Learning and Industrial Competitiveness.", *Cambridge Journal of Economics*, 23: 167-185.

Mbeki, T. 2003. *State of the Nation Address of the President of South Africa*. (Houses of Parliament, Cape Town)

Meiring Naudé, S. and Brown, A.C. 1977. "The Growth of Scientific Institutions in South Africa." in A.C. Brown (ed.), op. cit.

Merton, R.K. 1957. *Social Theory and Social Structure*. (Free Press).

Michie, J. and Smith, J.G. (eds.) 1995. *Managing the Global Economy*. (Oxford University Press).

Miyoshi, M. 1997. "Sites of Resistance in the Global Economy.", in Ansell-Pearson et al.

Moll, T. 1991. "Did the Apartheid Economy 'Fail'?", *Journal of Southern African Studies*, 17: 71-291.

Molteno, F. 1991. "The Historical Foundation of Black South Africans.", in Kallaway, P. (ed.), op. cit.

Morin, E. 1992. "The Anti-Totalitarian Revolution.", in Beilhartz et al., op. cit.

Motlhabi, M. 1984. *The Theory and Practice of Black Resistance to Apartheid: A Social-Ethical Analysis*. (Johannesburg: Skotaville Publishers).

Moura Roque, F. 1984. "Factor Endowment, Technology, and Foreign Trade.", *The South African Journal of Economics*, 52: 377-390.

Nattrass, N. 1991. "Controversies About Capitalism and Apartheid in South Africa: An Economic Perspective.", *Journal of Southern African Studies*, 17: 654-677.

Nattrass, N. and Ardington, E. 1990. *The Political Economy of South Africa*. (Cape Town: Oxford University Press).

Neale, W.C. 1987. "Institutions.", *Journal of Economic Issues*, 21: 1177-1206.

—. 1989. "The Evolution of Colonial Institutions: An Argument Illustrated from the Economic History of British Central Africa.", in Tool and Samuels, op. cit.

Nedbank Group Economic Unit. 1983. *South Africa: An Appraisal.* (Johannesburg: The Nedbank Group).

Nelson, R.R. 1959. "The Simple Economics of Basic Scientific Research." *Journal of Political Economy*, 67: 297-306.

—. 1982. "The Role of Knowledge in R&D Efficiency." *Quarterly Journal of Economics*, 97: 453-70.

—. 1986. "Institutions Supporting Technical Advance in Industry." *American Economic Review (Papers and Proceedings)*, 76: 186-189.

—. 1990a. "On Technological Capabilities and their Acquisition." in *Science and Technology: lessons for development policy*, eds. R.E. Evenson and G. Ranis (U.S.A.: Westview Press Inc.).

—. 1990b. "Capitalism as an Engine of Progress." *Research Policy*, 19: 193-214.

—. 1991. "The Role of Firm Differences in an Evolutionary Theory of Technical Advance." *Science and Public Policy*, 18: 347-352.

—. 1993. *National Innovation Systems: A Comparative Analysis.* (New York: Oxford University Press).

—. 1995. "Recent Evolutionary Theorizing about Economic Change.", *Journal of Economic Literature*, 33: 48-90.

—. 1996. *The Sources of Economic Growth.* (USA: Harvard University Press).

Nelson, R.R. and Nelson, K. 2002. "Technology, Institutions and Innovation Systems.", *Research Policy*, 31: 265-272.

Nelson, R.R. and Winter, S.G. 1974. "Neoclassical vs. Evolutionary Theories of economic Growth." *The Economic Journal*, 84 (336): 886-905.

Nelson, R.R. and Winter, S.G. 1982. *An Evolutionary Theory of Economic Change.* (USA: Harvard University Press).

Nelson, R.R. and Winter, S.G. 2002. "Evolutionary Theorizing in Economics." *Journal of Economic Perspectives*, 16 (2): 23-46.

Ngoasheng, M. 1995. *An Industrial Strategy for the Building Materials Supplies Sector.* (Cape Town: UCT Press).

North, D.C. 1981. *Structure and Change in Economic History.* (New York: W.W. Norton).

—. 1990. *Institutions, Institutional Change and Economic Performance.* (UK: Cambridge University Press, 2004 print).

—. 2005. *Understanding the Process of Economic Change.* (USA: Princeton University Press).

North, D.C. and Wallis, J.J. 1994. "Integrating Institutional Change and Technical Change in Economic History: A Transaction Cost Approach", *Journal of Institutional and Theoretical Economics*, 150/4: 609-624.

Norval, A. 1996. *Deconstructing Apartheid Discourse*. (UK: Verso).

Norval, A.J. 1962. *A Quarter Century of Industrial Progress in South Africa*. (Cape Town: Rustica Press).

OECD. 1992. *Oslo Manual: OECD Proposed Guidelines for Collecting and Interpreting Technological Innovation Data*. (OECD, Paris).

—. 1997. *National Innovation Systems*. (OECD, Paris).

Ogbu, O.M., Oyeyinka, B.O. and Mlawa, H.M. 1995. *Technology Policy on Africa*. (IDRC: Ottawa).

O'Meara, D. 1975. "The 1946 Mine Workers' Strikeand the Political Economy of South Africa.", *Journal of Commonwealth and Comparative Politics*, 13: 146-173.

Orford, J., Nattrass, N. and Kaplan, D. 1992. "Firm Size and Innovative Capability in the South African Electronics Industry: Schumpeterian Perspectives." in *Papers Submitted for the Competition to Promote Academic Research into Industrial Policy and Development in South Africa*, ed. J. van Pletsen and J.J. Hunter (Industrial Development Corporation of S.A. Ltd., South Africa).

Padayachee, V. (ed.) 2006. *The Development Decade? Economic and Social Change in South Africa, 1994-2004*. (South Africa, HSRC Press).

—. 2006. "Development Discources in Post-Apartheid South Africa." in Padayachee (ed.).

Pakes, A. and Schankerman, M. 1984. "An Exploration into the Determinants of Research Intensity." in Z. Griliches (ed.) *R&D, Patents and Productivity*, (University of Chicago Press).

Palda, K.S. 1986. "Technological Intensity: Concept and Measurement.", *Research Policy*, 15: 187-198.

Perez, C. 1988. "New Technologies and Development." in Freeman and Lundvall, op. cit.

Perez, C. and Soete, L. 1988. "Catching up in Technology: Entry Barriers and Windows of Opportunity." in Dosi et al., op. cit.

Perry, H. and Arends, F. 2003. "Public Schooling." in Kraak and Perold (eds.).

Peukert, H. 2001. "On the Origins of Modern Evolutionary Economics: The Veblen Legend after 100 Years." *Journal of Economic Issues*, 35 (3): 543-555.

Phillips, A. 1966. "Patents, Potential Competition and Technical Progress.", *American Economic Review*, 56: 310-310.

Pietrobelli, C. 1994. "Technological Capabilities at the National Level: An International Comparison of Manufacturing Export Performance., *Development Policy Review*, 12: 115-148.

Posel, D. 1983. "Rethinking the 'Race-Class Debate' in South African Historiography.", paper presented at a conference on *Southern Africa: Retrospect and Prospect*, (University of Edinburgh: Centre for African Studies).

—. 1991. *The Making of Apartheid, 1948-1961: Conflict and Compromise.* (Oxford: Clarendon Press).

Reinganum, J.F. 1989. "The Timing of Innovation: Research, Development, and Diffusion.", in Schmalensee and Willig, op. cit.

Republic of South Africa (RSA). 2003. *Towards a Ten Year Review: synthesis report on implementation of government programmes, a discussion document of the Policy Coordination and Advisory Services.* (Office of the President).

—. 2004. *Accelerated and Shared Growth Initiative for South Africa-AsgiSA*. (SA: Office of the Presidency).

—. 2005. *South African National Innovation Survey* (DST)

—. 2006. *Joint Initiative on Priority Skills Acquisition -JIPSA*. (SA: Office of the President).

—. 2007. *Development Indicators - Mid-term Review*. (SA: Office of the Presidency).

—. 2008. *National Survey of Research and Experimental Development (R&D) 2006/2007.* (DST)

—. 2008. *Towards a Fifteen Year Review.* (Office of the President).

Richardson, P. and Van-Helten, J.J. 1982. "Labour in the South African Gold Mining Industry, 1886-1914.", in Marks and Rathbone, op. cit.

Rosenberg, N. 1974. "Science, Invention and Economic Growth.", *Economic Journal*, 84: 90-108.

Ruttan, V.W. 1997. "Induced Innovation, Evolutionary Theory and Path Dependence: Sources of Technical Change.", *The Economic Journal*, 107 (444): 1520:1529.

Saul, J.S. 1991. "South Africa: between 'Barbarism' and 'Structural Reform'.", *New Left Review* I/188: 3-44.

Saunders, C. 1988. *The Making of the South African Past: Major Historians on Race and Class.* (Cape Town: David Philip).

—. 1976. "Research and Market Share: A Reappraisal of the Schumpeter Hypothesis.", *Journal of Industrial Economics*, 25: 101-112.

Scerri, M. 1990. "R&D and the International Competitiveness of the South African Manufacturing Sector.", *South African Journal of Economics*, 58: 341-356.

—. 1993. The Determinants of R&D Activity within the Context of the South African Manufacturing Sector, *PhD thesis submitted to the Faculty of Commerce, University of the Witwatersrand, South Africa.*

—. 1998. "The Parameters of Science and Technology Policy Formulation in South Africa.", *African Development Review (Special Issue: Information, Knowledge and Africa's Development)*, 10: 73-89.

—. 2003a. "The Competitiveness of the Southern African Customs Union within the Context of the Indian Ocean Rim." in Gwyn Campbell (ed.).

—. 2003b. "The Prospects for Regional Innovation System(s) Within Sub-Saharan Africa." in Mammo Muchie, Bengt-Åke Lundvall and Peter Gammeltoft (eds.), *Putting Africa First: The Making of African Innovation Systems*. (Denmark: Aalborg University Press).

—. 2006a. "Introduction.", in Blankley et al (eds.)

—. 2006b. "The Conceptual Fluidity of National Innovation Systems: Implications for Innovation Measures", in Blankley et al (eds).

—. 2008. "Provincial Systems of Innovation and Globalisation in South Africa", *International Conference on Apparent Antithesis: Globalisation and Local Development*, School on Local Development, University of Trento – Trento, 9th - 11th October 2008.

Scherer, F.M. 1967a. "Market Structure and the Employment of Scientists and Engineers.", *American Economic Review*, 57: 524-531.

—. 1967b. "Research and Development Resource Allocation Under Rivalry.", *Quarterly Journal of Economics*, 81: 359-394.

Schimank, U. 1988. "The Contribution of University Research to the Technological Innovation of the German Economy: Societal Auto-dynamic and Political Guidance.", *Research Policy*, 17: 329-340.

Schmalensee, R. and Willig, R.D. (Eds.) 1989. *Handbook of Industrial Organisation: Volume II.* (Netherlands: Elsevier Science Publishers B.V.)

Schumpeter, J.A. 1954. *Capitalism, Socialism and Democracy.* (London: George Allen & Unwin).

Simpson, L.C. 1995. *Technology, Time and the Conversations of Modernity.* (U.S.A.: Routledge).

Smith, M.R. and Marx, L. (eds.) 1994. *Does Technology Drive History?: The Dilemma of Technological Determinism.* (U.S.A.: MIT Press).

Spence, A.M. 1984. "Cost Reduction, Competition and Industry Performance.", *Econometrica*, 52: 101-121.

Stahl-Rolf, S.R. 2000. "Descendence and Social Genealogies: Toward an Evolutionary Conception of Economic History." *Journal of Economic Issues*, 34 (4): 891-908.

Stern, R.M. 1984. "Some Evidence on Factor Content of West Germany's Foreign Trade.", *Journal of Political Economy*, 84: 131-141.

Subotzky, G. 2003. "Public Higher Education." in Kraak and Perold (eds.).

Stigler, G.J. and Becker, G.S. 1977. "De Gustibus Non Est Disputandum", *American Economic Review*: 76-90.

Terreblanche, S. and Nattrass, N. 1990. "A Periodisation of the Political Economy from 1910.", in Nattrass and Ardington, op. cit.

Thompson, J.B. 1995. *The Media and Modernity: A Social Theory of the Media.* (Cambridge: Polity Press).

Thompson, L.M. 1985. *The Political Mythology of Apartheid.* (USA: Yale university Press).

Tiles, M. 1984. *Bachelard: Science and Objectivity.* (UK: Cambridge University Press).

Tool, M.R. and Samuels, W.J. (eds.) 1989. *State, Society and Corporate Power.* (U.S.A.: Transaction Publishers).

UNESCO. 1969. *Apartheid: Its Effects on Education, Science, Culture and Information.* (Paris: UNESCO).

United Nations Development Programme (UNDP). 2005. *Human Development Report 2005.*

Union of South Africa. 1955. *Report of the Commission for the Socio-Economic Development of the Bantu Areas within the Union of South Africa* (U.G. 61-'55) (Tomlinson Report).

—. 1956. *Government Decisions on the Recommendations of the Commission for the Socio-Economic Development of the Bantu Areas within the Union of South Africa.* (W.P.F.-'56).

Variava, R. 1989. *The Deployment of Racism in South Africa.* PhD dissertation. (Cambridge: Newnham College). http://www.sahistory.org.za/pages/pdf/deployment of racism.pdf

Veblen, T. 1898. "Why is Economics not an Evolutionary Science?" *The Quarterly Journal of Economics*, 12 (4): 373-397.

Wade, R. 1996. "Japan, the World Bank and the Art of Paradigm Maintenance: *The East Asian* in Political Perspective." *New Left Review*, 217: 3-37.

Waissbluth, M., Cadena, G. and Solleiro, J.L. 1988. "Linking University and Industry: An Organizational Experience in Mexico", Research Policy, 17: 341-347.

Wilson, M. and Thompson, L. 1971. *The Oxford History of South Africa, Vol. II: 1870-1966.* (London: Oxford University Press).

Woldendorp, J. 1990. "Technology Transfer to Circumvent the Oil Embargo.", in Hanlon (ed.), op. cit.

—. 1990. "The Oil Embargo Against South Africa: Effects and Loopholes.", in Edgar (ed.), op. cit.

Wolpe. H. (ed.) 1980. *The Articulation of Modes of Production*. (London: Routledge & Keegan Paul).

—. 1980. "Capitalism and Cheap Labour-Power in South Africa: From Segregation to Apartheid" in Wolpe (ed.), op. cit.

—. 1989. *Race, Class and the Apartheid State*. (Paris: UNESCO Press).

Wolter, F. 1977. "Factor Proportions, Technology and West German Industry's International Trade Patterns", *Weltwirtschlaftliches Archiv.*, 113: 250-265.

INDEX

Adam, H. 7, 8, 9, 149, 150
Adelzadeh, A. 215, 217, 224, 225
Advisory Board of Industry and Science. 110, 111, 113, 117, 123, 124, 126, 139, 145
African Explosives and Chemicals Industries (AECI). 107, 193, 194, 204
African Explosives and Industries Limited (AE&I) 107
African National Congress (ANC) ..71, 97, 127, 129-132, 150, 159, 161, 169, 177, 212- 214, 221, 230, 252, 253, 255, 257
Altman, M. 217, 246
Anderson, B 48
Angolan war 195, 196, 207
Archibugi, D. 22, 238
Ardington, E. 126
Arends, F. 236
Armaments Development and Production Corporation (ARMSCOR) 194, 197, 199, 201
Arrow, K. 30
AsgiSA 217, 218
Asheim, B. 50
Atomic Energy Board (AEB) 164
Atomic Energy Corporation (AEC) 206
Ballinger, M. 130-132, 134-136, 142-145, 162, 181
Bantu Education Act, 1953 156, 174
Bantu Education Commission, 1951 156
Bantustans 150, 156, 238
Basson, N. 93, 163, 166, 168, 170
Bauman, T. 202, 203
Bauman, Z. 42
Becker, G.S. 55, 76, 83
Bernstein, J.I. 31
Black Consciousness Movement 82, 212, 230
Black Resettlement Act, 1954 155
Blankley, W. 231
Botha, L. 88, 104, 113, 115, 116, 161
Brown, A.C. 10, 115
BTI 201, 202, 203
Carnegie Corporation Commission Report, 1932 116
Champion, A.W.G. 132
Chataway, J. 201, 202
Chesnais, F. 86
Christie, P. 177
Coase, R.H. 35
Cohen, W.M. 30, 31, 38, 39
Collins, C. 177
Colour bar 76, 105, 110, 114, 116, 118, 120-122, 133, 134, 156, 161, 173
Coloured Peoples Act, 1963. 174
Commonwealth 86, 113, 117, 139, 152, 153, 155, 158, 159, 163, 165, 193, 194, 282, 289
Communist Party of South Africa (CPSA) 130
Community Innovation Survey (CIS) 32, 33, 275
Congress of Non-European Trade Unions 131
Congress of South African Trade Unions (COSATU) 213, 252, 255
Cooke, P. 48, 49, 53, 63
Cordes, J.J. 44
Council for Mineral Technology (MINTEK) 169

Council for Scientific and Industrial Research (CSIR) 10, 93, 100, 128, 137, 138, 140-145, 159, 162-166, 168-170, 181, 189, 191, 193, 194, 198, 199, 201, 225, 231, 235, 275
Creswell, F.H.P. 100, 115, 120, 121, 122, 123
Crompton, R..................95, 204, 205
Dagut, J.......................114, 122, 124
Danziger, K.............................88, 89
Davenport, T.R.H.......102, 103, 127, 131, 132, 134, 136, 146, 155
Davies, R. 160, 161
Davis, D..................................80, 81
De Kiewiet, C.W. 115, 133
Department of Arts, Culture, Science and Technology (DACST) 94, 221, 222, 224, 225, 226, 228, 230
Department of National Education (DNE)....................................180
Department of Science and Technology (DST) 230, 231, 232, 233, 234, 249
Department of Trade and Industry (DTI) 179, 226
Dosi, G............18, 20, 24, 37, 58, 64
Dube, J. 132
Economic and Wage Commission, 1925 ....116, 120
Electricity Supply Commission (ESCOM) 117, 119, 122, 125, 126, 140, 175, 197, 201
Extension of University Education Bill, 1957 174
Feller, I.. 40
Feyerabend, P.K. 59
Fieldhouse, D.K. 97
Final Report of the Drought Investigation Commission, 1923 116
Fine, B. ..13, 44, 78, 79, 92, 96, 151-153, 175, 183-185, 190, 246
Fine, R. 80, 81
First World War.....12, 93, 100, 106, 121, 196, 221, 249
Foucault, M. 36, 58, 59, 72
Framework Autonomy 227, 228, 280
Federation for Research Development (FRD)...... 96, 168, 169, 275
Freeman, C.....18, 21, 24, 56, 57, 61, 86, 167
Gellner, E. 4-6, 9, 10, 12, 48, 70
Gertler, M.S................................. 50
Goode, R. 199
Goto, A. 31
Griliches, Z............................. 26, 31
Group Areas Act, 1950.............. 155
Growth, Employment and Redistribution: A Macroeconomic Plan (GEAR) ... 214-217, 220, 221, 223, 224, 230, 252-255
Hancock, W.K....103, 129, 132, 133, 135
Hare, P. 41
Hertzog, J.B.M. ...88, 100, 103, 104, 106, 108, 115, 120-122, 126, 127, 135
Hirsch, A.................................... 172
Hirschman, A.O............................ 46
Hodge, J. 192
Hodgson, G.M............................. 18
Hofmeyr, J.H.... 118, 127, 130, 133-135, 139, 142, 175, 177, 178
Holemans, B................................ 39
Horwitz, R.... 73, 102, 104-106, 115, 121
Houghton, D.H. 114, 122, 124
Howe, J.D. 44
Hulsman-Vejsova, M................... 91
human capital ..4, 26, 41, 42, 47, 51, 55, 75, 78, 80, 85, 91, 95, 98, 102, 137, 141, 142, 144, 146, 147, 157, 165, 171, 172, 175, 178, 180, 197, 201, 202, 207, 212, 215, 217, 219, 220, 222, 227, 228, 233-251, 254- 256

Human Sciences Research Council (HSRC) 169
Immorality Amendment Act, 1950 155
Indians' Education Act of 1965 ..174
Industrial Conciliation Act, 1924 ....103, 156
Industrial Development Corporation (IDC).... 126, 138, 140, 142, 175, 193, 201
Industries Advisory Board.. 109-112
Infant industry argument 46, 122, 145, 201, 238
International Development Research Centre (IDRC) ..32, 94, 223, 226, 227
Iron an Steel Corporation (ISCOR) 100, 117, 118, 122, 123-126, 137, 140, 179, 193, 201
Jabavu, D.D.T. 129
Jacobs, A......116-119, 125, 137, 138
Jaffe, A.B. 28, 31
Jensen, E.G...............................152
Joint Initiative on Priority Skills Acquisition (JIPSA).............218
Joffe, A. 160
Johnes, G. 41
Johnson, B.................35, 54, 55, 56
Jones, S. 128, 138
Kahn, M............. 221, 231-233, 236
Kamien, M.I...............................167
Kaplan, D.....................10, 199, 200
Keck, O..............................111, 112
Kingwill, D.G. 10, 93, 117, 142, 164, 165
Kleu report, 1983.........................168
Koekkoek, K.A. 91
Kozul-Wright, R...............50, 51, 52
Kraak, A.............................236, 240
Kros, J..........................10, 193, 204
Kuhn, T.S. 18, 24, 58, 59
Lall, S. 4, 21, 43, 45, 95, 171
Lancaster, K. 31
Landgren, S......10, 15, 192-195, 198
Levin, R.C........................28, 38, 39
Levinthal, D.A.......................30, 31
Levy, D.M. 39, 44
Liberal economics1, 6, 8, 11, 12, 45, 63, 73-75, 97, 147, 149, 153, 182, 183
Lichtenberg, F.R. 26, 39
Lipton, M. 78
List, F. 2, 18, 46, 238
Lodge, T. 129
Luke 83, 85
Lundvall, B-Å..... 18, 22, 51, 95, 96, 238
Luthuli, A. 132
Lyotard, J.F. 83
Malan, D.F. 126, 153
Malmberg, A. 50
Mansfield, E. 27, 31, 44
Marglin, S.A. 21, 35, 58, 59
Marxist theory 1, 6, 8, 11, 12, 66, 73, 74, 90, 182
Maskell, P. 50
Matthews, Z.K. 132, 134, 178
Mayer, M. 246
Mbeki, T. 218, 252, 253
McFetridge, D.G. 44
Medical Research Council (MRC) 169
Meiring Naudé, S. 115, 163
Merton, R.K. 54
Military-industrial complex.. 13, 44, 184, 190, 192, 207, 234, 238, 247
Mine and Works Amendment Act, 1926 121
Minerals-energy complex14, 44, 92, 153, 183-190, 199, 202, 207, 246
Mines and Works Regulation Act, 1911 105
Mining Industry Commission, 1907-1908 106
Miyoshi, M. 51
Moll, T. 89
Molteno, F. 177
Morin, E. 148
Mosaka, P. 132
Mossgas 204, 205
Motlhabi, M. 103

Moura Roque, F. 91
Msimang, S. 132
Müller, A. 128, 138
Musgrave 194
NACI...226
Nadiri, M.I.................................. 31
National Party 13, 74, 87, 88, 90, 93, 94, 101, 104, 126, 145-148, 153, 155, 158, 159, 161-164, 166, 213, 223
National Research Board............127
National Research Council.127, 139
Native Affairs Act, 1920............102
Native Affairs Commission Report, 1903-1905.............................104
Native Labour Regulation Act, 1911 105
Native Lands Act, 1913.............105
Native Laws Amendment Act 1952 155
Natives Representative Council 127, 131, 135, 136, 146
Natives (Urban Areas) Act, 1923 ....103, 136
Nattrass, N. 101, 126
National Chemical Research Laboratory (NCRL) 194
National Electrical Engineering Research Institute (NEERI) ..194
National Institute for Aeronautics and Systems Technology (NIAST)................................194
National Institute for Defence Research (NIDR) 194
National Institute for Telecommunications Research (NITR) 194
National Mechanical Engineering Institute (NMERI).................194
National Physical Research Laboratory (NPRL)..............194
National Research and Development Strategy (NRDS)...........231, 236
National Research Institute for Mathematical Sciences (NRIMS) 194
Neale, W.C..........34, 54, 56, 81, 114
Nelson, R.R... 18, 21, 22, 24, 28-30, 34, 40, 48, 50, 56, 62, 63, 67, 68, 158
Neoclassical economics.2-4, 10, 18-20, 25, 27, 32, 34, 35, 38, 45, 49, 53, 55, 56, 60, 63, 67, 68, 84
Neoliberal economics 37, 45, 51, 71, 73, 90, 97, 98, 169, 192, 213-216, 218, 220, 221, 223, 225, 233, 248, 251, 253, 254
North, D.C.....23, 35, 54, 60, 70, 129
Norval, A. 87, 88, 155, 175
Nuclear Development Corporation (NUCOR)............ 164, 201, 206
O'Meara, D. 76, 105, 120
Ogbu, O.M. 32
Organisation for Economic Cooperation and Development (OECD) 31, 209, 215
Pact coalition 120
Pakes, A. 26
Palda, K.S.................................... 29
Pan African Congress........ 159, 212
Perez, C................24, 56, 57, 61, 65
Perry, H...................................... 236
Phillips, A.................................... 27
Pietrobelli, C................................ 21
"poor white" problem 106, 116, 122, 181
Population Registration Act, 1950 155
Posel, D.70, 76-78, 83, 84, 154, 173, 174
Prohibition of Mixed Marriages Act, 1949 155
Promotion of Bantu Self Government Act, 1959........ 155
Reconstruction and Development Programme (RDP)214, 215, 221, 223
Reikert 1979 Commission......... 168
Reinganum, J.F................ 19, 38, 39
Report of the Low Grade Mines Commission , 1920............... 114
Research Grant Board........ 126, 127

Reservation of Separate Amenities Act, 1953 ... 155
Rosenberg, N. ... 27
Rustomjee, Z. .. 13, 44, 78, 79, 92, 96, 151-153, 175, 183-185, 190, 246
Saul, J.S. ... 169
Scerri, M. ... 31, 32, 91, 157, 222, 257
Schankerman, M. ... 26
Scherer, F.M. ... 28, 31
Schimank, U. ... 41
Schonland, B. ... 102, 138, 163
Schumpeter, J. 2, 24, 37, 66, 73, 167, 182, 183, 185, 189
Schwartz, N.L. ... 167
Scientific and Technical Committee ... 109-111, 113
Second World War ... 57, 71, 79, 83, 94, 102, 107, 108, 117, 128, 138, 184, 192, 193, 196, 204
Simpson, L.C. ... 20, 35, 82
Sleuwagen, S. ... 39
Smuts, J. ... 74-76, 87, 88, 100-104, 106, 108, 113, 115-118, 121, 126-130, 132, 134-136, 138, 145-147, 152, 157, 161-163, 175, 177, 181, 184
South African Bureau of Standards (SABS) ... 169
South African Coal and Oil - Suid Afrikaanse Steenkool en Olie (SASOL)107, 179, 197, 204, 205
South African Communist Party (SACP) ... 213, 252, 253, 255
South African Institute of Medical Research (SAIMR)107, 139, 140
South African Journal of Industries ... 109, 112
South African Native National Congress ... 129, 161
South African Party ... 104, 113
Spence, A.M. ... 31
Stern, R.M. ... 91
Stigler, G.J. ... 83
Suzuki, K. ... 31
Terleckyj, N.E. ... 39, 44
Terreblanche, S. ... 101
Thompson, J.B. ... 35, 49, 71
Tomlinson, F.R. ... 156
Uranium Enrichment Corporation of South Africa (UCOR) ... 206
United Nations Development Programme (UNDP) ... 224, 237
United Nations Educational, Scientific and Cultural Organisation (UNESCO) ... 175, 176, 180
Unionist Party ... 113
United Party ... 126
van der Bijl, H.J. .100-102, 116-119, 124-127, 137, 138, 147, 162, 181, 193
Variava, R. ... 72, 81, 82, 120, 175
Verwoerd, H. ... 7, 81, 149, 152, 154, 156, 159, 166, 171, 191
Victoria Falls Power Company Limited (VFP) ... 119
Wade, R. ... 45
Wage Act, 1925 ... 121
Waissbluth, M. ... 41
Wallis, J.J. ... 60
White Paper on Industrial Development Policy, 1983 ... 168
White Paper on Industrial Strategy, 1985 ... 168, 179
White Paper on Science and Technology, 1996.. 14, 161, 221-229, 233, 249
Wiehahn Commission Report, 1982 ... 168
Winter, S.G. ... 67, 68
Wolpe, H. ... 73-77, 80, 81
Wolter, F. ... 91
Wyatt, G. ... 41
Xuma, A.B. ... 130